M000239216

The Emerald Horizon

A BUR OAK BOOK

The Emerald Horizon

The History of Nature in Iowa

Cornelia F. Mutel

University of Iowa Press | Iowa City

University of Iowa Press, Iowa City 52242
www.uiowapress.org

Copyright © 2008 by the University of Iowa Press

Printed in the United States of America

Design by April Leidig-Higgins

The University of Iowa Press is a member of Green
Press Initiative and is committed to preserving natural
resources.

Printed on acid-free paper

Library of Congress Cataloging-in-Publication Data
Mutel, Cornelia Fleischer.
The emerald horizon: the history of nature in Iowa /
Cornelia F. Mutel — 1st ed.
p.   cm. — (A Bur Oak book)
Includes bibliographical references and index.
ISBN-13: 978-1-58729-632-1 (pbk.)
ISBN-10: 1-58729-632-2 (pbk.)
    1. Natural history — Iowa — History.   I. Title.
QH105.I8M875   2008   2007036106
508.777 — dc22

08 09 10 11 12 P 5 4 3 2 1

For Robert,
who with me calls this
beautiful land home

On the clay ridges the white oak flourished sometimes to the exclusion of all else. To one following some long clay ridge the trees opened on every hand as in a royal park, and out past their clean white weathered boles on a summer day the emerald prairie gleamed and shone to the horizon's edge.

— Thomas Macbride, 1895

Contents

Preface

I have always felt that to live most fully, people need to be in contact with the land. And to do that, they need to know something about its natural features. While Iowa now claims a growing number of publications on elements of our natural history, no single publication ties the state's natural features into a comprehensive whole. Indeed, only one earlier publication (Cooper 1982) describes the multiple natural features comprising Iowa's landscape.

This book is intended to fill the gap. It attempts to explain Iowa's natural history so that Iowans can better perceive and enjoy our native landscape. *The Emerald Horizon* is thus a book for my fellow Iowans, but it is also a book for the land, for I believe that Iowans who are knowledgeable about native species, communities, and ecological processes will better care for them.

While intended for a lay audience, this book is also appropriate for introductory coursework and may serve as a reference for experts knowledgeable about selected aspects of native Iowa. Because of its intended audience, terms that may not be understood are defined in the text, with definitions cited in the index. Although the book's details pertain specifically to Iowa, *The Emerald Horizon's* broader story can be equally well applied to surrounding states within the range of the former tallgrass prairie, which today is largely synonymous with the Corn Belt.

With so much of Iowa now transformed into a working landscape, understanding nature means comprehending the transformation process and its implications. Thus in chapters 1, 3, 4, and 5 I have included a great deal about the human history of the last 200 years as it relates to interactions with the land. Because of agriculture's dominance, its impact is emphasized, although urban transformation is also discussed. Chapter 1 also stretches back before modern human occupation to summarize the geological, ancient ecological, and archaeological features that helped shape our modern landscape, and it describes Iowa's climate.

Chapter 2 presents a picture of Iowa around 1800 just before Euroamerican settlement — the most recent period that native communities and ecological processes fully governed Iowa. Our knowledge of this period is somewhat con-jectural: the speed of Iowa's settlement and transformation means that we must now strive to understand Iowa's natural history through the altered fragments of native communities that remain. Although we can perhaps never know the full complexity of native communities once found here, historic records and modern techniques allow us to paint a broad picture of this once wild landscape.

Chapters 3, 4, and 5 examine the land transformation process, from settle-ment to the present, its influence on species and communities, and the native features that remain. Chapter 3 looks at species changes and focuses mostly on native animals; it includes detailed surveys of the four types of animals that have been best studied. Introduced plants and invasive species are also discussed. In chapters 4 and 5, the emphasis is on the plant communities that form the base upon which animals depend: Iowa's prairies, wooded lands, and the wetlands embedded within each of these.

Chapters 6 and 7 look toward the future. Chapter 6 defines techniques for restoring native communities — that is, for working to bring back their health and functions through reinstituting native species and ecological processes. Chapter 7 examines a broad variety of ways in which Iowans can nurture nature and human relationships with the natural world. The prologue and epilogue ad-dress the broader question of why we should be concerned about Iowa's natural world.

Scientific names of plants mentioned by common name in the text are in-cluded as an appendix because common names of many plants vary from region to region, and thus plant identification can be ambiguous. The list is limited to native and naturalized plants, that is, to species that today are not restricted to Iowa's gardens, croplands, and tree plantations. Taxonomy here and throughout the book follows U.S. Department of Agriculture 2007 as determined by John Kartesz of the Biota of North America Program. Scientific names of animals have not been listed, since identification of the common animals mentioned in this book is not problematic.

This book's story was pieced together from a great wealth of sources, includ-ing notes from numerous field trips, interviews with dozens of researchers and land managers, historic and modern literature, and discussions with researchers who greatly refined my perspectives. Because of the large number of informa-tion sources utilized, I have cited only those that provided the most significant or abundant information. Citations are given in one of three locations: detailed information and statistics are cited in the text as references or as personal communications, broader sources of information are listed in the bibliographic acknowledgments, and references that require explanation are cited in the notes. Web citations were accessed prior to July 2006 unless otherwise noted.

This book differs from my earlier book, *Fragile Giants*, which synthesized a wealth of established information about western Iowa's Loess Hills. In *The Emerald Horizon* I felt I was stepping onto new ground, piecing together a larger picture that is sometimes based on established research, but that also includes subject areas that have not received the research they deserve and are inadequately discussed in the literature. This is true particularly of Iowa's wooded lands. *The Emerald Horizon* emphasizes the characteristics and restoration of our native upland oak woodlands, subjects that are little discussed elsewhere but are a primary focus of today's conservation efforts. While I believe that my book represents the best of current knowledge, it is presented in part as an invitation for future explorations, with the full expectation that concepts explained herein will evolve and more refined syntheses will appear as additional Iowa-based field research is performed.

Although I had intended this book to be a comprehensive natural history, length limitations forced me to delete discussion of several worthy topics. Thus this book's coverage is uneven. Terrestrial ecosystems are stressed at the expense of aquatic ecosystems, for example, and Iowa's most unusual ecological features, such as algific talus slopes, are mentioned only in passing. Discussion of water quality, a major environmental concern, is brief. Fortunately, readers can refer to other texts for information on some of these subjects, such as Iowa's geology and archaeology.

Readers will come to know two of Iowa's classical natural historians whose quotations are sprinkled abundantly throughout the text. Thomas Macbride (1848–1934) served the University of Iowa for nearly forty years as its first professor of botany and later as university president. Macbride became one of Iowa's earliest and most eloquent spokesmen for conservation. (His last name, variously spelled in his publications, has been represented in a single manner in this book.) Macbride's colleague Bohumil Shimek (1861–1937) was likewise devoted to conservation. Shimek taught at the University of Iowa as a botany professor for nearly fifty years but was also recognized for his work in geology, paleobotany, and zoology. Both Macbride and Shimek actively researched a breadth of natural history subjects, producing an abundance of publications that today are invaluable for their descriptions of Iowa's early postsettlement natural history. Others of the same period whose citations are less abundant in this book include Louis Pammel (1862–1931), professor of botany at Iowa State College (now Iowa State University), and Samuel Calvin (1840–1911), University of Iowa natural science professor, invertebrate paleontologist, and geologist for the state of Iowa.

Were any of these gentlemen to return to Iowa today, I have no doubt that they would be confounded by how much the state has changed since their lifetimes. But I also think they would be pleased by current efforts to restore the land and reestablish native species. In these efforts, I believe they would sense a culmination of the values they promoted a century ago. These men's spirits, as well as those of Iowa's thousands of native plants and animals, have energized my writing and given it a sense of purpose. They and the many other Iowans who have cared about nature in Iowa continue to pull our research and ecological restoration work forward.

Acknowledgments

This book began as a tribute to my homeland, Johnson County, but during preparation expanded first to cover the eastern half of Iowa and then the entire state. These changes meant that the expected duration of my research and writing doubled from around three to six years. There was plenty of time, and plenty of need, for friends and colleagues to share their knowledge and to express their emotional support and their long-term belief in my efforts. Dozens of Iowans have done so, to an amazing degree. My heart goes out to all of you.

I had neither the knowledge nor the wisdom to write this book on my own. Numerous scholars and content experts across the state were exceptionally generous with their time and patience, educating me by providing information and answering questions via e-mail, telephone, and in-person communications, and by sharing literature and citations. Many then reviewed portions of the expanding manuscript. Many but not all of these munificent people are acknowledged for their personal communications in the text or are cited in the bibliographic acknowledgments or the notes. To all who have been my mentors, listed and unlisted, many, many thanks. I will remember not only the times and ideas you shared, but also your kindness in doing so, the laughs and friendship that became part of the whole. This book should bear your names as coauthors — and in my mind it does.

A few deserve special praise. John Pearson bore the brunt of my questions, answering them with his profound understanding of Iowa's natural features. John, Wayne Petersen, Paul Christiansen, and Thomas Rosburg were instrumental in shaping the coverage and concepts in this book. In addition, they and Karl Delong, Mark Vitosh, Dave Wehde, Lon Drake, Richard Baker, Gail Clingerman, Daryl Smith, Laura Jackson, Stephen Hendrix, and several others visited field sites with me, sharing perceptions and insights as well as camaraderie. These field trips were crucial to my understanding of Iowa's native communities. The oak woodland restorations owned or managed by Karl Delong, Sibylla Brown, Grinnell College, the Indian Creek Nature Center, and Driftless Land Stewardship inspired and educated me. Susan Galatowitsch deepened my appreciation of the complexity of wetlands.

Others have provided a variety of crucial services. Holly Carver invested untold hours in reshaping the manuscript into a more accessible whole, and with the rest of the University of Iowa Press staff consistently applied high standards and professionalism along with friendly aid. Mary Swander provided a much needed getaway where I could focus and write. Deborah Lewis reviewed plant nomenclature. Susan Cowles helped me locate agricultural statistics. Laurie Eash, David Egloff, Claudia McGehee, Teresa Opheim, Christine Flagler, and other friends read selected chapters and commented on the manuscript's style. Many additional people have contributed to this project's success in manners too numerous to list. All have added greatly to the quality of the book, and I thank you.

My research and writing would not have been possible without the financial and logistical support of my home institution, IIHR-Hydroscience and Engineering, and the Center for Global and Regional Environmental Research, both at the University of Iowa. My gratitude extends beyond these amenities to the continued support of the directors of these institutes and my other university colleagues. Graphics were supported by a grant from the Iowa Science Foundation, administered by the Iowa Academy of Science, and by subvention funding from the Office of the Vice President for Research, University of Iowa. I am grateful for these funds, and also for the artistry of Carl Kurtz, Casey Kohrt, Mark Müller, and Will Thomson, and for Mary Bennett's assistance in helping me locate historic photographs at the State Historical Society of Iowa. These people not only have made my book beautiful, they also will help readers visualize Iowa as it once was.

My friends have supported me and this project with their questions, smiles, and genuine interest. Hugs of thanks to all you special people. And double hugs to my entire family, from the oldest to my grandchildren Sophia, Noah, Moses, and Matvei, all of whom joined our family during this book's preparation and give me much joy. You may never know how much your love and belief have urged me on. And of course thank-you to the land and the spirits of all who inhabit it, to the oaks and anemones and woodpeckers, the fungi and the soils, just for being there.

While this book would not have been possible without the contributions of dozens of others, I take full responsibility for any errors and misinterpretations made in merging this complex information into a new whole. I look forward to others preparing future publications that further refine our understanding of this beautiful land.

Prologue

This is a book about change. About landmasses drifting through oceans to form new continents, mountain chains rising, seas sweeping across flatlands, and climates warming and cooling. It's a book about natural communities colonizing bare grit, and plants and animals following receding glaciers northward. This book accepts Earth's fluidity and nature's inexorable flux as both natural and necessary, for without these features rigidity and death would be the norm. All living systems depend on their ability to adapt to the slow but constant shifts that define Earth's history.

This is a story about people on the move. About fur-draped humans colonizing North America's vast midcontinental grasslands and then shaping the landscape with their fires. And a later wave of human migration, this time flowing westward from the Atlantic. It's about the dreams and desires of nineteenth-century settlers who trudged onto Iowa's prairies leading their cattle and hogs, trusting that if familiar farming methods were applied to virgin soils, the earth would feed them abundantly — which it did.[1] It's about these settlers and their progeny toiling to transform Iowa into a land whose bounty was funneled into cattle and croplands rather than bison and butterflies.

This is a book about human expectations accelerating nature's changes to a bewildering whirlwind and our unspoken assumption that nature will always adapt — that the natural world, and Earth itself, can withstand whatever we demand of it. Today there are growing signs that nature is rejecting this assumption. Our collective impacts seem to have thrown Iowa's natural world severely out of balance. There are, for example, disturbing signs that even Iowa's most

1. Throughout the book, I use the term "settler" to refer to Euroamericans who first entered Iowa in the 1800s. Likewise "presettlement" and "settlement-era" ecosystems refer to native communities that predate and postdate the early 1800s. For the sake of simplicity, I do not always use the prefix "Euroamerican" when referring to these people or this period. This usage is not intended to ignore or trivialize the Native Americans who had initially settled this land thousands of years earlier, whose bonds to the landscape I recognize and respect.

common, most widespread native organisms like oak trees, bullsnakes, and blue jays are decreasing in number. These declines are indications that incremental pressures may be outweighing the ability of Iowa's life-support systems to function in a basic manner.

Some may ask whether this truly matters. We Iowans occupy some of the richest agricultural soils in the world. Isn't it right and good to focus our land on feeding an increasingly crowded and hungry world, rather than reserving some areas as habitat for Earth's native diversity?

There is little question that Iowa will remain primarily a working landscape, but natural communities and their biological diversity are vital to our working lands. This is most evident when considering nature's many ecological goods and services, those things that healthy natural ecosystems provide freely, every day, as a matter of course. Native birds, bats, and insects pollinate orchards and crops. They join spiders, viral diseases, and other natural enemies in destroying 99 percent of crop pests and weed seeds. Nature manufactures and purifies the air we breathe, cleanses water, generates fertile soil, and holds the earth in place. Natural ecosystems provide timber and meat, help stabilize climate, moderate droughts and floods and other weather extremes, and cycle water, energy, and nutrients. Nature detoxifies pollutants, renders pathogens harmless, and decomposes organic wastes (Daily et al. 1997).

These and countless other free ecological goods and services are fundamental to life, yet easy to take for granted. Their worldwide value is estimated at roughly $38 trillion annually (in year 2000 dollars), a figure similar to the annual gross national product of the entire globe.[2] As nature's services disappear, we attempt to replace them — with technologies to purify water and air and with chemical additives to fertilize soils, for example. But these replacements are usually less satisfactory than nature's originals, and they are expensive. The disappearance of nature's ecosystem services would lead to worldwide economic collapse and the dissolution of human society as we know it. In the long run, it will be easier to care for the natural world so that it can continue to nurture life, as it has done

2. Costanza et al. 1997, looking at over 100 attempts to value ecosystem goods and services, estimated their aggregated annual value at $18 to $61 trillion (updated by Balmford et al. 2002 to year 2000 U.S. dollars), a rough average of around $38 trillion. These figures were similar to the global gross national product. However, Balmford et al. 2002 prefer to express the economic worth of natural habitats in other terms — as the benefit:cost ratio of a global program to conserve what remains of wild nature, which they conclude is at least 100:1

since life began. This book suggests methods for doing so. It looks to historic natural ecosystems as models for future ecological wholeness and health, environmental sustainability, and long-term stability.

Readjusting the balance between Iowa's natural and intensively utilized lands will provide many additional amenities. Natural lands are crucial to the quality of life. They constitute major recreational sites, attract people to Iowa, stimulate tourism, and support the state's economy. Prairies, forests, and wetlands are part of our cultural heritage. They serve as living museums, refuges for biological diversity, and sites for education and scientific research.

The natural world also remains a source of intellectual stimulation and creative inspiration, delight, and challenge. Here we are confronted with ancient and seemingly permanent entities that make us feel both very large and very small. Many sense mystery and the unknown as well as beauty and wonderment in nature. Some find a spiritual connection and healing. Perhaps this sense of being embraced within something large and stable explains why many people return to nature for relaxation and solace. At a deep level, the need for intimate experience with the natural world seems to be built into the human psyche and is, some suggest, vital to mental health. And finally, safeguarding nature's systems and native species here in Iowa is a way of guaranteeing that those who follow will enjoy the delights that graced our own childhoods: chasing fireflies on summer nights, falling asleep to the chorus of frogs and katydids.

Native Iowan Aldo Leopold, father of the modern conservation movement, argued for nature's preservation not because of its benefits to humans, but rather on moral grounds. In *A Sand County Almanac*, Leopold expounded on other species' innate right to existence. There he also coined the term "land ethic" for a concept that "enlarges the boundaries of the community to include soils, waters, plants, and animals, or collectively: the land." The resulting ecological conscience, he believed, would reflect "a conviction of individual responsibility for the health of the land" (1949: 204, 221).

Iowa's Euroamerican settlers knew nothing about today's arguments for preserving the natural order. They listened to a different set of directives. Just as we cannot moderate the intensity of their land-transforming efforts, neither should we condemn their actions. These settlers provided us not only with the ability to feed and shelter ourselves today but also with a culture that has served Iowa and the nation well — one that values education, hard work, and high moral standards coupled with a strong impulse toward social reform and justice.

But with time comes hindsight and broader understanding. Today we can envision Iowa a hundred years from now. We can picture new beginnings, shaped by celebrating and nurturing nature's remaining gifts. Iowa still exudes beauty and life in abundance, along with wide-open spaces and connections to the earth and its elemental forces. While our actions have shrunken nature's grasp on the land, they have not wiped it clean. Most of our original native plants and smaller animals remain. Iowa's land has provided many examples of its ability to recover and heal. The earth has its memories, and given half a chance, will speak its mind freely. Hope and resilience remain.

Future possibilities can be sensed when visiting one of Iowa's nature preserves or better ecological restorations. Most are small. But go there and imagine times past when the wonders of nature were overwhelming. Picture yourself coming over a rise and finding a windblown meadow of wildflowers alive with the buzzing of nectar-feeding bees and seed-seeking goldfinches. Imagine a spectacle of scent, color, and song. Envision it blown up until it surrounds you. Throw in a bison, a stream with swans and cranes, a herd of elk. And listen to the wind, constant and true. Then, in your mind's eye, you will have a glimpse of what this land of ours once fostered. This book suggests that you take that glimpse and cast it to the horizon, using it to imagine what this land of ours once more can become.

The Emerald Horizon

1   Setting the Stage

Iowa's broad acres, "fair as a garden of the lord," spread from river to river before a human foot had pressed the surface of the planet. … Seasons rolled by the same as now. … The struggle for life … was here yearly carried to the final issue. Man at last joined the struggle, and long before there were any historians, events of historical importance were enacted within the limits of Iowa.
— Samuel Calvin, 1893

We think that we walk on solid ground, that the earth under our feet is inviolable. But this rectangle of land we today call Iowa has always been restless turf. Only the rate of its ceaseless transformation has changed with time. While in past millennia the landscape was modified at glacial speeds, now the character of our planet is transformed at ever-faster tempos, speeded onward by technological innovations and the cravings of growing numbers of people.

Today the speed and magnitude of Earth's ongoing transformation have reduced the ability of nature's systems to function with integrity. And we search for methods of regaining the environmental stability that once was afforded as a matter of course. To plot future directions with wisdom and coherence, we must try to understand our landscape's genesis and historic capabilities — commencing with the creation of the land we now inhabit.

A Brief History of Land and Life

Iowa's origins might be traced to the birth of our planet around 4.5 billion years ago, when Earth coalesced from dust and gasses swirling in the solar nebula. Geologists believe that the major continental crusts emerged about 600 to 700 million years later, when lighter components of the molten mass cooled and solidified. Soon thereafter, these continental shields began their ceaseless wander of the planet's surface, migrating as huge discrete slabs of rigid rocks (tectonic plates) that slid over deeper, more pliable layers. Time and again the shields merged to form a single landmass, only to break into large pieces that sometimes reconfigured the borders of the tectonic plates. During its wanderings, our embryonic state spent considerable time near or south of the equator.

By the Cenozoic Era, or Age of Mammals, which began about 65 million years ago, Iowa had reached its modern location on the planet and nestled into the heart of the North American tectonic plate. Periodically advancing seas that had flushed the midcontinent for about half a billion years, leaving behind layers of limestone and other sedimentary rock thousands of feet thick, were giving way to dry ground that was reshaped by eons of weathering and erosion. Simple life-forms that first appeared perhaps 3.5 billion years ago had evolved into diverse mammals and flowering plants. North America's climate was changing, in part because the rising Rocky Mountains were drying midcontinental air by blocking the flow of moist Pacific air. The stage was set for the appearance of North America's drought-adapted midcontinental grasslands.

Grasses developed and spread across the dry interiors of most continents during the Miocene, becoming firmly established over vast tracts of mid North America by five to seven million years ago or even earlier. In northeastern Nebraska, the discovery of large concentrations of animal and grass seed fossils reveal that savanna-like grasslands covered the region about twelve million years ago. Communities were likely very similar to those of today, although species differed. The expansion of the world's grasslands was accompanied by the development of fast-running grazers and small burrowing animals. In North America, three-toed and one-toed horses, llamas, camels, mastodons, and rhinoceroses were among the common mammals, with fossils of all of these found in Iowa (Ashfall Fossil Beds State Historical Park 2006; Risser et al. 1981: 26, 31; Holmes Semken, personal communication).

About 2.5 million years ago, a dramatic change in course was signaled: the climate became cooler and wetter, and the amount of snow falling surpassed the amount melting each year. This shift triggered periodic massive glacial advances. Continental ice sheets thousands of feet thick usurped enormous amounts of Earth's water, lowering coastline sea levels by 300 to 400 feet. Glaciers crept southward across Iowa and into northern Missouri many times between 2.5 million and 500,000 years ago. Later glacial advances were less extensive in Iowa. Around 150,000 years ago, the leading edge of a continental ice sheet nudged its way from the east into southeastern Iowa. More recently, a broad tongue of advancing ice (the Des Moines Lobe) lapped southward into north-central Iowa, advancing to today's city of Des Moines. This occurred several times, the most recent such advance being around 15,000 years ago. The melting back of that ice around 12,000 years ago signaled the termination of Iowa's glaciation.

Each advance of massive ice sheets scraped the land's surface, leveling hills and filling valleys. The receding ice also left its remains: uneven deposits of unconsolidated boulders, gravels, and smaller particles. Rocks of all sizes collected by glaciers from shield rocks that were exposed farther north were carried into Iowa or laid down by melting ice. In addition, voluminous meltwaters flowing from receding glaciers carried particles from rocks that had been pulverized by glaciers. Loess — silt particles deposited in broad river valleys that were picked up by the wind and redeposited on uplands — covered much of Iowa and became the basis of modern soils. Iowa's glacial deposits in places exceed 600 feet in depth.

Glaciers, their deposits, and water's subsequent erosion created the distinctive landforms that shaped native prairies, woodlands, forests, and wetlands as well as Euroamerican settlers' subsequent land-use patterns. Iowa's youngest and most recently ice-covered terrain, our state's north-central Des Moines Lobe, remains fairly flat with poor surface drainage. Lakes and wetlands abounded here in presettlement times. In contrast, the steeply rolling southern half of Iowa, last covered by glaciers over half a million years ago, has had sufficient time for water and wind to dissect glacial deposits. Here even-topped hillcrests reveal the approximate level of the once-continuous glaciated land surface, which now is interspersed with deeply incised drainage networks. Broad regions to the east and west of the Des Moines Lobe are characterized by their generally gently rolling, open topographies. These sweeping landscapes are thought to have been massively eroded and vigorously planed by the cold, harsh conditions spun from nearby glaciers: turbulent winds, extensive freezing and thawing, and the slumping and washing of surface materials. Iowa's far northeastern corner and the Loess Hills (found in a thin north-south belt in western Iowa, just east of the Missouri River floodplain) claim the state's greatest topographic relief and variation. The Loess Hills' loose powdery loess, up to 200 feet in depth, has been carved by water and wind into the highly dissected landscape we see today. Northeastern Iowa, the state's "Little Switzerland," is dominated by outcroppings of sedimentary bedrock, which is abundantly displayed in bluffs bordering deeply incised streams. Bordering and dissecting Iowa are broad, flat river valleys, some of which were widened tremendously by the great volumes of glacial meltwater they once carried (Prior 1991).

The grassland complexes that were present by 5 to 7 million years ago dominated much of the midcontinent until glaciation commenced about 2.5 million years ago. Then, as ice and cold climates repeatedly pulsed southward, plant species today typical of colder, more northerly locations did the same. Tundra and coniferous forest organisms moved southward and established themselves in the Midwest. Whenever the climate moderated, many of these cold-region plants and animals followed the retreating glaciers back to the north and recolonized newly bared land. During warmer interglacial times, grasslands may have moved back into the Midwest from southerly regions, their return fostered by dry air masses.

Such a story of migrating vegetation is told by the plant, small mammal, and snail fossil record that commenced about 33,000 years ago. These fossils reveal that, in Iowa, from that time until about 25,000 years ago, modern prairie species were present in open parklands of aspen, willow, and spruce, which were probably analogous to the aspen parklands of today's northern Great Plains. Then as the climate started cooling once again, wetlands with spruce abounded (resembling the modern boreal forest of southern Canada), joined by larch in eastern Iowa. The climate continued to cool, and glaciers again flowed toward Iowa. When the cold reached its maximum, around 21,000 to 16,500 years ago, parts of Iowa claimed an open arctic environment with tundra animals and plants and widely scattered spruce trees.

As the climate moderated and the last swells of glacial meltwater receded, Iowa's plant communities started their return to a semblance of today. First the tundra was replaced by spruce-larch forests, then about 11,000 years ago these gave way to a succession of deciduous trees (first black ash and birch, later oak, elm, basswood, ironwood, and others), and finally to grasslands.

Ice Age fossils tell us of a succession of diverse mammals that roamed the midcontinent, some evolving in place, others immigrating here from South America (for example, sloths and their relatives) or Eurasia (for example, horses and bison). Many, collectively called the megafauna, were exceptionally large. Of animals present in Iowa toward the end of the Ice Age, a portion — bison, elk, bears, white-tailed deer, wolves, and many smaller species — remained here into modern times. Other animals — caribou, reindeer, musk ox, moose, and smaller affiliates — are now found in colder climes and presumably followed the melting glaciers northward. And still other ancient Iowa residents — elephant-like mammoths and mastodons, giant beavers, giant ground sloths, peccaries, camels, and horses — passed into extinction in North America, many suddenly around 10,000 years ago. While major extinctions occurred around the world about this time, none were as severe as North America's. With the departure of many of the Ice Age animals, a greatly impoverished grassland fauna replaced the diverse assemblage of glacial times (Holmes Semken, personal communication; Alex 2000: 41–44; Anderson 1998: 343–344).

Pollen records tell us that by 9,000 years ago, the modern prairie was creeping back into western Iowa, nurtured by a warming climate and dry air masses. As prairie plants pushed eastward across the state, they displaced deciduous woodlands. By 8,000 years ago, the prairie extended eastward approximately to a north-south line passing through today's Iowa City. Then curiously the prairie's migration halted, probably held at bay by moist air sweeping northward from the Gulf of Mexico. Oaks and other deciduous trees maintained their dominance of more easterly lands. This pattern was broken around 5,500 years ago, when grasslands again surged eastward to cross the Mississippi River and dominate a dry, tongue-shaped extension that reached through Illinois and beyond, a vast prairie peninsula that represented modern tallgrass prairie at its maximum expanse. By 3,000 years ago, the return of a moister climate was shrinking that prairie tongue by allowing patchy oak woodlands to reclaim territory as far west as eastern and southern Iowa. Thus was formed the shifting prairie-woodland mosaic found by Iowa's Euroamerican settlers (Baker et al. 1992; Richard Baker, personal communication).

The prairie's eastward surge 5,500 years ago was correlated with the expansion of an especially warm, dry climate that favored drought-tolerant grasslands. But another factor may have encouraged this eastward extension and almost certainly favored the easternmost tallgrass prairie's survival into modern times: fire. Lightning-ignited fire was likely a routine summertime component of midcontinental grasslands since their first appearance. Here, as around the world, grasslands and wildfire evolved together, living out a congenial codependency: flames stimulated growth of grasses and their fire-dependent associates, with the grasses providing abundant and readily ignitable fuel. Burn frequency surely increased when prehistoric big-game hunters brought knowledge about igniting fire to North America. As was true of nomadic peoples around the globe, midwestern Native Americans routinely set fires knowing these would ease travel, open woodlands, increase visibility, decrease dangerous wildfires near villages, control pests, and produce lush vegetation that would attract game. They executed carefully planned fires to control animal movement during bison and deer hunts, clear areas around campsites, and remove trees from garden plots. Fire in woodlands, they knew, aided the gathering of acorns and nuts and stimulated fruit and nut production. Native Americans extended the midsummer burn season to spring and fall, and may have burned some areas annually. They fired the midwestern landscape as naturally as we mow lawns today (Richard Baker, personal communication; Anderson 1990; McClain and Elzinga 1994; Brose et al. 2001).

Fire remained a spectacular landscape component well into Euroamerican settlement. Thomas Macbride described autumnal settlement-era fires in this way:

> Sometimes their coming was announced by smoke which filled the air by day with filmy haze, and at evening rolled in cloudy masses down the low watersheds. . . . More frequently by night a pale red tint appeared along the horizon's edge. . . . [At length] we saw the painted flames, like distant choppy waves on a sunrise-tinted sea; so slowly they came on, the very poetry of combustion, as tuft after tuft of tall blue-stem went up in lambent blaze. . . . But if once upon a prairie-fire the wind should rise, then came the storm, a fiery blizzard of destruction. The flames sped along the ground with marvelous rapidity, the air was burdened with ashes and flying sparks, and great smoke wreaths were rolled along in ever increasing volume, darkening the sun. Whole hill-sides burned as by a single blaze, and down in the valleys where the grass was high the flames were higher still and the roar terrific. No living creature could stand before the storm. (1895: 347–348)

By the time Macbride wrote these words, Iowa's ecosystems were already being altered by Euroamerican settlers. How then are we to detail the character of nature in Iowa just before settlement and trace its subsequent changes?

Clues come from a number of sources, including early records (settlers' journal descriptions, sketches, and photographs), logging and game records, sequential maps, and scientific surveys. These investigatory tools can often be used in tandem to decipher a site's ecological past (see Egan and Howell 2005).

Especially significant are the earliest site-specific vegetation descriptions, those of the General Land Office's (GLO) survey notes. All of Iowa was surveyed by the U.S. government between 1832 and 1859 to aid in the disposal of land. Surveyors traveled the boundaries of each mile-square section, taking scant field notes and recording the boundaries of prairies, swamps, and tree groves. They also identified and recorded distances to witness (or bearing) trees at the corners of each section. These surveys were not perfect (Thomson 1987). Surveyors' records included inconsistencies, errors, subjective assessments, and undecipherable terms. Imagination is required to understand terms such as "barrens," which have no known correlate in modern Iowa. Some sites were surveyed after wooded areas had already been cleared. And scant attention was given to prairies. Despite their inadequacies, GLO records provide a valuable broad-scale tool for understanding Iowa's settlement-era plant communities.

Modern soil maps provide a far more detailed picture of the location of pre-settlement prairies and wooded areas. Nearly all soils in Iowa were formed from the same parent material: unconsolidated deposits left by glacial activity, wind-deposited loess, or water-deposited alluvium. However, prairies and trees each added organic matter to these mineral deposits in a distinctive manner and, by doing so, produced characteristic traits that distinguish resulting soils. Prairie soils display a rich black color throughout the thick topsoil and a dark subsoil layer. The dark color is due to large quantities of organic matter from decomposing roots, fungi, and soil organisms. Native prairie soils have a granular structure, have little acidity, and hold their component particles firmly in place.

Soils formed under woodlands and forests, in contrast, have a dark gray, very thin topsoil of only one to four inches, immediately above a grayish brown layer (four to ten inches thick) from which the clay has been leached. These overlie a distinct lighter layer. The soils contain far less organic matter, and this entered primarily from the ground surface via decomposing leaves plowed in by earthworms. Woodland and forest soils are less granular, less fertile, and more acidic than prairie soils (Oschwald et al. 1965; Michael Sucik, personal communication).

Maps of Iowa's soil types, historic vegetation based on GLO records, and more recent vegetation are now available on the Iowa Geological Survey and Iowa Department of Natural Resources Web sites (see also Anderson 1996).

The First Humans

Changes in Iowa's landscape were tempered by human occupation for thousands of years before Euroamerican settlers speeded and intensified the land's transformation. The first humans wandered into today's Iowa at least 13,000 years ago, when climate and vegetation reflected the diminishing presence of the last ice sheets. Small tribes were presumably drawn toward North America's midcontinent by abundant large-animal herds. These people, along with many other animals and plants, had entered the New World from northeastern Asia by traipsing eastward across Beringia, a land bridge to modern Alaska. Beringia, now underneath the Bering Strait, had emerged as expanding glaciers claimed oceanic waters and lowered sea levels around the world. The small, highly mobile bands used stone-tipped spears and darts to kill the large Ice Age animals then present — mammoths, camels, early horses, and bison, among others, which provided meat, fat, skins, sinew, and bone — and to hunt smaller game as well.

The diffuse human bands were forced to deal with tumultuous environmental changes: evolving landscapes, major climatic shifts, migrating plant communities, and massive animal extinctions. During the next several thousand years, as the Midwest's climate warmed and drier grasslands slowly reclaimed their dominance, humans developed a variety of new subsistence patterns. Their foraging and hunting efforts expanded to include waterfowl, fish, and shellfish. They increasingly collected, preserved, and stored acorns and other wild nuts, fruits, greens, seeds, and tubers. Plant-processing equipment such as grinding stones appeared. Dogs were domesticated. People established trade networks that brought the first metallic artifacts as well as stone tools into today's Iowa.

With time, regional adaptations became more pronounced, with peoples of eastern Iowa's open woodlands utilizing deer and numerous smaller animals and plants, while those of western Iowa's open prairies continued the big-game traditions and communal bison hunts of earlier periods. As human populations grew, small nomadic units slowly gave way to integrated semipermanent villages. Seasonal hunting and gathering forays continued to provide various foods. By 3,000 years ago, a few native plants were being cultivated in Iowa. Groves of hickories and oaks near human habitations may have been managed to increase their nut production.

In the following centuries, cultivation of plants expanded to include gourds and squash, common sunflowers, and several small native grains (for example, goosefoot, little barley, knotweed). Some of these were domesticated — that is, new genetic strains emerged as their growers purposefully selected seeds with desirable traits, such as large size. Agriculture's gradual intensification permitted human population growth, a more sedentary life-style, and larger permanent villages. Corn dominated Iowa's agriculture, providing a reliable, storable food source just as it does today. It grew well in the period's warm, moist climate. Other food supplies also were becoming more dependable; production of native seed crops increased, and people collected an increasingly diverse assemblage of wild plants, game, and aquatic animals. Hunters now used bows and arrows to kill bison and other game. Seasonal hunting and gathering forays continued.

About 1,000 years ago, between 950 and 1200 or so, tribal societies and distinct village cultures emerged across Iowa. Their relatively large permanent villages shared several traits. All relied primarily on intensive horticulture of corn and other crops, although residents also hunted and utilized wild plants for food and medicine. The tribes located their villages near river bottoms with easily worked, fertile alluvial soils where crops could be cultivated and protected. In western Iowa, villagers also planted raised garden beds. Some fortified their villages with earthen embankments or ditches and palisades, a probable indication of increasing warfare resulting from growing populations, the desire for new territory, and attempts to protect garden produce and trade items. Trade networks tied the villages to Cahokia, an influential community near present-day St. Louis, which with its surroundings held perhaps 10,000 to 15,000 residents and is thought to have been administered by complex religious and political hierarchies. Western Iowa's horticultural villages were mysteriously abandoned by 1300. Village horticulturalists may have migrated elsewhere or been integrated into other cultural groups.

What remained across Iowa were Indians collectively called the Oneota, a poorly understood group of Native Americans appearing in today's Iowa around 1200 who were widespread throughout the tallgrass prairie region. The Oneota utilized virtually all available avenues of food production: they hunted bison, deer, elk, and numerous smaller animals; harvested fish and mussels; foraged for wild plants; grew and dried wild fruits; and intensively cultivated corn, squash, beans, and sometimes small native grains — foods that they stored in abundant storage pits. They lived in both diffuse settlements and compact villages.

The Oneota are thought to have been ancestral to historic tribes such as the Oto, Winnebago, Missouri, and Ioway. All four ranged into Iowa, with the Ioway (who gave Iowa its name) dominating territories and living throughout the state well into historic times. About 1,000 Ioway are estimated to have inhabited Iowa in 1700 (Alex 2000: 220). Their life-style closely resembled that of the prehistoric Oneota, with dependence on both hunting and horticulture of corn, beans, squash, and tobacco. Permanent villages were seasonally emptied for bison hunts. The Ioway's acquisition of firearms and horses by the mid 1700s aided their mobility and hunting efforts.

This stream of people and evolving cultures invoked many changes on the land. The sudden demise of much of the Ice Age megafauna 10,000 years ago was likely caused in part by nomadic big-game hunters overkilling these large meat sources, with disease and environmental upheavals also playing a role. In later millennia, human-set fires probably encouraged the eastward spread of prairies into the prairie peninsula. Later, when the climate became moister, fire certainly helped maintain these prairies and the open character of interspersed oak woodlands. People also reshaped the composition and distribution of plant communities through horticulture, which both introduced and produced new varieties of cultivated plants. By 1500, garden plots throughout the Upper Mississippi valley specialized in four crops, none of which were native to the region: corn (with origins in south-central and western Mexico), garden or common beans (then only recently introduced, originally from Central or South America), squash (with probable origins in the Gulf Coast region), and annual sunflowers (originating in the southwestern United States or Mexico) (Lentz 2000: chaps. 4, 9; Delcourt and Delcourt 2004).

Iowa's landscape was locally subjected to other, lesser human manipulations. Native people cleared land for gardens and villages and pocked the earth with middens, hearths, and storage pits. They littered the landscape with discarded tools and broken pottery. They may have overexploited local resources when gathering wild plants, hunting and fishing for wild animals, and cutting trees for fuel and building purposes. Disturbed sites were prime for invasion by weedy species, which must have proliferated near habitations. People transported species when traveling, trading, and foraging. They likely tended wooded areas to increase nut-producing trees and shrubs. Village and garden sites may have eroded and released sediment into streambeds. As populations increased and settlements became more compact and permanent, human impacts surely grew more intense.

However, excluding their use of fire, Native Americans possessed neither the numbers nor the technologies to alter vast biological communities substantially. Disturbed areas remained relatively localized and small, and were embedded within a matrix of native communities ready to reinvade and restore the land. Thus, on the whole, Native Americans were part of a sustainable, stable, and self-sufficient system, one where the rivers ran clean, the prairie soils grew thicker and richer, and thousands of plants and animals continued their reproduction and massive annual migrations.

Columbus's 1492 voyage initiated a series of traumatic events that broke down Native Americans' social and political life and reshaped their interactions with the land. Native Americans were forced to deal with the destruction and dislocation of their settlements, massive migrations, depopulation, formation of new economic and political alliances, and creation of new economic patterns.

Perhaps most destructive was the spread of European infectious illnesses to

Native Americans, who had no natural resistance. Of the four million or more people inhabiting North America prior to 1492, 90 percent may have died from smallpox, measles, influenza, and other diseases that were passed from one village to another (Delcourt and Delcourt 2004: 163). This massive depopulation certainly altered land-use and hunting pressures, possibly allowing bison herds to increase in size and large game to expand eastward, which in turn would have altered native vegetation.

The initiation of formalized trade networks created an export economy that fed midwestern skins, hides, robes, and furs primarily to Europe. The desire for control of fur-bearing resources caused warfare to break out among eastern tribes. Conflicts sent waves of Native Americans fleeing westward as far as Iowa. About this time, European trade goods first appeared in Ioway villages, concrete signs that long before the Ioway ever saw a white face, European influences radiated westward like a series of shock waves. With time, Native Americans abandoned traditional tools fashioned from nature for items imported from the East. They replaced pottery vessels with kettles, animal skins with blankets and cloth, stone cutting tools with iron knives, and native weapons with guns.

The first known face-to-face contact between the Ioway and Caucasians, in this case a French Jesuit, occurred in 1676 in an eastern Wisconsin village where the Ioway had come to trade. A few years later, a French trader visited an Ioway village in northeastern Iowa. These contacts initiated Iowa's historic period, with its relentless press of westward-moving white populations and their intensifying effects. Soon thereafter the Ioway were drawn into the beaver pelt trade with the French and then into direct contact with traders, trappers, explorers, and missionaries. The Ioways' subsequent migrations across Iowa were shaped in part by the search for abundant bison and other trade animals.

In all, as many as eighteen different Native groups pulsed into Iowa during the historic period, nearly all originating in territories to the east and moving west in response to ongoing hostilities, the competing interests of Europeans and Americans, and the press of growing eastern populations. Native groups remained in Iowa only until they were pushed farther westward. One exception was the Meskwaki (or Fox), who with their allies the Sauk first fled into Iowa in the 1730s when they were pursued by a French force that threatened to annihilate them. Unlike most other tribes, the Meskwaki and Sauk remained in Iowa and gradually displaced the Ioway. The Meskwaki combined hunting, gathering, and horticulture with trapping and trading. They also mined, smelted, and traded lead along the Upper Mississippi River, activities that had been carried out by other Native Americans since the late 1600s. A century later (1788) the Meskwaki granted mining rights to the French Canadian trader Julien Dubuque, who commenced large-scale lead operations near the city that today bears his name.

The lure of trade goods and the new fur trade–focused economic order instigated profound changes that played out in the treatment of the land. Trapping and hunting for export replaced subsistence use of native animals and signaled a shift away from self-sufficiency. Native Americans became increasingly dependent on Euroamerican traders and their goods. The trade economy likely led to overexploitation and declines of fur-bearing species such as beaver, the backbone of the North American fur industry. Such declines could have altered natural processes — the removal of beaver and beaver ponds, for example, causing significant hydrological alterations. Other trade items included honey, meat, feathers, finished clothing, and maple sugar. Native Americans tapped sugar maple trees by cutting deep Vs into their trunks, a practice that eventually killed the trees and may have helped limit their spread.

However, alterations of native systems remained sufficiently limited to allow Euroamericans to enter a land of abundance with diverse native species, communities, and natural processes. Today we tend either to use land very intensively, reshaping it for extensive agriculture or housing, or to leave it alone. Either extreme changes the vegetation dramatically. But Native Americans used the entire landscape with moderation. They nudged native species, communities, and processes to meet human needs without eliminating or replacing them. Thus for around 13,000 years both humans and natural communities were sustained.

This balanced interplay between humans and nature has disintegrated rapidly during the last two centuries, commencing with the departure from Iowa of most Native Americans. In the early 1800s the Ioway were gradually pushed westward as the Meskwaki and Sauk competed for trading sites and increasingly pressed their own claims for Iowa territory. Growing American interests and settlements following the Louisiana Purchase of 1803 (which made Iowa's land part of the United States) also forced the Ioway to relocate multiple times. Finally in 1838 the Ioway signed a treaty ceding all their lands between the Mississippi and Missouri rivers, and they were moved onto reservations to the west. They were followed shortly by the Meskwaki and Sauk, who since the early 1800s had ceded more and more land to the American government. The Black Hawk War in 1832 comprised an unsuccessful and tragic Sauk attempt to resist the American incursion. While many of the Meskwaki and Sauk were formally relocated outside Iowa in 1845, in 1856 the Iowa legislature voted to approve the Meskwaki tribe's request to purchase land along the Iowa River for tribal occupation and use. For decades hence, Meskwaki who lived on the Iowa settlement continued their traditional hunting, foraging, and maple sugaring throughout the larger eastern Iowa countryside. Today the Meskwaki land near Tama remains an independent Native American settlement.

Land Transfer and Transformation

In the mid 1800s authority over Iowa's land was removed from the dominion of natural systems and Native peoples and placed under the governance of Euroamerican immigrants. This transfer of power, which signaled an accelerating transformation that eroded traits that had characterized Iowa's landscape for eons — long-term biological diversity, stability, and sustainability — initiated many of the environmental problems we face today.

The earliest Euroamerican settlers built and heated their homes and fenced their livestock with Iowa-grown wood, obtained food and medicines locally with a shotgun and gathering basket, drank crystalline water from any stream, and grew crops on soils so rich that they required no fertilizers. All human necessities were free for the taking. However, the self-sufficient frontier homestead was short-lived, indeed nonexistent in parts of the state. Only a short distance to the east lay a settled landscape with an abundance of factories, technological innovations, and raw materials. Within a few years of arrival, settlers tied themselves to this eastern meshwork of civilization and imported diverse supplies with ease. Thus Iowa's settlement was faster, easier, and more predictable and uniform than that of states to the east and west.

Equally rapidly, farmers started producing sufficient excess so they could market agricultural products and export meat and grains to eastern populations. Even before settlers shipped expendable agricultural products eastward, the exported skins of native animals tied our land to the world economy, thus initiating the mining of Iowa's wildlife, soil, and water reserves for profit. Ties to eastern states allowed settlers to superimpose economic and cultural operating systems developed in distant locales, rather than forcing site-specific applications more closely melded to Iowa's unique native resources and environments.

Iowa was officially opened to pioneer settlement on June 1, 1833, and permanent settlers started to surge across the Mississippi River. The Sauk and Meskwaki had ceded eastern Iowa the previous year by agreeing to the Black Hawk

Purchase, a land transfer to the federal government that was conceived as punishment for inciting the Black Hawk War. Indian inhabitants were to vacate the purchased land by June 1.

The earliest new arrivals were squatters. They were unable to purchase land legally until it had been surveyed by the federal government, a process that commenced in 1836. Two years later the government offered land for sale and opened the first of Iowa's government land offices. Land sold at $1.25 an acre, a price that was maintained through much of the century. About a third of Iowa's land was dispersed through cash purchase from the federal government. Other major land dispersements included military land warrants granted to soldiers for wartime service (40 percent of Iowa's land) and land grants to railroad companies to help them finance the construction of tracks across the state (12 percent) (Bogue 1963: 30).

Once settlement had begun, its speed was fostered by the press of a land-hungry population in eastern states. Iowa's first census, taken in 1836, recorded 10,531 residents, a number that more than doubled (to 22,859 residents) by the time Iowa acquired independent territorial status in 1838. Early settlers spread inland along major watercourses and from there onto uplands. Settlement generally swept from east to west, with northwestern Iowa being settled last. By 1846, when Iowa acquired statehood and assumed its present boundaries, the state boasted 96,088 residents (Schwieder 1996: 48). Five years later, the last of Iowa's lands passed from the hands of Native Americans into those of the federal government.

By 1870, Iowa had come to the end of the frontier era and had clearly demonstrated its potential as a major agricultural region. Iowa was by then mostly settled: its 1,194,020 residents were scattered in farms and small towns throughout the state. Population density had soared to 21.5 persons per square mile, up from just 3.5 in 1850. By 1900, Iowa claimed about 2.2 million residents, a number that then crept upward more slowly to 2.6 million in 1950 and 2.9 million in 2000. Since 1960, Iowa's population density has hovered around 50 people per square mile (State Data Center Program 2006).

The rapidly burgeoning population's actions were shaped in large part by the settlers' attitudes and desires. From the start, these pivoted around profit-driven principles that had governed land development across the continent. Settlers' expectations reached beyond reaping a subsistence. They approached land as a commodity that could be owned, a raw material to be manipulated for producing surpluses that would increase personal wealth. This approach is significant because it assumed transformation of the land and its native communities into something defined as useful — a transformation that occurred in Iowa more intensely and completely than in any other state. In rural areas, usefulness equated with agricultural productivity; settlement-era land speculators applied the same ethic to town development schemes across the state, in the hopes of reaping fabulous profits.

While agricultural productivity soared and towns coalesced, the state's game was depleted, large trees were cleared, native pastures were decimated, waters were sullied, and soils were washed downslope and downstream (fig. 1). For the most part, these environmental costs went unrecognized or ignored. The assessment of one settler — that he had "transformed a wilderness into a garden of wealth and beauty" — seemed to be the generally accepted viewpoint (Wilson 1901: 22). Sometimes environmental costs were seen as the necessary price of development. And sometimes the transformation was approached as a moral imperative, as imposing fulfillment on a presettlement landscape perceived as "just as it was at creation's dawn, lonely, desolate, still," a land hungering for the "labor in subduing and cultivating the rich soil of Iowa" (Patterson n.d.: 88). But all in all, justification for nature's transformation and its costs was not required. The short-term benefits were so great, the profits so immediate, that losses in the landscape's long-term stability simply paled in comparison.

Not all voices favored the land's total domestication. "About all we have done with the wild fruit of Iowa is summed up in its destruction," wrote the settler John Springer in his reminiscences (1924: 12). In response to such sentiments, Iowa in 1857 passed legislation to protect prairie-chickens, and soon thereafter legal measures and private efforts were adopted to restrict wasteful fishing and preserve wild animals. But nineteenth-century game laws and private efforts were not enforced and thus had little effect. This situation was reversed toward the end of that century, when the nation was shocked by the evaporation of the tremendous bison herds and widespread slaughter of birds for feathers and meat. Iowa then joined the nation in a back-to-nature movement and in promoting legislation focused on conserving the birds and game that remained.

In the twentieth century, our state demonstrated creativity in multiple conservation strategies. During the 1920s and 1930s, Iowa became a leader in the nation's then-vibrant state park movement and was selected for hosting the first national conference on state parks. Because of its ambitious long-range conservation plan, Iowa in 1933 received the first federal Civilian Conservation Corps camps west of the Mississippi. This New Deal program, initiated during the

Fig. 1. The transformation of Iowa's sweeping prairies and wooded lands into dissected agricultural lands occurred within a few years. The environmental costs of this transformation started to appear almost immediately. Note in this 1875 sketch, for example, that an eroded streambed has already replaced what a few years earlier would have been a sedge-covered, slowly seeping swale. Source: Andreas 1875: 265.

Great Depression, funneled unemployed workers into state park development, soil erosion control, and reforestation. And in the 1940s Iowa and Wisconsin were the first states to establish prairie preserves. Iowa's 1989 Resource Enhancement and Protection (REAP) program was greeted as one of the nation's most progressive pieces of state environmental legislation (Conard 1997).

Iowa also has boasted a number of nationally significant conservation champions. The writings and teachings of Aldo Leopold, born and raised in Burlington, reshaped the nation's concept of nature and helped initiate the modern conservation movement. Iowa's congressman John Lacey, initiator of federal game legislation, championed national conservation efforts to halt market hunting and establish forest and wildlife refuges and national parks. His Lacey Act (passed in 1900) served as a forerunner to legislation protecting declining species. And J. N. "Ding" Darling, longtime *Des Moines Register* cartoonist and conservationist of national stature, helped create the national wildlife agenda in the 1930s, cofounded the National Wildlife Federation in 1936, and for a time headed the federal Bureau of Biological Survey, forerunner of the U.S. Fish and Wildlife Service (Conard 1997; Penna 1999). However, as strong and visionary as Iowa's conservation leadership efforts have been, on the whole the voices for intensive land use and financial gain have been more powerful.

Necessary Amenities

The vast majority of settlers had been attracted to Iowa by glowing reports of its physical resources and the opportunity to improve their economic lot through agriculture. Farmers found the optimal conditions they were hoping for: deep, rich soils; limited need to clear the land of trees or stones; relatively flat terrain amenable to plowing and raising livestock; and lack of American Indian hostilities.

Last and crucially important, the settlers found a climate that, along with Iowa's soils, was ideal for raising cultivated grains as well as prairie grasses. Iowa's growing season is long (162 days in central Iowa), and summer days are sunny and warm. Nearly three-fourths of the thirty-two inches of average annual precipitation drops during the growing season (late April through September) when it is most needed, but much falls at night, leaving sunny days to foster plant growth. Summer temperatures are adequate for optimum crop growth (July temperatures range from an average 83°F maximum to 68°F minimum; the statewide average for the entire year is 48°F), but not usually high enough to stress crops. And fall days are normally dry, allowing optimal dry-down of grains and ready access to fields for harvest. It is true that winters can be harsh, and summers sometimes bring severe weather. Thunderstorms, most abundant in June, can spawn hail, high winds, torrential rains, and occasionally tornadoes or floods. Precipitation cyclically dips and causes drought. However, Iowa's climatic benefits outweigh the potential damage caused by these perturbations (Hillaker 2005a).

Climate, along with soils (discussed in chapter 2), was crucial to Iowa's agricultural prowess. Today we describe Iowa's climate as continental, meaning that its marked seasonal fluctuations are not moderated by a nearby ocean. Iowa's yearly climatic cycles are produced by the patterns of flowing air masses. Summertime's warm, muggy days are brought on by moist air moving northward from the Gulf of Mexico, a feature more prevalent in eastern than western

Iowa. That pattern reverses in winter, when cold, crisp days are shaped by dry Canadian air masses flowing down from the northwest. Perturbations in this pattern result when Pacific air masses move in from the west, bringing milder weather — events that cause, for example, October's Indian summers — or when hot, dry, desiccating winds blow in from southwestern deserts.

Regional climatic variations occur from one part of the state to another. Iowa's southeastern corner has the longest growing season (182 days), highest average annual temperature (52°F), and greatest average annual precipitation (thirty-eight inches). Southeastern Iowa's climate thus most closely resembles that of the eastern United States' deciduous forests; southern native species are most likely to move into this corner of the state. These climatic traits gradually decline toward the north and west. Northern Iowa's growing season is 147 days, its average annual temperature is 45°F, and snow cover is significantly greater than toward the south. Northwestern Iowa claims the state's lowest average annual precipitation (26 inches) as well as its most frequent and severe hailstorms. Climatic conditions in this corner of the state approach those of the drought-prone, arid Great Plains to the west, a feature conducive to western species but one that restricts growth of plants that depend on more moisture (Hillaker 2005a).

Temperature and precipitation also change from year to year. Iowa's wettest year was 1993 (48 inches of precipitation), and its driest was 1910 (20 inches); drought was most severe in the 1930s. Taking a broader look at climatic trends, Iowa's long-term average annual precipitation of 32.13 inches (1873–2005) has risen to 34.08 inches in recent decades (1971–2000). Temperatures were low in the 1880s, warmed rapidly into the 1930s, dropped in the 1970s, and since then have been rising (Hillaker 2005b; Harry Hillaker, personal communication).

With Iowa's favorable climate and soils and a rapidly growing population of willing farmers, only ties to fully settled eastern states were needed to jump-start the state's entrance into the global economy. These ties were provided by the rapid development of transportation systems. Evolving boat, road, and train networks flooded Iowa with all the tools needed for landscape transformation: a continuing flow of workers, investors with energy and ideas, imported raw materials and finished products, and ever-diversifying modern agricultural (and other) technologies. With ever-easier transportation, residents of the hinterlands gained access to everything from commercial cloth and clothing, white pine lumber, furniture, candles, books, and drugs to purebred livestock and housing materials; even materials for ready-made houses were being shipped by train from Chicago as early as the 1870s.

Transportation networks fed Iowa's growing economy with new agricultural machinery, purebred livestock, and experimental crops. Equally important, transportation networks tied Iowa to Chicago, St. Louis, and points east, stimulating the export of products to commodity markets and to larger populations hungry to absorb any excess production. Ready access to distant markets encouraged farmers to utilize new agricultural technologies to maximize production and potential exports. Thus transportation was crucial to developing Iowa's export-driven agriculture.

Iowa's transportation systems evolved with breathtaking speed. Rivers were the first highways. Already in 1823 steamboats plied the Mississippi River, the heartland's major transportation artery, carrying soldiers and provisions upstream and returning to St. Louis with pelts and lead. Flatboats and canoes floated skins of wild animals and Indian trade goods along inland routes. A decade later, oxen hauled covered wagons over rough trails through the prairies, and smaller steamboats started chugging up the Mississippi's tributaries. Large flatboats soon floated Iowa's agricultural surpluses (mainly corn, wheat, cured pork, and lard) downriver to thriving towns along the Mississippi and from there to larger commodity markets. Road building was one of the first and most important tasks of Iowa's newly formed government. Dirt or plank roads, which commonly followed old Indian trails, soon were frequented by wagons carrying produce and merchandise and by stagecoaches running between emerging towns. Rivers were forded or crossed via ferries, until the toll bridges replaced the ferries.

By 1855, when tracks first connected Davenport to Iowa City, the state was being swept by railroad fever. Twelve years later the first cross-state railroad line was completed. By 1870, four lines stretched across the state, and trains had replaced steamboats and stagecoaches as the primary means of shipping agricultural goods and transporting people in Iowa. Railroad feeder lines then were constructed to the north and south. By 1880, no one in Iowa lived more than eight miles from a railroad line. And by 1900, Iowa was one of the best-tracked states in the nation, boasting 9,185 miles of railroad tracks.

The Iron Horse not only carried people with greater comfort and speed, it also promised the first year-round transportation to and from markets. In addition, the 1860s and 1870s saw the development of refrigerated railroad cars and the construction of grain elevators in every Iowa town. Refrigerated cars set the stage for the massive exportation of dressed beef and fresh pork to eastern markets and advanced the market hunting and export of Iowa's prairie-chickens, shorebirds, and waterfowl. Elevators, coupled with the developing practice of futures trading, fed Iowa's grain in an orderly fashion into more elaborate storage facilities in Chicago and St. Louis and from there to the world. By 1870, market connections provided by railroads also poised Iowa for major industrial expansion. Many of the resulting factories — for example, widespread pork-packing plants, oat-processing plants, and, after 1900, agricultural implement industries — reflected Iowa's agricultural focus.

In the twentieth century, an expanding network of highways traveled by automobiles and trucks, later supplemented by airlines, replaced the railroad systems of the previous century. Today's speedy climate-controlled transportation systems and the globalization of food markets have created a bewildering circumstance: Iowans, including farmers, live on the world's finest soils, but we purchase most of our food from distant locations. Conventional fresh produce, for example, is imported from an average of 1,500 miles away (Pirog and Benjamin 2003).

Shifting Cities and Suburbs

In 1900 all but 3 percent of Iowa was occupied by farms, leaving scant land for any other purpose (U.S. Census Bureau 1900). Yet the villages and towns sprinkled throughout Iowa were vitally important. Urban and rural areas have always depended on each other for survival. The two complement one another, creating a partnership that allows each type of landscape to do its own business. Rural areas provide food and natural resources that maintain urban populations. They house natural systems that decompose the cities' wastes and purify their air and water.

In return, towns traditionally have provided supplies to farmers, processed their products, and supplied markets for their wares. Urban areas have been sites of cultural and industrial innovation as well as financial, political, educational, commercial, and manufacturing centers. During economic downturns, Iowa's towns have provided rural citizens with jobs and income. In the days before radio and television, cars and paved roads, and the telephone, when farming was synonymous with isolation and hard work, towns tempted farm children to lives of relative ease. As Iowa's farms became more mechanized and increased in size, towns swelled with surplus populations no longer needed to grow food.

Iowa's rural population continued to grow until 1900, when it reached a high of 1.66 million people. Rural residency, which includes inhabitants of communities under 2,500 as well as farms, then started a slow but steady decline until 1990, when 1.1 million of Iowa's residents (39 percent) were rural. Meanwhile the urban population grew steadily, from 9,700 people (5 percent of the state's total population) in 1850 to 1.8 million (61 percent) in 2000. The slow but steady shift from rural to urban dominance reached a crucial transition in the 1950s, when Iowa's urban population outstripped rural residents for the first time (State Data Center Program 2006). About that time, the open countryside became increasingly attractive to urban residents, and suburbs started expanding, the expansion fueled by rising levels of affluence, good roads and cars, and people's desire to escape urban commotion and social problems.

Iowa has traditionally maintained a healthy balance between rural and small-town society and the urban industrial sector. However, today the nurturing interplay between rural and urban areas is being lost as lines delineating town from country blur and the distinct functions of each are lost in diffuse suburbs. Around Iowa's cities and larger towns, suburbanites are replacing farmers, and rural populations are again pulsing upward. Between 1990 and 2000, even as the number of farmers continued to shrink, Iowa's rural population increased by 45,000, growing for the first time in a century (State Data Center Program 2006).

Consideration of Iowa's land use dictates that the state's cities and towns should be growing inside their boundaries and extending upward, not outward. Instead, low-density and rural subdivisions, with their associated commercial, road, and other developments, are spreading over the world's richest topsoils even as many Iowa town centers decline. Between 1986 and 1997, an average of 26,227 Iowa acres per year were transferred from agricultural to nonagricultural zoning classes, with the rate of transfer increasing each year. Rates were considerably higher than average near urban centers, particularly in Pottawattamie, Polk, Johnson, Jasper, and Dallas counties, where subdivisions often leapfrogged far beyond the city limits. The land base of Iowa's metropolitan areas has been expanding far faster than their populations, leading to decreased average urban density. The trend has been toward bigger suburban homes built on larger suburban lots. In the Des Moines metropolitan area, for example, between 1952 and

1995 the population and land base both grew steadily while density dropped from 5.7 to 3.6 residents per acre.[1]

Even as Iowa's vast agricultural lands are picked away by urban sprawl, a far higher percentage of our remaining natural areas is being lost to suburban housing developments. Consider that Iowa's oldest and now largest towns were all built on rivers — first the Mississippi, then the state's inland waterways and the Missouri — because rivers were the settlers' initial means of transportation and power. Land near rivers, carved by numerous tributary streams, is far hillier and more rugged than land distant from rivers, and thus riversides have received less intensive agricultural use than flatlands. Riverside hills have become sanctuaries for Iowa's native plants and communities. In particular, land near rivers is often covered by mature oak woodlands and diverse forests and, in the Loess Hills, our largest remaining prairies.

Urban sprawl is increasingly funneling housing developments into these attractive riverside wooded lands and Loess Hills prairies. Zoning policies often favor development of riverside forests as a way of preserving cropland elsewhere. This is now occurring, for example, in Johnson County along the Iowa River north of Iowa City. Such land-use policies preferentially target areas with our greatest biological diversity and those increasingly rare natural areas with multiple environmental values, landscapes that many think should be preserved for future generations as well as for their environmental richness and functions. While agricultural lands are indeed deserving of preservation, doing so at the cost of our sparse high-quality natural areas will, in the long run, be detrimental to both farms and cities.

Tilling the Soil

Agriculture, more than any other factor, has redefined nature in Iowa, but its influence has not been static. When Iowa's first settlers arrived in the 1830s, sowing, cultivating, hay raking, grain reaping, and most other farm chores

1. Data on Iowa's loss of agricultural zoning are from Iowa State University Extension 1998: xi, xvi, 27, 36. Information on Iowa's expansion of metropolitan land and decreased urban density is from Iowa State University 2000: 8. Information on larger suburban lots and lower density of residents near Des Moines is from Iowa Natural Heritage Foundation 1996, which reports that in 1952 the population was 186,770 and the land base was 32,960 acres, while in 1995 the population was 291,494 and the land base was 80,960 acres.

Fig. 2. Iowa's settlement and agricultural transformation occurred just as the Industrial Revolution was revolutionizing farming technology. This two-horse riding mower greatly eased and speeded the cutting of alfalfa. It was one of many nineteenth-century innovations that signaled the abandonment of traditional subsistence farming. Courtesy State Historical Society of Iowa, Iowa City.

were laboriously completed by hand, just as they had been around the world for preceding millennia. Oxen pulled wagons and plows, but other activities were performed with the scythe, flail, hand rake, and other basic tools powered and often manufactured by the farmer. Coincidentally, at that very time the Industrial Revolution was being applied to agriculture. The 1800s saw the invention of numerous horse-drawn mechanized devices, among them John Deere's steel plow, the McCormick reaper, the grain drill and thresher, the corn planter, the two-row cultivator, and the portable steam engine for farm use (fig. 2). Although these devices usually were not adopted immediately, their appearance signaled the shift from labor-intensive to capital-intensive agriculture and from traditional subsistence practices to mechanized commercial agriculture.

Agricultural devices and scientific research have continued to revolutionize farming. Farm machinery has grown steadily larger, faster, and more powerful, even as new implements to perform tasks such as picking and shelling corn and combining wheat have been invented. In the first half of the twentieth century, the internal combustion engine and imported oil largely replaced animal and human power, and tractors started to pull farm implements. The 1920s marked the appearance of hybrid seed corn, which increased the vigor, yield, and disease resistance of Iowa's primary crop. Efforts to reduce labor and increase productivity were promoted through research and education provided by the U.S. Department of Agriculture, state agricultural extension services, and land-grant colleges from the Civil War onward. However, this did not halt agriculture's periodic economic downturns. The farm crisis of the 1920s helped initiate the federal government's complex, ever-changing crop-subsidy and acreage-reduction programs under the leadership of Iowa's Henry A. Wallace, secretary of agriculture during Roosevelt's 1930s New Deal administration. Today many farmers could not survive without federal subsidies.

Immediately after World War II, the massive adoption of synthetic chemicals — pesticides, livestock feed additives, and commercial inorganic fertilizers — altered farming techniques and products dramatically. And in the 1980s science developed the ability to modify organisms in the most profound manner possible — by transferring selected genetic material and its associated attributes from one species to another. Transgenic organisms, commonly referred to as genetically modified organisms, or GMOs, are created to modify a plant's or animal's growth patterns, chemical makeup, insect or disease resistance, or response to pesticides. Transgenic organisms, which first worked their way into agriculture in the 1990s, have been incorporated into Iowa's croplands at an impressive pace that exceeds national averages. By 2005, 60 percent of Iowa's corn was genetically modified to resist insects or herbicides, and 91 percent of Iowa's soybeans were modified for herbicide resistance (National Agricultural Statistics Service 2005a: 71).

These technological developments have produced bewildering consequences. With mechanization's steady relief from backbreaking hand labor, each farmer could tend more land and produce more food, more rapidly and easily than before. The number of labor hours required to produce 100 bushels of corn, for example, fell from an estimated average of 147 in 1900 to 3 by the mid 1980s (Gardner 2002: 18). Perhaps most enticing of all, the yield per acre steadily increased. Again looking at corn, yields of 30 to 40 bushels per acre remained common in Iowa from the mid 1800s well into the twentieth century. But by early in the twenty-first century, the average yield was 160 bushels per acre.[2]

These trends have placed Iowa in the nation's vanguard for agricultural pro-

---

2. Changes in corn yields are from National Agricultural Statistics Service, USDA-NASS Quick Stats (Crops), Iowa Data — Corn field, retrieved June 29, 2006.

ductivity. By early in the twenty-first century, Iowa had routinely led the nation in the production of corn and hogs for over a century and had recently claimed that position for the production of soybeans and eggs.[3] Its cash receipts from farm commodities in 2004 totaled $15.9 billion, the third highest in the nation (Iowa Department of Agriculture and Land Stewardship 2006).

The state's tremendous agricultural potential should have ensured the farmer's economic security, but ironically the opposite happened. Mechanization's higher productivity has routinely caused overproduction, which quickly became a chronic problem that drove down prices, lowered unit profits, and pushed farmers to plant more acres, causing more overproduction. Simultaneously, increasing operating costs from the purchase of equipment, energy, hybrid seeds, and chemical products expanded the typical farmer's capital investment and indebtedness to creditors. Farmers became ever more closely tied to the whims of the market economy and agricultural cycles of boom and bust.

Mechanization and its corollary, increasing capital investment, have favored large operators while steadily eliminating the small and midsize farms that have defined Iowa's traditional family-farm culture. In the last quarter of the twentieth century, the number of 50-to-499-acre farms was cut in half, while the number of farms above 1,000 acres more than quadrupled. Iowa's farm number peaked at 228,622 in 1900. But after World War II, as mechanization intensified, Iowa's farm number started a steady decline — dipping below 100,000 in 1996 and dropping to 89,000 in 2005. This decrease is explained by Iowa's declining land in farms (down from 34 million acres between 1900 and 1975 to 31.6 million acres in 2005) and steady rise in average farm size — from 151 acres in 1900 to 355 acres in 2005 (with many farms being much larger than the average).[4]

3. Iowa's rank in various agricultural commodities was provided by personal communication with Susan Cowles, July 18, 2006, National Agricultural Statistics Service — U.S. Department of Agriculture Iowa Field Office, Des Moines, from Census of Agriculture publications.

4. Data on the drop in small farms and rise in large farms are given in National Agricultural Statistics Service 2002: 6, which states that the number of farms between 50 and 499 acres dropped from 96,838 to 48,969, while the number of farms over 1,000 acres increased from 1,796 to 7,534. Changes in farm numbers, land in farms, and average farm size are from National Agricultural Statistics Service, USDA-NASS Quick Stats, Iowa Data — Farm Numbers, retrieved June 29, 2006. Data on these three changes for the half-century preceding 1950 are from the Census of Agriculture. Loss of farms and increase in average farm size are much greater if hobby farms and nonworking acreages are excluded (Fred Kirschenmann, personal communication).

Fig. 3. The small, diversified farms that characterized Iowa to about the mid-twentieth century maintained some native animals, plant communities, and environmental features. Note, for example, the prairie in the foreground of this 1910 photo of Clermont, Iowa, and wooded lands in the background. Courtesy State Historical Society of Iowa, Iowa City.

The above broad trends have defined agriculture in Iowa and across the United States for over a century. They have also defined evolving agricultural impacts on natural and human communities. The greatest impact — the loss of vast wilderness — resulted from the initial imposition of an agricultural landscape on Iowa's prairies, woodlands, forests, and wetlands. However, as dramatic as that transformation was, it resulted in small, diversified farms that were far more economically and ecologically sustainable than today's industrial-style operations (fig. 3). Our first farmers experimented with a variety of crops before settling down to a rotation of small grains (often oats), hay (often legumes that incorporated soil nitrogen), and corn. This rotation protected and maintained the soil and retarded the spread of weeds, insects, and diseases. Hogs and cattle were integral to the system's tight cycling of nutrients and energy. They turned the crops into meat and manure fertilizer. Milk cows, chickens, orchards, and vegetable gardens were common. Scattered prairie plants survived in pastures, hay meadows, and other uncultivated pockets. Perennial grasslands mimicked the prairie's ability to absorb and purify rainfall and protect soil. The entire system of small fields, mixed croplands, and pastures interspersed with pockets of wildness afforded habitat for some native animals.

This self-maintaining, diverse crop-rotation system characterized Iowa's farms for nearly a century. Its demise commenced with the appearance of the tractor. Horses had become common beasts of burden in the mid 1800s, replacing oxen that were too slow to operate mechanized farm implements. But by the end of the nineteenth century, horses were criticized as too costly and slow. They were gradually replaced by gasoline-powered tractors that became more powerful and versatile. Tractors dominated the farm scene by the 1950s.

World War II provided additional tools for moving full speed toward more simplified, specialized farming systems. Wartime's labor shortages and need for food were addressed by intensifying the mechanization process and by greater use of hybrid seeds, fossil fuels, and synthetic farm chemicals. These inexpensive, readily available compounds seemed to offer farmers a miraculous future free of weeds and problem insects. They were rapidly integrated into agriculture and used in increasingly large quantities. Immediately after the war, factories built to supply nitrogen for munitions shifted to producing nitrogen-based agricultural ammonia. Its low price and dramatic effect on yield led to soaring rates of use.

Since 1980, the use of many pesticides and nitrogen-based fertilizers has leveled off or decreased. However, Iowa still claims some of the highest application rates in the nation. In 2005, 1.7 billion pounds of nitrogen (more than in any other state except Illinois) were applied to Iowa's corn (National Agricultural Statistics Service 2006a: 8). That year nearly 25 million pounds of herbicide (most commonly atrazine) were applied to Iowa's corn, and 11 million pounds were applied to Iowa's soybeans (mostly glyphosate). Nearly 700,000 pounds of insecticides were applied to these two Iowa crops, which are some of the nation's most pesticide dependent (National Agricultural Statistics Service 2006a: 18, 96; Gardner 2002: 25).

Adoption of the tractor had wide-ranging environmental repercussions. It divorced farmers from a locally produced, sustainable energy source and helped launch agriculture's and the nation's dependence on imported oil. In addition, more tractors meant fewer horses and thus less need for pastures and for the hay and oats they ate. This switch, along with the adoption of chemical pest controls, set the stage for the abandonment of traditional diversified farming operations and crop rotations. Lands previously dedicated to prairie-mimicking hayfields and pastures, and rotations with sodcrops of small grains and hay, were converted to monocultures of row crops, with their typically high soil erosion rates and heavy dependence on fertilizers and pesticides. Oat harvest, for ex-

Fig. 4. Corn and soybeans, in 2002 grown on areas indicated in black, cover about two-thirds of Iowa — a figure that approaches the 80 percent coverage by diverse tallgrass prairies a few centuries ago. In fact, the distribution of these two row crops and of Iowa's presettlement prairie lands is almost identical (see fig. 6). Map by Casey Kohrt, Iowa Geological Survey, from 2002 satellite imagery.

ample, declined from around 6 million acres to 130,000 acres between the mid 1950s and the early twentieth century. Harvested hay dropped from nearly 5 million acres in the early 1900s to 1.6 million acres a century later.[5]

These two declines have been nearly totally absorbed by increased soybean row crops. While Iowa's corn plantings have mostly remained between 10 and 13 million acres throughout the twentieth century, soybean plantings did not exceed 1 million acres until 1942; by 2006, soybeans covered 10.1 million acres in Iowa.[6] With this cropland transfer from hay and oats to soybeans, diverse corn-hay-grain rotations gave way to simplified rotations of soybeans and corn. Crop-

5. Data on oat harvest changes are from National Agricultural Statistics Service, USDA-NASS Quick Stats (Crops), Iowa Data — Oats, retrieved June 29, 2006. Data on harvested hay changes are from National Agricultural Statistics Service, USDA-NASS Quick Stats (Crops), Iowa Data — Hay All, Dry, retrieved June 29, 2006.

6. Data on the rise in soybean plantings are from National Agricultural Statistics Service, USDA-NASS Quick Stats (Crops), Iowa Data — Corn field, Soybeans, retrieved June 29, 2006.

land traditionally divided between equal coverage of sod-forming crops and row crops shifted to nearly all row crops, with major environmental repercussions.

The second half of the twentieth century pushed the trend toward specialization and simplification of Iowa's rural landscape to an ever-greater extreme. This completed the conversion of family-centered diversified operations into businesses striving to maximize production of one or two uniform commodities and increasingly fewer strains of major crops. Farmers grew what was profitable, guided by economies of scale and governmental policies that promoted expanses of corn and soybeans, which in 2005 covered about two-thirds of Iowa's surface (see fig. 4) (National Agricultural Statistics Service 2005b). Once the infrastructure was designed to accommodate a two-crop system, it became almost impossible for farmers to diversify. Croplands became ever more vast as fields were merged, fencerows were eliminated, and marginal lands and pastures were plowed by larger, more powerful, more expensive equipment.

The decoupling of livestock and land continued as the rise of large western feedlots and low profit margins prompted farmers to sell off their cattle. Iowa's total cattle number, which rose to a high of nearly 8 million head in the 1970s, shrank to 3.8 million by the early twenty-first century. During that time, Iowa's total pastureland declined by 38 percent. Equally important, the number of farms with cattle dropped by more than 50 percent.[7]

Shifts in hogs and chickens were equally profound. Iowa's hog population has remained consistently robust. In 2005 the hog slaughter approached thirty million. But while their predecessors had run in the fields, the vast majority of twenty-first-century pigs were concentrated in large automated confined animal feeding operation (CAFO) buildings, some holding thousands of animals. CAFOs have turned voluminous manure, once a soil-replenishing resource, into a threat to air quality, nearby streams, and human health. Meanwhile the number of Iowa farms raising swine plummeted from around 60,000 to 10,000 between 1974 and 2002. And eggs, once a product of every Iowa farm, were by

7. Data on Iowa's decline in the number of cattle are from National Agricultural Statistics Service, USDA-NASS Quick Stats, Iowa Data — Cattle All, retrieved June 29, 2006. Data on Iowa's decline in pastureland are from U.S. Census Bureau 1978: Table 3; and National Agricultural Statistics Service 2002: Table 11, Pastureland All Types. The decline in farms with cattle is outlined in National Agricultural Statistics Service 2002: 6, and is true for cattle and calves, beef cattle, and milk cows (which dropped over 75 percent).

2002 sold by fewer than 2,000 farms. The eggs then produced in Iowa — nearly thirteen billion in 2005 — came primarily from CAFO operations.[8]

The environmental and social repercussions of all these changes have been profound. While yields continued to soar, the landscape's actual and functional diversity decreased greatly as grasslands, remaining prairie patches, and pockets of wildness were plowed to cropland. With expanding row crops, soil erosion remained high despite increased conservation measures. Dependence on nitrogen fertilizers soared along with surface and groundwater pollution and unsustainable use of greenhouse gas–producing fossil fuels, used in the manufacture of agricultural chemicals as well as transportation. Reliance on chemical pesticides reduced natural pest controls and pollinators and added additional pollutants to the air, water, and soil. Some effects of chemical use remain unknown and perhaps unknowable — for example, the health effects of long-term exposure to low concentrations of the multiple pesticides that drift through Iowa's air and water.

The trend toward fewer farms and farmers and the concentration of production in larger operations have made parts of Iowa's flattest, most intensively cultivated landscape appear uninhabited. By 2000, Iowa's farm population comprised a mere 5.9 percent of the state's total population and 15 percent of rural dwellers (State Data Center Program 2006).

Today population declines are threatening the economic and social viability of small communities, a cultural mainstay of our state. The farmers who remain are an aging population, and many earn the bulk of their income at off-farm jobs. While the largest, most technologically astute farming operations have been financially rewarded, many farms continue to be economically vulnerable because of reliance on a few crops, high production costs, and sizable indebtedness.

The result of all these trends — toward larger size, specialized machines, standardized processes and products, and greater efficiency and yield — has been

8. Data on Iowa's hog slaughter are from National Agricultural Statistics Service 2006b, All Hogs and Pigs, December 1, 2005, and Commercial Hog Slaughter 2005. Data on the decline in farms raising swine are from National Agricultural Statistics Service 2002: 6, Hogs and Pigs Inventory, Farms. Data on the decline in farms selling eggs are from National Agricultural Statistics Service 2002: Layers 20 weeks old and older — farms, number. Data on changes in the number of eggs produced in Iowa are from National Agricultural Statistics Service 2006b, Egg Production 2005.

termed the industrialization of Iowa's agriculture. Since the late 1900s, industrialization has been joined by other trends that put new pressures on natural lands and processes. Modern agriculture has created conditions that are concentrating land, money, and control over technology and markets in fewer and fewer hands. Multinational and multidimensional agribusiness corporations have been consolidating and using vertical integration to gain centralized control of production, processing, marketing, and distribution of certain agricultural commodities. This often includes corporations contracting with farmers to produce large quantities of a uniform farm commodity (in Iowa, mostly eggs and swine) by using very specific management techniques. While this arrangement guarantees a market and some financial stability, farmers providing the labor are removed from the decision-making process. They become essentially wage laborers who have lost their autonomy and control of the land.

Following these trends to their logical conclusion, Iowa's farmlands could become a few mammoth "factory farm" food complexes managed by distant multinational corporations and worked by minimum-wage employees, rather than by on-site owners with an understanding of the land. What such management by profit-driven corporations bode for environmental safeguards, and for the farming community itself, remains unknown. Also worrisome are the political and economic implications of concentrating global food production in the hands of a few corporations.

Expanded use of biotechnology presents additional environmental concerns. Although disputed by research, some claim that transgenic or GMO crops could reduce environmental hazards — for example, by reducing pesticide use. The driving force behind their adoption is management simplicity that once again allows the cultivation of more acres. However, researchers have called the adoption of GMOs "one of the largest uncontrolled experiments ever conducted in field community ecology" (Banks 2004: 540). Possible spin-offs include the unanticipated transfer of GMO genes to related wild species — for example, from GMO corn or trees bred for reduced lignin to their native wild precursors. The escape of GMO genes that impart herbicide resistance also could create aggressive superweeds that would be difficult to control. And widespread planting of herbicide- and insecticide-resistant GMO crops could accelerate the natural development of resistance to the chemicals in question. In addition, injury could occur when nontarget species come in contact with GMO crops. Beneficial insects, for example, might be killed while feeding on crops that have had insecticides incorporated into their genome. Any of these scenarios could dramatically affect native species and communities, as could scenarios we cannot predict or imagine. Once self-propagating GMO genes or organisms have escaped from croplands into the wild, they could be impossible to retrieve. The widespread effects of GMOs remain largely untested, even as Iowans and multinational corporations continue to adopt and promote GMO crops.

Current agricultural practices have been justified primarily through their increased efficiency, productivity, and short-term profit, without consideration of their long-term costs. However, for decades some voices expressed concern about the long-term sustainability of highly mechanized, high-input, industrialized, chemically based corporate farming. These voices emerged in the 1930s as the permanent agriculture movement, which was championed nationally by Iowa's Henry A. Wallace and other leaders of Roosevelt's New Deal. Morphing into the sustainable or ecological agriculture movement of the 1970s, alternative agriculture concerns have taken the name of organic agriculture (which avoids the use of synthetic pesticides and fertilizers), permaculture (which emphasizes small-scale technology on individual farms), perennial polyculture (tillage-free mixed crops), and agroecology (emphasizing natural ecosystems as examples), among other approaches.

As a group these approaches have emphasized the crucial values of human, societal, and environmental health and the long-term sustainability of human communities, the farming economy, nature, and the land itself. Alternative agricultural systems attempt to use technology to maintain economic and cultural vitality, and the land's health and complexity, into the indefinite future. They call for low-input approaches that conserve energy and nonrenewable resources, integrate biological processes, and are themselves self-regulating and self-renewing. They point out that healthy agriculture depends on diversity in crops, cropping systems, and nature. They emphasize ecological integrity and stability through efforts such as comprehensive soil conservation and land-use planning. They consider farmland as a national trust and raise questions about economic justice for farmers, the quality of life, and the continuity and stability of rural communities and lifestyles. They accept material and human limitations and value smaller-scale farming and ecological stewardship and responsibility. They ask for an accounting of agriculture's hidden costs, such as lost natural diversity, soils, cultural stability, and inherent farming knowledge (Beeman and Pritchard 2001).

Today alternative and mainstream agricultural practices often mix in varied manners. For example, many farmers are trying to use fewer chemicals and employ more natural pest-control methods, reduce tillage, and grow alternative crops. Practical Farmers of Iowa is one of the nation's most vocal and successful organizations promoting the integration of sustainable agricultural techniques.

This summary of agriculture's complexities does not do justice to the efforts of many thousands of Iowans who have poured their lives into feeding the world. Each farm family could tell its own story of gains and losses. Each native community and species could do the same. But the bottom line remains the same: evolving agricultural practices have created a continual struggle both for farmers and for nature. Our agricultural heritage and our prairie heritage are sources of pride, elements that define our past and present. And both have lost many of their finer qualities.

Today voices argue strongly for further implementation of industrialized agriculture and for alternative farming systems. Too often these voices are pitted against one another, as are the voices of some environmentalists and farmers. Such dissension is unfortunate and counterproductive. All these groups have as their base concern the survival and long-term sustainability of Iowa's land. If we are to address many of the problems outlined in this book, the environmental and farming communities need to work together for a more positive future.

Here in Iowa, nature and agriculture are forever wed. The high value of Iowa's soils dictates that most of our state will continue to be working farms. However, this does not mean that nature's species and processes must be eliminated. If anything, perpetuating native plants and animals and nature's safeguards will become more important here, where our economy is so closely tied to the land's response, than in wilder states.

2 A Miracle of Sight, Scent, and Sound

Undoubtedly one of the most captivating features . . . of the upper Mississippi valley, is the unique and beautifully diversified Prairies, or unwooded tracts. They are, in fact, the gardens of nature. . . . Sometimes they are spread out in boundless plains; at other times they are gently rolling, like the swell of the sea after a subsiding storm. . . .

These meadows of nature are covered with a rich coat of natural grass, forming excellent grazing for cattle; and, in the season of flowers, present the most captivating and lovely appearance. The traveler now beholds these boundless plains, untouched by the hand of man, clothed with the deepest verdure, interspersed here and there with beautiful groves, which appear like islands in the ocean. The writer has often traveled amidst these enchanting scenes, on horseback, for hundreds of miles.

— John Newhall, 1846

At first the Euroamerican settlers could not fathom the tall-grass prairie. Stepping into it from cropland-speckled woodlands to the east, they entered a land of sky and horizon, wind and light, flower and scent, a surging sea of grasses that staggered the imagination. The prairie grasslands seemed to stretch on forever, a landscape that promised no enclosure, only intensity and exposure. Nothing like this lay behind the settlers, not in their experiences, not in their memories or those of their grandparents. The wind strummed ceaselessly through the grasses, reshaping fields of color and putting the prairie into motion. The air was buzzing, humming, whirring with inexhaustible life. Insects by the millions flitted and whirled about reedy stems. Flocks of birds dove through the sky and whistled overhead, casting shadows over the land for hours on end. Elk and bison snorted and stomped, then thundered over the rise. Wolves and cougars circled and crouched, readying for the spring. In the end, the remains of all were incorporated into one of the richest soils on Earth, a deep, loamy topsoil that ironically would become the demise of the prairie. Settlers' journals described the vast prairie in the only terms these newcomers knew: as an inland ocean of storm-tossed waves, as a billowing sea.

Today, standing among fields where bumper crops have been coaxed from the earth for over a century and a half, it is nearly impossible to imagine the rich wilderness that overwhelmed Iowa's Euroamericans, the miraculous fecundity and fearful mystery of the land. The earliest settlers could have walked across Iowa without exiting the prairie that cloaked four-fifths of the state. But not all of Iowa was prairie. Portions of the state were dominated by trees and shrubs. Open oak woodlands and savannas climbed the hills and lined ridgetops, especially in eastern Iowa, giving way gradually to open treeless grasslands toward the drier west. Denser floodplain forests filled river bottoms everywhere. Prairies varied as well. The moistest valley-bottom soils, for example, shot up grasses that could hide a herd of cattle, while shorter, sparser growth typified high, dry hillsides. Across the state, wetland communities redefined portions of both prairie and wooded land. These vegetation patterns were roughly true for thousands of years prior to Euroamerican settlement.

This was the land we now call Iowa, a sublime land of abundance and grandeur that remains only in historic descriptions and our imagination. If we are to understand the places we call home today, we must first envision this ancient self-maintaining landscape before it was targeted and transformed by the plow, cow, and saw.

Wind and Rain, Fire and Tooth

Presettlement Iowa was a harsh land of life lived on the edge, a land that constantly tested the survival ability of its inhabitants. Exposure to destructive forces was as routine as the life-giving rain. Iowa's many thousands of native species had nearly 10,000 years to adapt to racing wildfire, simmering heat and intense sunshine, frigid winters, drying winds, jaws that devoured, and hoofs that trampled. With time, these stresses came to define Iowa: our native communities stepped from being disturbance-prone into being disturbance-dependent. They thrived in the harsh midcontinental environment. Routine disruptions became part of the landscape's fabric and shaped its character. Disturbances transitioned from being agents that destroyed into being agents that rejuvenated.

Take fire, for example. Prairies and interspersed oak woodlands forged a longstanding allegiance with wildfire, which cleansed the land of debris, opening both woods and grasslands to sunshine. Prairie fires could race with ease across the Midwest's open, gently rolling topography, their ferocity amplified by the annual production of a thick flammable thatch of dead plant parts that dried to a crisp each fall. Where it burned its hottest, fire killed many species of trees and shrubs and suppressed growth of fire-tolerant oaks, thus allowing tall grasses to maintain their dominance. Less intense flames crept through upland oak woods and even reshaped wetlands. As the early settler Solon Robinson wrote, "The streams are often broad and nearly covered with vegetable growth, in some instances to the degree that sheets of water many rods wide actually burn over with autumnal fires" (1842: 15).

Or consider climate. While Iowa's warm, moist summers were and are on the whole conducive to lush prairie growth, the annual statewide average of 32 inches can vary greatly from locale to locale and year to year (see chapter 1). Prehistoric climatic extremes determined what lived and what died. Periodic drought ensued when temperatures soared and precipitation declined. Drought's effects were multiplied by the prairie's constant wind and intense sunshine. Drought was (and is) most pervasive and severe in western Iowa, where precipitation is lower than in the eastern part of our state, and drought occurred most commonly in summer (Hillaker 2005a, 2005b).

Periodic drought, like fire, was crucial for maintaining grassland dominance by helping to cleanse prairies of infiltrating trees and shrubs. Iowa's prairie plants have deep roots, and their leaves and biochemical processes are adapted to drought's harsh demands. Prairie leaves are finely divided or narrow in shape (to lower wind resistance), silvery or light in color (to reflect the bright sunlight), or covered with hairs, scales, or leathery or waxy surfaces (to deflect wind and lower water loss). Most prairie plants are classified as warm-season species, implying metabolic adaptations to hot, dry conditions. These plants flourish in summertime, carrying out photosynthesis using a distinct chemical pathway that operates most efficiently at warmer temperatures, and use water and nitrogen more efficiently than cool-season plants. In fact, native prairies often can be recognized by their gray "dead" look in early spring, when surrounding farmlands (with their cool-season species) are greening up.

Broad-leaved trees, on the other hand, require more precipitation and are killed by severe drought. Periodic drought, where strongest, thus led to the loss of trees and other woodland species on uplands and their restriction to sheltered streambed locations. It also decreased the productivity and diversity of prairie plants. The effects of multiple-year droughts were most profound. During the prolonged drought of the 1930s Dust Bowl, shorter, sparser prairies to the west of Iowa moved eastward into tallgrass prairie territory over a broad 100-mile-wide zone (Costello 1969: 200; Weaver 1954: 8). During especially wet years, in contrast, prairie productivity and diversity increased, and wetland plants climbed higher on slopes.

Now consider the grazers. With the clamp of the jaw, wandering herds of large herbivores could devour the hard-earned products of months of photosynthesis. Bison, which are primarily grazers, would have reduced tallgrass dominance and thus favored a greater number of forbs — nongrasslike or broad-leaved flowering plants. But bison may not have been abundant enough to strongly influence the easternmost tallgrass prairie. However, elk, which are generalist feeders that both browse woody and graze herbaceous plants, were more ubiquitous. White-tailed deer and millions of smaller animals joined in the feast. Crickets and grasshoppers constituted the major aboveground insect herbivores. Herbivorous activity underground was led by the nematodes, which numbered in the millions per square yard. The many additional invertebrate plant-eaters included beetles, caterpillars, ants, leafhoppers, and scale insects, often found in abundance. In addition to devouring foliage, these small animals sucked sap and fed on pollen, nectar, and seeds (Risser et al. 1981: 470; John Pearson, personal communication).

Herbivores were as crucial as fire and drought to maintaining the landscape's biological diversity, or biodiversity — that is, the number of species forming a community within a given area. Along with the burrowing of small animals, wallowing of bison, construction of ant hills, and other disturbances that overturned earth, grazing created a patchwork of diverse environments: bare and vegetated soils, sunny and shaded sites, short and tall plant growth, and transitory and mature communities. The resulting mosaic of habitats fostered a diversity of species and maximized ecological stability. Without a variety of disturbances and habitats, native plant biodiversity and the land's stability and sustainability would have declined.

Environmental stresses worked in tandem to produce local variations in Iowa's living landscape. For example, during drought the impact of grazing became more intense, and fires were larger and hotter. Fire spread most rapidly when winds were strong. Fire also interacted with grazing. Newly burned prairies produced lush, nutritious forage preferentially grazed by bison and other large herbivores. And fire magnified the patchy heterogeneity produced by grazing because fire strength was shaped by local variations in fuel, moisture, topography, and wind.

Interacting stresses also shaped broader vegetation patterns. At the time of settlement, just as today, eastern Iowa's moister climate could support both prairie plants and trees — a fact true throughout the prairie peninsula that bulged from southern Minnesota, Iowa, and northern Missouri through Illinois into Indiana and on into sites in central Ohio (fig. 5). Eastern Iowa and the prairie peninsula were thus a broad transitional zone and blending ground for two of the continent's major biological regions: North America's widespread eastern woodlands and forests and its vast midcontinental grasslands. The line between the two was neither sharp nor permanent. Tallgrass prairies graded into savannas and savannas into open oak woodlands, the communities and their borders constantly shifting in response to changes in the environment. Historically, in this region, fire's importance was proportionately more significant than drought, which (as one moved eastward and precipitation increased) was progressively more restricted to the driest uplands. Fire maintained the prairie, limited the moderately fire-tolerant oaks to sites with less intense burns, and eliminated many species of fire-sensitive trees from the uplands. Fire created the patchy prairie-savanna-woodland communities seen by eastern Iowa's first settlers. In contrast, in western Iowa, intense periodic droughts joined the fires fanned by a drier climate and other stresses to eliminate trees and produce sweeping treeless prairies (Anderson 1990; McClain and Elzinga 1994).

Climate and disturbances also placed Iowa in the middle ground of a broad climatic and vegetational gradient that reached from the Atlantic Ocean (where average annual precipitation often exceeded forty-five inches) to the base of the Rocky Mountains (where it fell to fifteen inches or less). Proceeding eastward through the prairie peninsula toward the Atlantic, moisture steadily increased and prairies grew smaller and more confined to uplands, until they eventually disappeared. Deciduous woodlands and forests assumed dominance. Many of the continent's eastern woodlands were dominated by oaks, as they had been for thousands of years. White oak reigned supreme. Being very long lived and thriving on a broad range of sites, white oak was the most abundant eastern oak. It also possessed the largest range: it was found in every state east of the central plains (Abrams 2003).

West of Iowa, as moisture decreased, rich, lush, tall grasslands faded into equally vast but sparser Great Plains grasslands, the two merging to form a vast grassy sea that covered around 400 million acres of midcontinental North America (Samson and Knopf 1994: 418). The Great Plains grasslands became gradually shorter, transitioning into midgrass and short-grass prairies toward the base of the Rocky Mountains. There the height of scruffy grasses was measured in inches rather than feet. A tremendous variety of uniquely adapted plants and animals mingled and migrated through each type of prairie, affording the grassy sward stability and resilience in the face of inevitable climatic shifts and physical disturbances.

Take the variations of fire, compound them with climate, grazing, and other landscape complexities, and it becomes obvious that Iowa's vegetation exhibited a delightful variety. Iowa's native communities were an amalgamation of fluctuating patches, each with its own members and dynamics, each a product

Fig. 5. Tallgrass prairies once stretched from Manitoba into Texas. The eastward-extending prairie peninsula blended prairie grasslands with oak savannas and open oak woodlands, which increased in dominance as precipitation rose toward the east. To the west, the tallgrass prairie gave way to shorter grasslands that stretched across the Great Plains. Iowa is the only state to have once been completely surrounded by tallgrass communities. This map shows the extent of tallgrass prairies at the time of Euroamerican settlement. Source: Runkel and Roosa 1989, as adapted from Risser et al. 1981 and Transeau 1935.

of the climate and environment playing out at that particular time. The patchwork was constantly in flux. A slight increase in precipitation might boost tree growth and simultaneously subdue fire intensity, thus sending trees on forays into grasslands. Subsequent severe droughts would stress trees and fan wildfires that might become intense enough to destroy woodlands, pushing them back toward the edges of creeks and rivers. The march of the plant world, although slower than that of animals, was constant. Iowa's changing landscape was as dynamic as that of any place on Earth.

Prairie Seas, Earth Oceans

In 1830 prairies comprised the crown jewel of Iowa's landscape, draping a full 80 percent of today's state with a diversity of plant species unknown to their interfingering oak woodlands and bottomland forests (Smith 1998: 97). Iowa's 28.6 million prairie acres constituted the heart of the tallgrass prairie biome, one of North America's most diverse and productive biological regions, which cut a swath covering an estimated 142 to 169 million acres across the continent's center (Risser et al. 1981; Samson and Knopf 1994: 419). North America's midcontinental tallgrass prairies, in combination with the more westerly mid- and short-grass prairies, joined the Eurasian steppes, African veldt, and South American pampas in defining the world's major grasslands.

Iowa's prairies sprouted on all types of soils and landscapes, from wet, deep-soiled alluvial bottomlands to dry, thin-soiled rocky bluffs. The majority of the prairies, and those that were most lush and diverse, were found on broad rolling uplands that were mesic: they received sufficient moisture throughout the growing season but were neither exceptionally dry nor wet (see color plate 2). These were the prairies where big bluestem, Indiangrass, and many of the common tall prairie forbs reached their maxima.

Prairies were most expansive on the relatively flat terrain of north-central Iowa and in the western third of the state, where river valleys paralleled the dominant southwesterly winds (fig. 6). Both of these topographies encouraged hot, frequent fires that promoted grasses and discouraged trees. These prairies also were favored by western Iowa's dry, windy climate.

In all, nearly 1,000 vascular plant species comprise North America's modern tallgrass flora. Many of these occupy only certain parts of the tallgrass region: Iowa claims around 300 different prairie plants.[1] Fewer species would be found in any one locale. Grasses define the prairie just as trees define a forest. However, a prairie is not a haphazard assemblage of grasses and other species, and not any grass-dominated community constitutes a prairie. True prairie grasses have evolved together with myriad other plants, animals, and their microbial, fungal, and their other living associates. Together they form a complex, integrated community uniquely adapted to the midwestern environment.

Nowadays, across Iowa's remaining prairie landscape, a total of six dozen or so specific prairie grasses occupy more space both below and above the ground than all other prairie plants combined (fig. 7). Perhaps a third of them will be found in any given high-quality remnant (Cooper 1982: 166, 168). Chief among these is big bluestem, the most widespread and abundant tall grass, which produces a thicket of stems and blades that commonly reach up six to nine feet by autumn

1. The number of species in North America's tallgrass prairie is from Ladd 2005, which also lists those species. Iowa's prairie species count is from John Pearson, personal communication, as based on counts taken from Eilers and Roosa 1994.

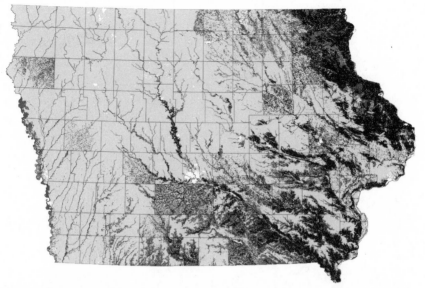

Fig. 6. In 1800 prairies covered the vast majority of Iowa, while trees were concentrated in eastern and south-central Iowa and flourished along water courses. Abundant wetlands were scattered throughout wooded and prairie lands. On this map, which uses soil traits to locate plant communities, prairie-derived soils are light gray. Soils developed under heavy and consistent tree cover are black. Dark gray areas indicate soils with transitional or intermediate characteristics. These may have been brushy areas, open savannas, mixed patches of grassy and woody species, or sites with advancing and retreating woody cover. Sharp-lined differences between counties probably reflect variations in mapping convention, date, and scale. Map prepared in 2007 by Casey Kohrt, Iowa Geological Survey, from statewide soils geographical information system coverage, including the Iowa Co-operative Soil Survey ISPAID data.

and under optimum conditions grows to ten or twelve feet. Big bluestem is easily identified not only by its height and abundance but also by its rich bluish or russet waxlike color and by its turkey feet: large three-pronged seedheads produced in September. Indiangrass, little bluestem, and various sedges (grasslike plants with triangular stems in the Cyperaceae family) are also nearly ubiquitous.

While grasses visually dominated the prairie, forbs with their many colors and shapes captured the eye, drawing praise for their intense beauty. The growing season's floral display stretched from April into October as a stately procession of prairie forbs budded, blossomed, and then succeeded to other blooms, this sequence paralleling the changing activities of insects and other animals.

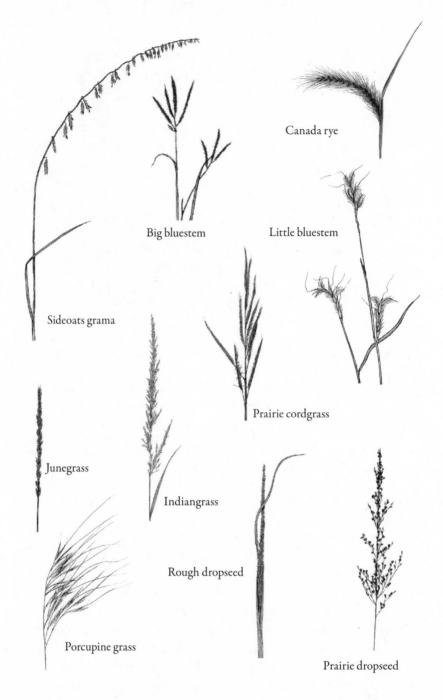

Canada rye

Big bluestem

Little bluestem

Sideoats grama

Prairie cordgrass

Junegrass

Indiangrass

Rough dropseed

Porcupine grass

Prairie dropseed

Fig. 7. Dozens of native grasses can be found in tallgrass prairies, with these being some of the more common species. Drawing by Mark Müller.

Wave after wave of flowers colored the grasslands crimson, cream, golden yellow, indigo, and lavender. Never during the growing season was the prairie dull. Bohumil Shimek described the prairie's seasonal changes:

> With opening spring the ponds and lakes were soon gilded with the water crowfoot, and the hills and higher prairies were dotted with . . . a variety of rapidly succeeding spring flowers. . . . Soon the grasses covered the surface with a great carpet of green painted with puccoons, prairie phlox and other flowers of late spring. But the real rich beauty of the prairie was developed only after mid-summer when myriads of flowers of most varied hues were everywhere massed into one great painting . . . but endlessly varied in delicate detail. In the fall this in turn was followed by the rusty-red or brown expanse of drying grasses which portended the coming of the terror and the splendor of that scourge of the early prairie settlers, the prairie fires. (1911: 170)

The seasonal sequence generally progressed from plants a few inches high in spring to increasingly taller plants as the season advanced, each successive wave of bloom reaching higher than the foliage and dried seedheads of the previous wave. Increasing plant height allowed pollinating insects to reach blossoms and the breeze to disperse windborne seeds with ease. Early-blooming short plants included prairie violets, prairie blue-eyed grass, and (in northern Iowa) pasqueflower. May heralded the slightly taller shootingstar (in eastern Iowa) and hoary puccoon, followed by golden Alexanders, prairie phlox, prairie ragwort, and, later still, pale purple coneflower. Midsummer brought an increase in the variety of flowers. By July, blackeyed Susan, gray-headed coneflower, butterfly milkweed, and prairie clover extended upward a few feet. In late summer a diversity of sunflowers, blazing stars, and other composites intermingled with blooming tall grasses, which reached upward seven feet or more. The growing season closed with blossoms of many species of goldenrods, asters, and gentians, which flowered until killing frost. Then rust and golden tall grasses captured the view and afforded color to winter's encroaching white and gray.

In some locations, this rich mixture of prairie grasses and forbs marched uninterrupted across Iowa's presettlement landscape for miles on end. Elsewhere prairies formed vague and shifting borders with wooded lands. Prairie species commonly fingered their way underneath open oak canopies, and prairie openings intermittently dotted extensive woodlands. Conversely, grasslands sometimes surrounded extensive thickets of bur oaks and hazelnut shrubs that had been reshaped by frequent fire into gnarled dwarfs.

On the whole, most of Iowa's immense prairielands looked remarkably similar. Bohumil Shimek stressed this point, stating that despite the prairie's varied topography and substrata, "the flora is practically the same, and this flora is the best ear-mark of the prairie" (1911: 187). It is true that prairie plants share a number of traits. For example, the vast majority (about 95 percent) are perennials with a long lifespan, probably ten to twenty years or more (Risser et al. 1981: 468). In addition, the same tall grasses grow on all but the most extreme sites. The prairie's sense of homogeneity was enhanced by the dominance of certain showy forbs — often members of the composite or sunflower (Asteraceae) and legume (Fabaceae) families. Composites ranged from small-flowered asters and goldenrods to large yellow sunflowers and oxeye and also included thistles, fleabanes, coneflowers, and the tall purple-spiked blazing stars. Legumes were represented by wild indigos, white and purple prairie clovers, and ticktrefoils, among other flowers.

But modern studies of Iowa's prairie remnants reveal that distinct prairie communities exist in the midst of apparent homogeneity, just as they must have in the past. Diverse discrete communities, often defined by subtle variations among forbs, are shaped primarily by soil moisture, which relates to a site's drainage patterns, exposure, and hillside position. Community composition also is affected by each plant species' natural geographic range and by each site's history of use and disturbance (White and Glenn-Lewin 1984).

Consider today's various dry prairies, for example. When compared to the mesic prairies described above, modern dry prairies are typified by shorter plants, sparser growth, more open space, and relatively more forbs than their counterparts on moister ground. Tall grasses often remain, but they relinquish dominance to midheight grasses such as little bluestem, which reaches upward a mere one to three feet. Sideoats grama, Junegrass, porcupine grass, and rough and prairie dropseed proliferate on many dry sites, as do leadplant (one of Iowa's few prairie shrubs) and forbs such as Missouri goldenrod, prairie coreopsis, prairie sunflower, pussytoes, and many species found on mesic prairies. Because of the dominance of shorter grasses, Iowa's driest prairies resemble the midgrass prairies found farther west on the Great Plains, and some publications refer to them as such or as mixed-grass prairies.

Dry prairies once swept over droughty hillsides, gravelly hummocks, and other sites with highly permeable soils or gravels. They still proliferate in a few special locales, especially on exposed upper hillsides. In past centuries, such dry prairies graded into taller, moister prairies on lower slopes, on slopes facing north and east, and in valleys; today dry grasslands often fade instead into wooded areas or cropland. In rugged northeastern Iowa, very dry hill prairies, or goat prairies, still abound on hilltops and steep upper hillsides facing south and west, which receive the full blast of southwesterly winds and hot afternoon sunshine. Common and widespread species here include the grasses big and little bluestem, prairie dropseed, and sideoats grama; sedge species; and the forbs leadplant, prairie coreopsis, and skyblue aster.

In western Iowa's Loess Hills, dry prairies abound on steep bluffs adjacent to the Missouri River floodplain and on upper ridges facing south and west. Here, where exposure to drying sun and wind is extreme, the dominant midgrasses little bluestem and sideoats grama mix with other drought-resistant plants and with species with western affinities such as blue grama, skeleton weed, yucca, purple locoweed, and animals such as the plains spadefoot toad and prairie rattlesnake. These Great Plains species differentiate Loess Hills communities from prairies farther east. Some Great Plains plants are also found in dry gravel hill prairies of northwestern Iowa, but many do not extend east of the Loess Hills and today are considered rare in Iowa.

Sand prairies, another dry prairie variant, survive on the sand deposits and dunes alongside eastern Iowa's major rivers. These provide homes for a sparse covering of grasses such as sandreed grass and sand dropseed and for nitrogen-fixing legumes (such as leadplant, round-headed bush clover, and American vetch) that are capable of colonizing the unstable, shifting, nutrient-poor substratum. More typical prairie species may take over sandy areas where soils become stabilized.

At the other end of the spectrum, wet prairies and associated flood-tolerant communities once abounded wherever flowing water or groundwater saturated the soil. Here varied associations of wetland plants greened meadows, fens, bottomlands, and shallow or deep marshes, giving way to submersed or floating aquatic vegetation in deep waters. Switchgrass and bluejoint increased as prairies moistened, the latter forming dense, solid patches. Native genotypes of reed canarygrass were once part of this moist matrix. The arching leaves of sedges formed a thick blanket covering many wet meadows. As Thomas Macbride described, "In the lowlands . . . sedges covered thousands of acres with a mantle of deepest green, whose lustrous sheen went waving in the breath of summer like the rolling of the tropic sea" (1895: 345). Prairie cordgrass covered wet river bottoms and shallow upland swales, its dense eight-foot-tall blades and thick, woody rhizomes excluding all other species over large areas. Soils that were shallowly flooded into the summer provided habitat for tall coarse-stemmed herbaceous vegetation such as cattails, bulrushes, larger sedges, bur-reed, and arrowheads. The many colorful wet prairie forbs included sawtooth sunflower, sneezeweed, cup plant, prairie ironweed, blue flag iris, swamp milkweed, Canada anemone, and common boneset.

Disturbance and use patterns dictated the age and thus also shaped the character of any given prairie community. Prairies included a suite of native weeds, opportunistic plants such as common evening primrose, common milkweed, eastern daisy fleabane, hairy aster, Canada goldenrod, ragweeds, field thistle, and Canada wildrye. These plants produced abundant seed that spread with ease and grew rapidly on bare, sunny soils disturbed, for example, by the diggings of badgers or pocket gophers or the wallowing of bison. Such short-lived annuals and biennials held the soil and produced shade until more discriminating, slower-growing prairie plants reclaimed dominance, many doing so through vegetative spread. Eventually more competitive, longer-lived perennials regained stature, and a disturbed prairie plot once again melded into its surroundings. Compassplant, rattlesnake master, cream wild indigo, prairie Indian plantain, green milkweed, leadplant, the prairie clovers and blazing stars, and lady's slipper orchids are signatures of mature prairies.

WHILE THE ABOVEGROUND tallgrass prairie was impressive in its height, density, and obvious richness of life, these traits paled when compared to the diversity, abundance, and adaptations of life underground. A prairie's roots are far bulkier than its aboveground plant parts, with as much as two-thirds of plant biomass resting below the soil surface (Miller 2005: 23). Much-branched fibrous and fine prairie rootlets permeate every cubic inch to a depth of several feet, threading soil and root systems together in an intricate living network, each holding the other in place (fig. 8).

These roots ply deep into the soil, often stretching farther down than the plant's foliage reaches upward. Roots of big bluestem extend to depths of five to seven feet or more, those of prairie cordgrass to nine feet, and those of switchgrass to eleven feet, with depth seeming to increase in drier climes and more porous soils (Weaver 1954: 116). Some forbs grow significantly longer roots, extending down twenty feet or more. These depths enable prairie plants to access moisture and thrive, even when upper soils become parched by drought.

Just as layered prairie plants aboveground take turns catching the sun's rays

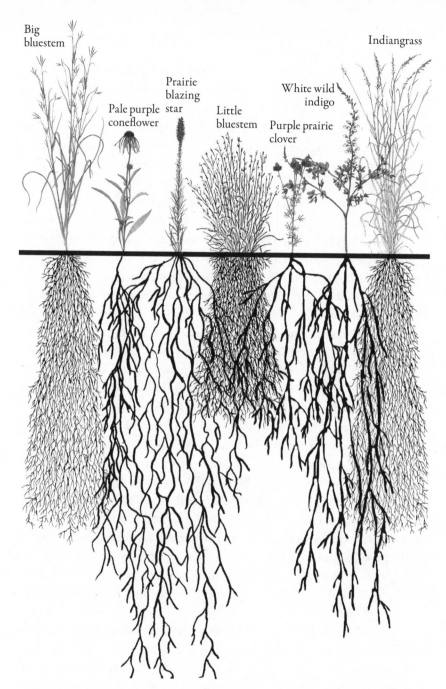

Big
bluestem

Indiangrass

Pale purple
coneflower

Prairie
blazing
star

White wild
indigo

Little
bluestem

Purple prairie
clover

Fig. 8. Roots of tallgrass prairie plants possess more biomass, and greater length, than the aboveground plant parts. These amazingly massive, deep root systems allow the plants to access moisture during drought, comprehensively utilize nutrients, build and hold rich soils, and provide habitat for a tremendous diversity of underground insects and microorganisms. Drawing by Mark Müller.

and blooming, so prairie root systems divide the soil's bounty. Each plant species occupies a specific portion of the soil profile, some spreading their roots outward while others stretch straight down. The resulting root layering enables each species to absorb water and nutrients within a particular soil area, thus encouraging a proliferation of plant species that would be otherwise impossible.

Many prairie plants also produce rhizomes, or underground stems. Shallow rhizomes sprout new shoots that are nourished by the parent plant, enabling grasses, sedges, and forbs to colonize disturbed areas. In addition, the growth points of rhizomes — like the tubers, bulbs, and corms produced by many prairie forbs — lie just below the soil's surface. The soil's safeguarding of these growing points allows them to resprout rapidly after disturbance and thus survive moderate grazing, fire, and other aboveground disturbances.

Consider wildfire, for example. Prairie grasses invite fire. They produce abundant fuel annually and, if sufficiently dry, can explode into flame any time of year. However, the fire's intense heat skirts the soil surface, reducing aboveground thatch to ash but leaving soils and underground plant structures unscathed. The sun warms the fire-exposed, darkened soils, and the warmth stimulates soil microbial action that results in a flush of nutrients. Following a conflagration that seems to have obliterated all life, prairie perennials return thicker, lusher, and with more blossoms and seed production than before. Plant vigor increases, senescence is delayed, and species diversity is maximized. If the fire occurred in early to midsummer, plants may resprout and green the landscape within a few weeks. One of Johnson County's first settlers, Abigail Irish, witnessed this magical cycle of death and resurrection. "When I first saw Iowa" in 1846, she later wrote, "it was a vast expanse of brown and blackened prairie, strewn thickly over with the bones of many animals that had been victims of prairie-fires that had recently consumed them while burning the rank grasses of the prairie. The deep snows of that winter and the warm, gentle rains of the following spring obliterated this gruesome scene by scattering beautiful verdure and flowers over these remains" (1922: 21–22).

Prairie soil also harbors an unbelievable diversity and abundance of microscopic creatures. A tenth of an ounce might hold as many as 50 million bacteria, the most numerous of prairie organisms. The top half-cubic-yard of soil may house 135,000 arthropods and 6.5 million nematodes, numbers that exceed aboveground invertebrates by ten times or more (Risser et al. 1981: 287, 470; Costello 1969: 78). Fungi, protozoa, algae, and other microorganisms are joined by amoebas, chief predators of the unicellular world, and by mites and springtails that wander up and down roots in search of a meal. Pseudoscorpions, assorted larvae, beetles, wasps, bees, spiders, and a large number of other life-forms join the subsurface menagerie — ants and earthworms, burrowing moles and badgers, snakes, lizards and toads, and many more. Because of this wealth of underground life, prairies are sometimes called tropical rainforests turned upside down.

Add to the dark, moist, churning mass a complexity of soil-bound interactions. Mycorrhizal fungi living partially inside plant roots bring soil nutrients to their hosts and in return are fed complex carbohydrates by the plants. Deep roots siphon buried nutrients and moisture to the surface, where they are transposed into leaves and stems that capture the sun's energy, which is used to produce complex molecules that are exuded by plant roots to foster soil microbes. These microorganisms feed one another and also nourish larger organisms, all of which eventually die. Bacteria and fungi transpose the dead, along with withered plant parts, into decomposed organic matter. Life's disintegrating remains are churned into the soil's mineral matrix by ants and earthworms, which aerate the soil as they build tunnels and bring vast stores of nutrients from deep underground for deposition near the soil surface. Through this process, the plethora of underground prairie life not only inhabited the soil, it became the soil.

These myriad interactions created an extraordinary soil structure. The crux lay in the clumps of mineral and organic particulates — although still minuscule, relatively large aggregates bound together by a slimy film produced by feeding bacteria. These macroaggregates, held in place by the intricate web of roots and fungi, help explain prairie soil's miraculous properties. Countless pores and openings between the aggregates, roots, and fungal strands provided abundant niches that housed the unusually diverse microscopic life. These spaces also decreased soil density and made it "fluffy." They allowed for ready percolation of water and air into the root zone, which enabled prairies to function like enormous sponges. Meanwhile the water-stable, tightly held macroaggregates resisted erosion. Aggregates released their nutrients slowly, as needed, to hungry users. Because storage of carbon-based organic matter exceeded its use, prairie soils sequestered organic carbon rather than releasing it all to the atmosphere as carbon dioxide. The buildup of organic matter created the thick, velvety black topsoil that originally averaged around sixteen inches on mesic uplands (Michael T. Sucik, personal communication).

All this biological activity culminated in a single glorious result: Iowa's black gold, its nutrient-rich, porous, well-aerated, and moist prairie-derived soils that are among the most fertile in the world. For century upon century, they held prairies that purred along, capturing the sun's energy, hoisting Earth's minerals from the deeps, and concentrating them into a thin skin of life that coated the Midwest's surface and held it in place. These soils and their inhabitants epitomized Earth's life-generating capacities.

Wooded Strips and Patches

Iowa's oceans of grasses were interrupted by trees growing in a variety of woody communities that collectively covered about 6.6 million acres, or 18 percent of the state (Smith 1998: 97; Jungst et al. 1998: 62). Savannas, woodlands, and forests, craving more moisture than prairies and being less tolerant of intense fire, draped over hilltops, slopes, and bottomlands where, for whatever reason, drought and fire were moderated. Where trees and grasses met, they formed a constantly shifting belt that blended traits of both larger communities.

Most of Iowa's trees grew in the eastern half of the state and in south-central Iowa (see fig. 6). Bottomland forests and oak woodlands were especially extensive in Iowa's northeastern and southeastern corners. Eastern Iowa's abundant tree growth was advanced by the region's relatively moist and mild climate. The precise distribution of woody growth was then shaped by the prevalence of fire, which was determined by the landscape's topography, among other factors. Consider, for example, that major rivers in eastern Iowa flow from northwest to southeast, perpendicular to the southwesterly winds that fanned many wildfires. This fact effectively turned the rivers into firebreaks. Wooded lands were thus most extensive north and east of waterways, lands that may have burned but did not receive the full brunt of racing prairie wildfires. Here trees covered riverside hills and swept onto adjacent uplands, becoming less dense and eventually disappearing as they merged with the flatter upland prairie's more intense fire regime.

Iowa's rivers also had carved their adjacent lands into hills and drainageways. Hilly landscapes on the whole harbored moister, more fire-sheltered sites than flatlands and thus were more conducive to tree growth than to prairies. However, the rugged topography played with fire's intensity and frequency. Fires generally race uphill, then creep downslope, and hills as well as trees moderate the winds that fan fire. In addition, ravines and slopes facing north and east are sheltered from the most intense sunshine and wind and thus are moister, cooler, and less fire prone than slopes facing south and west. The bottoms of slopes also share these traits. These factors resulted in variations in environments and fire regimes, which caused a diversity of types and densities of woody communities within the hilly landscape. Generally speaking, tree growth would have been most prolific on the moistest, most sheltered sites: bottomlands, ravines, slopes facing north and east, and the bottoms of slopes.

In rugged northeastern Iowa, trees were favored both by topography and climate. An abundance of steep slopes stymied wildfire, and a wealth of north- and east-facing hillsides remained shady, cool, and moist throughout the growing season. Some of Iowa's most unusual natural elements are found here: cold spring-fed streams; ice caves that exhale cold air throughout the growing season, creating algific talus slopes and habitat for rare species such as northern monkshood, Iowa golden saxifrage, and Ice Age land snails; clusters of the conifers balsam fir, white pine, and American yew; and many other plants and animals today classified as rare (Glenn-Lewin et al. 1984).

Throughout the state, woody growth interrupted prairies on river bottomlands and floodplains, stringing in linear fashion alongside drainages where the additional moisture stimulated tree growth and stymied wildfire. And trees were found on isolated knolls and pockets embedded within upland prairies, wherever topographic breaks, decreased fuel, or seeping soils tipped the competitive advantage toward woody species. Isolated islands, copses, and linear ridgelines of trees surrounded by expansive prairie were commonly cited by early settlers, especially in eastern Iowa, where such wooded interruptions of the prairie could be extensive.

Moving from central into western Iowa, conditions became less conducive to tree growth: precipitation decreased and drought increased. Wildfires found it easier to sweep across western and north-central Iowa's relatively flat terrain and eliminate trees, making these the state's least wooded regions. Tree growth was also discouraged by western Iowa's river system, which (unlike eastern rivers) ran toward the southwest, parallel to the prevailing winds. These rivers thus funneled and fanned the hottest racing wildfires.

For all these reasons, woodlands and forests diminished on a gradient from east to west, becoming less numerous, smaller, more isolated, and more limited to topographic breaks (stream valleys, valley hillsides). Individual trees and shrubs lost height and became more stunted. The far northwestern corner of the state essentially lacked wooded areas, with its prairie-favoring dry, windy, cold climate and shorter growing season. However, groves and savannas were found in the ravines and sheltered north- and east-facing hillsides of western

Iowa's Loess Hills. Woody growth was most prevalent in the moister southern Loess Hills, and the diversity of trees and shrubs was greatest in the south and decreased to the north.

In parallel fashion, the diversity of trees and shrubs decreased from eastern Iowa to the west. Forest and woodland species had long ago migrated into Iowa from rich forests to the east and south. The state's woody plant diversity remained greatest in Iowa's southeastern corner. For example, a dozen species of oak grew in southeastern Iowa, but only hardy drought- and fire-tolerant bur oak tolerated the state's northwestern corner. Of the five Iowa hickories, only bitternut extended almost (although not quite) into that distant corner. And Iowa's ash species dropped from three to one, green ash (van der Linden and Farrar 1993: 4).

The decline in diversity from east to west also was true of woodland and forest understory plants — forbs and ferns, mosses and fungi. This drop influenced the community structure of western woodland and forest communities, creating entities that might mimic but could not replicate those in eastern Iowa.

These patterns describe woodlands and forests that were far more prescribed than those of today. Trees were limited to predictable, discrete sites on the landscape. Occasionally a renegade might penetrate the grasslands — note the town of Lone Tree in Johnson County, named for an isolated American elm that served as a landmark for Native Americans as well as later settlers. But such a prairie-bred tree was the exception rather than the rule.

A CLOSER EXAMINATION of early records paints a picture of two very different types of tree-dominated communities: diverse forests on riverside bottomlands, streamside terraces, and moist draws, and oak woodlands primarily on hillsides and uplands (fig. 9). Describing the bottomland forests, Thomas Macbride wrote:

> Down by the streams the wild plum, wild cherry, box elder, soft maple and elm made with the grape and Virginia-creeper thickets almost or wholly impassable, with shade so dense that the ground beneath was absolutely bare.... Where the flood-plain was widened with richer alluvial soil, walnuts, hackberries and cottonwoods with an occasional bur-oak gave to the woodland more the appearance of an eastern forest. (1895: 343)

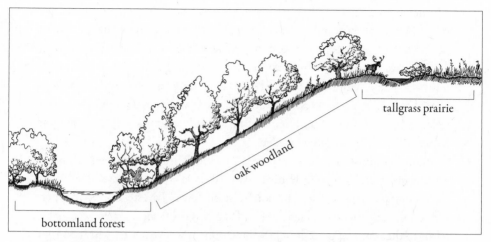

tallgrass prairie

oak woodland

bottomland forest

Fig. 9. Wooded communities were well defined and predictable in presettlement Iowa. Trained by drought, fire, and other stressors, they consisted primarily of diverse multilayered forests on moist bottomlands and open oak woodlands on hillsides, which decreased in density wherever fire and drought increased, such as on upper hillsides. Flat uplands, with their racing prairie fires, were dominated by prairies with occasional shrubs or oaks. This pattern was most prevalent in southern and eastern Iowa, within the range of white oak, where wooded lands abounded. Drawing by Will Thomson.

Bottomland forests were dense and multilayered. Their many fast-growing tree and shrub species took advantage of the diverse habitats and frequent disturbances created by flooding rivers and shifting riverbanks. Willows (peachleaf, black, and others), silver maple (soft maple), and cottonwood sprouted on wet sands and bare substrates alongside rivers and streams across the state, prospering until water swept them away and the cycle began again. These trees — plus American and slippery elm, green ash, boxelder, and black walnut — characterized bottomland forests, covering river terraces and floodplains throughout Iowa. Any of a diversity of additional species might be present — hackberry, sycamore, river birch, and others — although most of these were limited in range and did not extend throughout western Iowa. Other woody wetlands included willow thickets, shrub swamps dominated by buttonbrush, shrub-dominated fens, and ephemeral ponds in shallow, woody basins. Contrasting with the dense, diverse bottomland forests, swamp white oak formed an occasional lowland savanna, as did black oak.

Many bottomland trees utilized fast growth and easily dispersed seeds to advantage on their periodically disturbed sites, colonizing open ground with speed. Although bottomland species might occasionally populate an upland pocket or surround seeps and springs perched higher on hillsides, for the most part they were restricted to waterlogged lowland floodplains, oxbows, and shallow backwaters, with broad forested strips becoming narrower and more interrupted toward the drier west. Bottomland trees were mostly eliminated from uplands by more intense and frequent fires that were quick to penetrate their thin bark and kill off young invaders.

In stark contrast to the rich mixture of trees in dense riverside forests, hillside and upland woodlands were dominated by oaks. Oaks were the most ubiquitous and abundant trees in Iowa. In northeastern Iowa's Fayette County, 72 percent of the early surveyors' General Land Office (GLO) witness trees were oaks, while to the south 74 percent of Jackson County's were oaks. In other counties next to the Mississippi River, two-thirds of all trees were oaks. In east-central Iowa, 80 percent of Johnson County's GLO witness trees were oaks. The vast majority of other witness trees were either upland hickories or members of bottomland forests (Miller 1995: 90, 95; Dick-Peddie 1953; James Martin, personal communication).

Oak dominance implies a great deal about presettlement woods. Oak seedlings are slow-growing plants that do not tolerate shade. Although a woodland floor may be covered with young oaks, all will die or remain small and stunted if they do not receive sufficient direct sunlight. Since midwestern oaklands had flourished for at least 3,000 years, we can deduce that across the Midwest, they must have been far more open than anything we know today. Only sun-streaked, open-canopied tree stands could have provided a constant stream of thriving young oaks to replace their dying progenitors.

Historic descriptions of settlement-era oak woodlands support this supposition. "The most striking peculiarity of the Iowa upland [oak] forest was its openness," wrote Thomas Macbride (1895: 343). Elsewhere, he wrote that "one could drive [a wagon] or ride anywhere through the primeval woods of Iowa, except, perhaps, immediately along the borders of streams" (1897: 170).

Because of the airy openness of these upland communities, in this book oak-dominated communities collectively are referred to as "woodlands." Savannas, the most open oak woodlands with only a few trees per acre, are included in this nomenclature. The term "forest" is reserved for diverse, dense bottomland communities.

What maintained this openness, allowed the oaks to dominate the landscape, and determined their locations? The same force that maintained prairies: fire. While fires in presettlement oaklands were likely cooler and tamer than prairie fires, the low, steady creep of flame through oak-leaf litter was equally crucial for the survival of these woodlands and their dependent plant and animal associates. "Fire-swept groves are by no means always reduced to prairie," expounded Bohumil Shimek. "[They] are often soon restored, if indeed they do not remain practically uninjured, the destruction of the underbrush often probably being of advantage to the trees" (1899: 49).

Fire's positive role in maintaining native oakland biodiversity is becoming increasingly clear today. Oak woodlands are superbly adapted to fire. Their fallen leaves dry rapidly, curl, and crinkle, inviting and enhancing combustion. (Compare this to the unburnable soggy mats formed by leaves of maples or other fire-intolerant native trees.) Squirrels and jays preferentially bury acorns on soils bared by fire, and oak seedlings emerge more easily here. Insects preying on acorns are decreased by fire. Young oak trees may be burned back repeatedly but rapidly return by vigorously sprouting new shoots from buds near ground level. And older oaks, especially bur and white oaks, possess a thick bark that shields their sensitive inner tissues from fire's heat (Van Lear 1991).

Fire not only stimulated the oaks and created the openness they craved, it also eliminated or suppressed competing shrubs and trees. Because their seedlings and saplings were killed by regular fire, the fast-growing, thin-barked species of diverse bottomland forests were unable to proliferate on uplands and overtake the slow-growing oaks. Fire pruned oaklands into uncluttered communities with an airy two-layered structure, a canopy high above and a diverse and flourishing ground layer of flowering plants.

Mentally reconstructing Iowa's presettlement oaklands requires consideration of the several species of oak present. Deep-rooted, thick-leaved bur and white oaks were well adapted to dry sites, as they were to the fires that flashed more regularly through upland woods than through lower, moister woodlands. These two oaks were Iowa's most abundant trees. In Allamakee County, 32 percent of all witness trees were white oak, and 30 percent were bur oak (Dick-Peddie 1953). In Fayette County, 27 percent were white oak, and 25 percent were bur oak (Miller 1995: 90). In Johnson County, about 32 percent of witness trees were white oak, and 29 percent were bur oak (James Martin, personal communication). White and bur oaks clearly ruled the open woodlands and the upland savannas in the southeastern half to two-thirds of the state, that is, in eastern, central, and southern Iowa excluding the Loess Hills. Beyond here, to the north and west, white oak largely disappeared, and bur oak assumed dominance, becoming the most abundant tree in much of western Iowa, where it often grew in pure stands.

White and bur oak savannas are thought to have been especially abundant. The GLO surveys allocate roughly one-third of Iowa's presettlement woody cover (2.4 million acres, or 6 percent of the state) to savannas and two-thirds (4.2 million acres, or 12 percent of the state) to "forests" (presumably denser upland oaklands as well as bottomland and ravine forests) (Smith 1998: 97; Jungst et al. 1998: 62). Savanna parklands boasted massive, widely spaced trees that topped knolls and ridges. Because side branches of open-grown oaks received an abundance of sunshine, they extended far outward to produce broad, bulbous-shaped crowns. On rolling uplands and hillsides, savanna trees and their associated shrubs sometimes formed a broad belt between lower, denser woodlands and the treeless prairies, a dynamic tension zone that was constantly shifting in response to climate and fire. Regular fires of moderate to high intensity (along with the browsing, stomping, and rubbing of bison and elk) cleared savannas of shrubs and saplings. With their mature open-grown oaks and dense ground cover of grasses and forbs that bloomed sequentially throughout the summer, savannas were acclaimed as profoundly beautiful (see color plate 1).

In the southern and eastern halves of Iowa, black oak sometimes joined upland woodlands, especially on the driest sites, and also formed savannas on dry or sandy, very well drained stream terraces, bottomlands, and knolls. On Iowa's eastern and southern bottomlands, swamp white oak mingled into streamside forests and formed open, fire-maintained savannas on floodplains of major rivers. The Nature Conservancy's Swamp White Oak Preserve (along the Cedar River in Muscatine County) is one of the few surviving examples.

Bur oak, which grew throughout the state, occasionally joined bottomland savannas. But it was most abundant in the uppermost, driest woodlands and savannas, sites from which it strove actively to invade adjacent upland prairies. Here the trees withstood frequent and intense droughts and fires, surviving in part by shooting a taproot as deep as five feet by the end of their first growing season (van der Linden and Farrar 1993: 60). The harsh environment commonly reduced these prairie-invading bur oaks to grubs, thick and aging root bases that continued to grow and sprout vigorous new shoots despite being repeatedly burned back. Bur oak grubs (and those of other oaks or shrubs) dotted many brushy prairies, awaiting spans of a few fireless years when their shoots might develop a thick protective corky bark and spurt upward. The resulting scrub woodlands of multiple-trunked, stunted, gnarled bur oaks, examples of which can still be found in the Loess Hills, were not particularly impressive. Thomas Macbride described them in this way:

> The spread of timber was prevented by prairie-fires. Where the grass was heavy these were excessively hot, so that trees could maintain themselves only where the grass was scanty; that is, where the soil was thin or barren. Moreover, the trees were for the most part scattered.... The greater number of the trees were old; they were low, often scrubby, storm-tossed, often scarred by fire, of little value. (1897: 170)

Shagbark hickory was a regular, although far less abundant, member of upland savannas and open oak woodlands. Characteristic shrubs included hazelnut, smooth sumac, and gray dogwood. Like bur oak, they served as woody invaders of prairies. They might burn back to the ground, but escape from fire allowed thickets to proliferate.

Researchers now believe that Iowa's light, dry oak woodlands and savannas housed an abundance of animals and distinctive fire-adapted, semi-shade-tolerant understory plants that bloomed throughout the growing season, in parallel fashion to the ever-changing prairie flora (Packard 1988, 1993).

Take these varied open upslope and ridgetop oak woodlands, trace them downhill, and other patterns emerge. Wherever fire intensity and frequency decreased (because of slope exposure, moisture content, or fuel load), oaklands likely became denser. Species less able to tolerate drought and fire, such as the more shade-tolerant red oak, joined the white and bur oaks and shagbark hickory. A shifting mosaic of tree density might have covered hillsides and ravines of varying slope and exposure, with canopy coverage increasing in places to as much as 75 or 80 percent. Research in Wisconsin has indicated that most oaks can reproduce under canopy coverage of 80 percent or less, although other present-day environmental factors may hamper such reproduction (Curtis 1959: 146). While fire would have remained crucial, its decreased intensity on lower slopes might have allowed small numbers of other mesic trees to creep in — white ash, basswood, black cherry, and ironwood being likely candidates. A few sturdy American or slippery elms or other trees might have slipped onto lower hillsides from diverse bottomland forests.

Toward the west and north, beyond the range of white oak, oak woodland patterns would have reflected the disappearance of many woody species. In western Iowa's harsher, drier climes, bur oak was the dominant woodland tree species, likely forming savannas or open woodlands wherever topographic breaks interrupted the prairie's dominance. Moister, more sheltered sites — lower hillsides and ravines — were probably covered by denser stands of red oak (found up to, but not in, Iowa's far northwestern corner) and/or basswood (found throughout Iowa), possibly with an understory of plants characteristic of eastern Iowa's moister oak woodlands.

In the Loess Hills, moister woodlands likely existed low on north- and east-facing hillsides and in ravines. Here red oak and basswood may have mixed with other oaks and hickories or with trees moving up from narrow streamside forests, especially in the southern Loess Hills with its greater tree diversity. These gave way to bur oak woodlands and savannas on upper drier slopes and in the northern hills. Early records state that although prairies were expansive, especially in the northern Loess Hills, scattered bur oak grubs were common in these grasslands.

Might any oak woodlands have approached 100 percent canopy coverage in Iowa? We can only guess. Oak's promotion of fire and need for sunlight would argue against such closed-canopy oaklands. However, occasionally a stand-replacing fire, windstorm, or disease outbreak might have cleared a woodland segment, allowing a cohort of young oaks to form a dense, even-aged stand. Elsewhere smaller patches of oaks, filling in clearings created by the death of trees, presumably formed mixed-aged woodlands.

Two additional tree species common throughout the eastern two-thirds of Iowa demand attention. "Here and there on rocky banks were groves of hard maple rivaling those of Pennsylvania and Vermont," wrote Thomas Macbride about our presettlement wooded lands (1895: 343). Hard maples (sugar maple in the eastern third of Iowa, giving way to less aggressive black maple in central Iowa) are in some ways the antithesis of oaks, being highly tolerant of shade and intolerant of fire. As such, during presettlement times, these maples (with associates such as basswood, red oak, and white ash) would have been restricted to steep-sloped ravines and sheltered lower slopes facing north and east, moist sites that repelled fire. Here these trees likely formed shady self-perpetuating stands that were far denser than nearby oaklands, possibly with a characteristic understory of moisture-loving herbs. Indeed, examination of the GLO records of Mississippi River counties reveals that presettlement maple–basswood–red oak communities were three times as dense as nearby oak-hickory communities. Mature maple-basswood communities are thought to have been most expansive in the rugged terrain of northeastern Iowa. However, GLO records reveal that even here they were not common; only 6.5 percent of the witness trees in Fayette County were sugar maple, a figure that dropped to 5.4 percent in Jackson County and to under 1 percent in Johnson County (Miller 1995: 90, 95; Dick-Peddie 1953; James Martin, personal communication).

We thus can patch together an image of Iowa's trees and shrubs, based on historic records. But while woody plant records are sketchy at best, historic records of their understory plants are nearly nonexistent. How, then, can the grasses, sedges, and flowers underneath presettlement trees be imagined? About all we can do is extrapolate from what we see today. For example, the spring-blooming wildflowers must have been glorious then, as they are now. The sun-loving grasses must have given way to sedges and forbs as woodlands became denser, but some grasses (such as bottlebrush grass, long-awned wood grass, and broad-leaved panic grass) surely remained in open oak woodlands, as they do today.

Savannas provided sites where shade-adapted herbs of the denser oak woodlands could mingle with sun lovers of the prairies. Savannas also possessed herbs that grew best in these sun-dappled sites, plants that helped define a distinctive savanna flora different from that of either prairies or denser oak woodlands. Within their ranges mayapple, poke milkweed, elmleaf goldenrod, and the horse gentians may have been a few such savanna plants in Iowa (Delong and Hooper 1996). Certain plants now found in open woodlands also grow in prairies, examples being shootingstar, purple milkweed, cream gentian, Culver's root, pale-leaved sunflower, and prairie grasses such as Indiangrass and big bluestem. The quantity and vitality of such plants must have been greatest in the sunnier, more open oak woodlands.

In contrast, many ferns, mosses, and more shade-tolerant forbs such as hepatica, the trilliums, white trout lily, Dutchman's breeches, and bishop's cap well may have occupied moister, shadier wooded lands and perhaps thrived in northeastern Iowa's maple-dominated stands. And wet bottomlands likely held flowers such as toothwort, cardinalflower, Virginia bluebells, honewort, and many sedges within their respective ranges.

But did groups of such understory plants form distinct associations allied with specific woodland and forest communities, or did each species act more independently? We simply don't know. Many understory plants now occupy a broad range of habitats, but present-day associations of woodland and forest herbs may be misleading. The extent to which alliances of similar species predictably characterized specific presettlement oak woodlands and bottomland forests thus remains a mystery.

Trickles and Seeps

This chapter began by describing the fires, grazing, and climate that molded Iowa's presettlement communities. One crucial factor remains, a gentler but equally profound element that coaxed rather than shoved nature into shape: the flow of water through the landscape. Native tallgrass prairie largely controlled this flow, the dense and deep-rooted vegetation pulling water into the soil and counteracting water's tendency to pass over the surface of the ground and slip rapidly away.

The prairie's infiltration and storage system was quite unlike anything we conceive as normal today. The process began with the first droplets of rain, whose fall onto vast mesic prairies was broken by dense leaves and litter. The surface area of overlapping prairie leaves formed an intercepting layer five to twenty times as large as the underlying ground surface. Prairie leaves caught and held a significant amount of the rainfall, much of which evaporated and moistened the air (Weaver 1954: 120, 140).

Water that escaped evaporation dropped onto a rough-textured mat of unde-cayed plant litter that nearly eliminated surface flow and instead coaxed liquids downward into the waiting soil. There a maze of minute pores awaited the per-colating water, a network of open spaces that constitute about half the volume of a healthy tallgrass soil, the other half being a web of particulates and organic material.

Tallgrass soils thus functioned as a gigantic sponge, soaking up and holding unimaginable quantities of water. Thomas Macbride described the prairie's infiltration hydrology in this way: "The prairies were wet, and in all low places staid wet. Very rarely did the surplus water pass off by anything like a ditch as now, but every valley was a bog, utterly impassable to man or beast. The waters did not seem to run at all, but gradually evaporated or sank to lower and lower strata. . . . Over the oozy sloughs the sedges waved head-high, and into their treacherous depths horses, oxen or even men ventured at peril of their lives" (1895: 344–345).

The shallower soils of woodlands and forests absorbed and held moisture to a lesser degree. Nevertheless in 1952, when prairies had all but vanished, Iowa botanist Henry Conard boasted that "the oakwood [is] our greatest conservator of rainfall and our best insurance against floods," citing in particular the red oak's soft, loose, leafy mull, which is "so absorbent that the rain never moves it" (1952: 19).

Fig. 10. Both prairies and wooded lands supported abundant wetlands, a sign that the entire landscape was far wetter and its water table much higher than today. This south-central Iowa wetland displays the intermingling of grassland, wooded land, and wetland that must have characterized parts of presettlement Iowa. Photograph by Carl Kurtz.

With the entire landscape soaking up rather than shedding precipitation, the land was far wetter than it is today (fig. 10). Seeps and springs abounded. The high water table reshaped vegetation and fed settlers' wells. Even upland wells reportedly filled at depths of only twenty or thirty feet (Newhall 1841: 14). However, eventually the gigantic soil-sponge demanded release. While some of its contents continued a downward journey and replenished deep aquifers, and some was pulled through the plants' transpiration back into the air, a portion eventually seeped back to daylight to feed wetlands (areas governed by saturated or inundated soils) or track an aboveground course to the sea.

Discharging groundwaters ran clean, free of sediment: soil particles were tightly held within a mesh of prairie roots and fungal threads. The steady discharge of clear groundwater produced slow, stable, perennial streams that may have pulsed gently but lacked sudden changes in water level. Thus both floodwaters and droughty streambeds are thought to have been uncommon. Steady, shallow, meandering streams and other watery areas supported complex habitats replete with diverse and distinctive species. Animals could depend on the constancy of the water's quality and flow.

Prairie, shrub, woodland, and forest wetlands varied greatly in location, defining characteristics, and resident species. Some were seasonal and intermittent; others retained moisture year-round. Some were defined by still pools of varying depths, others by waterlogged soils. Sometimes groundwater hit an impervious layer of glacial till and then, moving horizontally, seeped out onto gentle slopes. Elsewhere underground flows spouted as springs, which along with ponds were abundant on uplands. As Thomas Macbride described, "Instead of grass-grown mead[ow], sometimes occurred a lake of greater or less extent.... Such morasses were not infrequent in the woods on the hill-tops forty or fifty feet above the surrounding prairie lowlands" (1895: 343). Water meandered through grassy swales. It trickled over the land to fill poorly drained bottoms and abandoned stream channels, streams, and rivers. Wherever it surfaced, Iowa's waters eventually flowed into the massive Mississippi River and meandering Missouri River and their tributaries, there creating additional wetlands by filling abandoned oxbows and interbraided backwater sloughs and overflowing onto riverside floodplains and lower terraces that often were covered with bottomland forests. These assorted wetlands provided nesting sites and resting and feeding stopovers for a rich abundance of migrating waterfowl, shorebirds, and other animals.

Some types of wetlands were abundant, while others such as fens were probably always uncommon. Fens are small boggy areas characterized by quaking organic soils (mucks of decomposed plant parts) and fed by cold, mineral-rich springs (see color plate 6). Found in both prairies and wooded areas, they are often dominated by sedges but may include woody plants. Usually located on hillsides, they also form on low stream terraces and in small basins. Fens, which may vary in their water's alkalinity and nutrient content, are united in providing habitat for uncommon plants and a rich variety of insects and other small animals.

In all, Iowa's varied presettlement wetlands covered about 8,936,000 acres, or 25 percent of the state.[2] This figure is based on the current extent of hydric

2. Presettlement wetland coverage was calculated from digitized soil maps first available in 2003. These maps permitted calculations of Iowa's hydric soil coverage, which is thought to provide the most accurate estimate of presettlement wetlands (Susan Galatowitsch, personal communication). Hydric soils were defined as in the text and were computed in 2005 by Casey Kohrt, research geologist at the Iowa Geological Survey, from a soil grid (30m pixels) of all Iowa soils, with metadata available at ftp://ftp.igsb.uiowa.edu/GIS_Library/IA_State/Geologic/Soils/soils.htm. Prior to the availability of these digitized maps, Dahl 1990 estimated Iowa's wetland coverage for the National Wetland Inventory. Using aerial

soils in Iowa, which underlie today's wetlands but also are found in sites that are now drained. The soils of both existing and drained wetlands display signs of having been saturated, flooded, or ponded long enough to have developed anaerobic conditions in the upper layer and of having supporting moisture-loving prairie, woodland and forest, or wetland vegetation. Earlier estimates, based on less comprehensive survey techniques, limited Iowa's wetland coverage to about 4,000,000 acres (Dahl 1990).

Iowa's wetlands were least abundant in the hillier southern and northeastern parts of the state, where well-developed drainage networks had evolved over the past half-million years. Here wetlands were associated with the waterlogged bottomlands of streams and rivers and with hillside seeps. Rugged northeastern Iowa also possessed cold, spring-fed streams.

The flatter expanses of northern Iowa, in contrast, boasted abundant wetlands — poorly drained depressions comprising prairie swales, sedge meadows, marshes, and forested floodplains. Soil maps suggest that these covered 20 to 60 percent of many northern Iowa landscapes (Galatowitsch and van der Valk 1994: 16). They were most abundant in the prairie pothole (Des Moines Lobe) region of north-central Iowa, which was covered by glaciers until a mere 12,000 years ago. Here, where the prairie landscapes had not yet evolved a stream drainage system, the land was pocked with potholes, kettleholes, and shallow and deep lakes. These north-central marshlands formed a veritable waterfowl factory. They constituted the southeastern terminus of the midcontinental prairie pothole complex, which provided the nation's most important nesting sites for dabbling ducks and was crucially important to additional breeding and migrating ducks, geese, shorebirds, and other birds.

Altogether, Iowa's hydrologic complex formed a self-regulating system whose widespread effects brought both heterogeneity and remarkable stability to the landscape. As the early settler Andrew Hyde recorded retrospectively, "The [prairie] soil had a wonderful capacity for [with]standing drouth.... The sloughs and hollows and damp spots [in] eastern and central Iowa ... used to grow a big

---

photographs from the 1980s and including as best he could those wetlands embedded within the original prairie and woodland matrix, he estimated that presettlement wetlands covered an estimated 4 million acres, or 11.1 percent of the state. Dahl's figures exceeded those of the GLO surveys, which reported only 489,096 acres (1.36 percent) of Iowa as wetland (Smith 1998: 97). GLO numbers are thought to be low because surveyors often did not define wet prairies or woodlands/forests as wetlands and because many original wetlands were small and overlooked.

crop of high rank slough grass. Its roots matted together and held water like a sponge. One of these sloughs would hold water in soak through a long dry spell. It would drain out slowly, forming a little stream through a long dry season; watering the stock along a little valley and helping to keep the creeks and rivers running" (1902: 20–21).

Untethered to the Soil

A great diversity of animals leaped, crawled, fluttered, and dug their way through Iowa's vegetation (fig. 11). Loose groups of elk commonly roamed the prairies in summer, gathering into larger herds and seeking shelter in wooded acres or marshes during winter storms. Gray wolves followed the bison that speckled tall-grass prairies, their numbers a pittance of the tremendous herds that blanketed the short-grass prairies farther to the west. Hungry badgers dug out Franklin's ground squirrels, plains pocket gophers, and other burrowing rodents. Prairie voles, meadow jumping mice, short-tailed and least shrews, and deer mice rustled through the grasses. Muskrat, beaver, and river otter constructed dens in or alongside wetlands, while semiaquatic mink slunk along their shores.

Within the sea of grass, nearly all birds nested on the ground or in structures nestled into grasses or held by low shrubs. Some, such as the loggerhead shrike, raised their young in interspersed shrublands. Nearly all prairie birds migrated south in autumn to feed and to escape winter's unforgiving blizzards and cold. Many traveled to tropical climes thousands of miles distant, leaving the prairie to sleep in silence through the winter. But in the summertime, birds were everywhere. Bohumil Shimek described them thus:

> The broad prairies were swept by great whirl-wind clouds of golden plovers, the long-billed curlew hovered between earth and space in marvelous manner, an easy mark for every pot-hunter in the land; the bobolink and the marsh blackbird made the welkin ring with their songs; the mournful "boom" of the prairie chicken resounded everywhere; and soon countless nests were occupied by wild geese, ducks and prairie hens on all sides, giving promise of new generations in untold numbers to enliven these prairies in a fashion which will never again be known to this or coming generations. (1911: 170)

Many prairie birds — the bobolink, dickcissel, meadowlark, and horned lark, among others — sang loudly on the wing, courting mates and defending their

Fig. 11. Presettlement Iowa provided habitat for large as well as small mammals and birds, including large predators. All shown here disappeared with settlement, although a few are making a comeback. Drawing by Mark Müller.

grassy territories with visual displays as well as song. They rustled through the grasses eating insects and seeds. Northern harriers, American kestrels, short-eared owls, and other predators hunted low overhead, and an occasional peregrine falcon streaked through the sky. Turkey vultures picked clean the bones of those who died.

Interspersed wetlands supported large birds such as whooping and sandhill cranes and untold numbers of associated marsh- and shorebirds. Water birds were complemented by belted kingfishers, rails, marsh wrens, swallows, yellow warblers, and other songbirds that nested in brushy wet prairies or along the shores of creeks and rivers.

In wooded areas, black bears, gray foxes, and coyotes feasted on a variety of smaller animals as well as insects and berries. Cougars stalked white-tailed deer. The solitary bobcat roamed the river bluffs and heavy timber. The gray squirrel planted a variety of trees when it cached nuts for the winter and clambered through dense forests to its treetop leaf nests, while the larger and more bushy-tailed fox squirrel favored open woodlands and savannas. Flying squirrels glided as much as thirty feet from one tree to another, soaring through the night on flaps of skin stretched taut between their front and back legs. Woodchucks, eastern chipmunks, raccoons, woodland voles, skunks, shrews, weasels, and eastern cottontails all were common.

Birdlife was abundant and rich, with diversity being many times greater than that of grasslands. During mating season, the woodlands resounded with the gobbling of the wild turkey, which grew plump feeding on acorns (a mainstay of many woodland animals). "The drumming of the ruffed grouse . . . was one of the most familiar sounds in our woods," wrote Bohumil Shimek of the later 1800s, "and the passenger pigeon still came in great clouds to seek shelter amid the oaks of our uplands" (1948: 6–7).

In distinct contrast to their prairie cousins, most woodland and forest birds nested in trees or shrubs and defended their territories from perches. The majority migrated south to feed for the winter, many being neotropical migrants that traveled thousands of miles to Central and South America. These included not only numerous songbirds (species of wrens, warblers, finches, vireos, thrushes, flycatchers, and others) but also predatory hawks and owls. However, a distinctive set of birds — many woodpeckers, the tufted titmouse, the black-capped chickadee, nuthatches, and others — remained in Iowa's woodlands and forests through the winter, switching their diet from the insects and berries that abounded in warm weather to seeds available throughout the winter. Overwin-

Fig. 12. This massive flock of snow geese migrating along the Missouri River provides a sense of the millions of waterfowl and other prolific wildlife that once were commonplace in Iowa. Photograph by Carl Kurtz.

tering birds, then and now, relied on our oaks and other nut producers (for example, hazelnuts and hickories), sometimes caching acorns and nuts and other nutritious foods in cavities or crevices in the bark for later consumption. They also inspected trees for insects and larvae, removing them from bark and tunnels within dead wood. Many were cavity nesters who used holes in trees for winter shelters.

Additional birds inhabited savannas, woodland and forest edges, and shrubby thickets, communities that supported a high diversity of animals. These residents could shelter or nest in protected sites and forage in open prairies, thus combining the advantages of both community types. Savanna birds included the eastern bluebird, red-headed woodpecker, indigo bunting, and orchard oriole, while other species resided in shrubby borders and thickets (for example, northern bobwhite, whip-poor-will, gray catbird, eastern towhee, song sparrow, and American goldfinch).

Many of these animals proliferated in numbers beyond compare, especially in the prairie. Most productive of all were the interspersed wetlands. Early residents described skies filled with clouds of waterfowl, with millions nesting in or migrating through Iowa (fig. 12). Flocks of upland sandpipers, common and abundant prairie nesters, could be heard over early Iowa City for more than an hour at a time upon their return migration from South America. The flights of marbled godwits were described as vast rivers of birds flowing from an inexhaustible source. Prairie-chickens would glide low overhead in flocks of thousands or feed in wintering groups of 200 or 300. "The prairie-hens were a most common bird over the whole prairie," wrote Thomas Macbride. "All day long you could hear the rustling of their wings. . . . Every old resident must remember the abundant eggs with which the prairies were once strewn" (1895: 346). These and the bobwhite quail of woodland edges and savannas became common market stock: in December 1858, following the fall hunting season, a single Iowa City firm shipped out 767 dozen quail and a few tons of prairie-chickens. Even shorebirds were abundant enough to feed the market hunters, with American woodcocks shipped out of Iowa by the thousands (Dinsmore 1994: 136, 138; Aurner 1912: 443).

Most numerous of all were passenger pigeons, the most abundant land bird in North America, which reached the western edge of its migratory range in eastern Iowa. Flocks obscured the sun and cast shadows over the earth. Waves of tens of thousands stretched from horizon to horizon, a single flock passing overhead for two or three days. Feeding on acorns, the savanna-dwelling birds roosted so tightly that their combined weight broke oak branches five to six inches in diameter. Settlers not only shipped millions from midwestern states to eastern markets, they also fed the easily harvested birds to hogs (Dinsmore 1994: 90–100).

The prolific wildlife sated the hunger of Iowa's early residents. Abigail Irish wrote that in the mid 1800s, "large flocks of [wild turkey] came to the barnyards searching for food, and the farmers set traps there catching them in plenty. . . . In those days there was no need for anyone to go hungry" (1922: 21–22). Another settler, John Springer, recalled that during his boyhood in the 1850s, the Iowa City game market was sufficiently overstocked that wildlife became unsellable. Game dealers abandoned their traplines, prompting young children to wander the outskirts of town salvaging the prairie-chickens, quail, and eastern cottontails that were caught therein. The winter's abundance gave this settler "a distaste for game which I have not outgrown," he later wrote (Springer 1924: 6–7).

Even the waters abounded with life. In 1862 the Iowa River yielded catfish weighing nearly seventy pounds and a gar pike over four feet long (Anonymous 1883: 579). Such fish provided ready food: "of Fish there can never be any scarcity," recorded an 1839 Iowa guidebook. "Every stream is filled with them . . .

the pike, the pickerel, the catfish, the trout, and many other varieties. Immense quantities are taken about the several rapids, where they may be easily speared" (Plumbe 1839: 11).

Tiny animals also populated the land in unimaginable numbers. Modern measurements of aboveground prairie invertebrates record densities exceeding 4,000 per square yard. About half of these are insects. Underground insects are even more abundant. Numbers of mites, ants, and thrips are especially high, but many additional types of invertebrates abound in prairies: spiders, bees, ticks, butterflies, moths, wasps, beetles, flies, leafhoppers, dragonflies, grasshoppers, lacewings, and other life-forms too numerous to catalog (Risser et al. 1981: 470).

Insects were well adapted to the prairie habitat. Butterflies were mostly skippers: small brown insects that used their rapid, strong flight to survive the prairie's winds. With a few exceptions (monarchs, a few prairie fritillaries), the majority of other prairie butterflies (the blues, coppers, and sulfurs) were also small. The relatively calm woodlands and forests, in contrast, housed larger, slower-flying butterflies. Bark mimics such as the mourning cloak, eastern comma, and question mark overwintered in tree cracks. These and other springtime butterflies (spring azures and eastern tiger swallowtails) were followed by little wood-satyrs and giant swallowtails, among others, while hairstreak butterflies sunned themselves on oak leaves of open savannas.

Insects ate plants, parasitized them, and pollinated their flowers. Invertebrates scavenged animal carcasses, preyed on one another, and in turn were feasted upon by birds during the day and bats at night. Minute species by the thousands shaped the flow of food and energy through prairie, woodland, forest, and wetland, fostering the constant cycling of substance from life, through death, and back once again into life.

Moving Waves in a Stable Sea

Thus we have a picture of Iowa as the initial wave of Euroamerican traders and settlers might have seen it: a living moist skin of fecundity, of flitting butterflies and roaming beasts, of grassland seas clinging to Earth's richest soils, of waters seeping through tangles of roots and humus, and of trees inching upward wherever the prairies relinquished their grasp, all under a sky that reached toward infinity. A land of fire and wind, harsh in its expectations, tempering life with drought and blizzard, heat and ice.

Envisioning Iowa's grasslands, wetlands, oak woodlands, and bottomland forests from the back of a moving horse or the seat of a wagon, the earliest traders and settlers may have imagined these communities as fixed and unchanging. But had the newcomers been able to compress time, they could have observed slow and small but constant shifts. One community flowed into another, the prairie running into savannas and savannas into more closed woodlands, the location, density, and nature of each patch always on the go. More drought-resistant grasses would hide under leaves of larger grasses until the driest of years, when they increased in number and dominance. Oak woodlands expanded when droughts yielded to rain. A herd of bison churning the mud could form a wallow that beckoned nesting shorebirds. Passenger pigeons might carry away a woodland's acorns, a fire might skirt large patches of a prairie. A windstorm would fell one cluster of oaks but leave its neighbor standing. Each variation veered the community toward a slightly different future. Brushy prairies, left unburned, grew into woodlands. Drought fueled conflagrations that erased savannas. Oak woodlands fell to become hazelnut copses, while new oaklands sprouted nearby. The landscape was in reality a dynamic mosaic of communities superbly adapted to Iowa's climate and soils. No single patch provided constant haven for all species. But somewhere within the localized, measured flux, all species found a niche to reach into the future (fig. 13).

While the parts changed, the whole remained amazingly constant. The restless communities formed a self-sustaining, self-replicating mosaic, comprising one of North America's most complex ecosystems. Hundreds of plant species were home to thousands of animals that danced together interdependently, each becoming food or function for dozens of other organisms. The communities required no energy other than sunlight to sustain life and no raw materials other than local minerals, organic matter, water, and air. Yet they were tremendously productive, fully and efficiently utilizing the resources available.

These pre-1800s native communities, with their tremendous biodiversity, functioned in a balanced and predictable manner, nurturing life even in the face of environmental challenges. They maintained an environmental integrity that can only be dreamed of today. This integrity afforded native communities long-term stability and sustainability — the ability to persist and function for the indefinite future. A sustainable landscape is one capable of providing food, shelter, and other necessities not only for today's humans and Earth's millions of other life-forms but also for generations and centuries to come. While members

Fig. 13. Iowa's complex of presettlement plant communities flowed one into the next, with fire, drought, herbivores, and other stressors shaping the migration and intermingling of grassland and wooded land. The result was a diverse, dynamic, and self-sustaining whole. Drawing by Paul W. Nelson from Packard and Mutel 2005: xxxvi. Copyright 1997, 2005, Society for Ecological Restoration International. Reproduced by permission.

of sustainable communities may shift in location and reassemble in varied manners, the landscape and its inhabitants on the whole remain stable. Populations of plants and animals are adaptable and remain viable over the long term. Sustainable communities continue to function well, providing ecosystem services in abundance (Naeem et al. 1999).

Iowa's presettlement communities were exemplary models of a long-term sustainability that this landscape has not known since. Native communities and their adaptations to Iowa's environment still provide our best models for counteracting environmental degradation. Restorations of our presettlement prairies, woodlands, forests, and wetlands constitute a standard for health and wholeness against which other communities can be measured, a vision for the future. They promise, if allowed, to provide agricultural models and ecological services that can renew the earth in a miraculous manner. For all these reasons, whenever considering environmental or land-use choices, the natural world in 1800 and three watchwords — sustainability, stability, and biodiversity — provide us with a meaningful standard of comparison and a benchmark for decision making.

3   The Great Transformation

So completely has the whole State passed beneath the plow, so
quickly assumed the appearance of one vast farm, that one who
thus studies the Iowa of to-day realizes with difficulty the strange
picturesque wildness of fifty or sixty years ago. . . . The whole flora
of the prairie went down to rise no more, to give place to plants of
man's selecting and to weeds. . . . Hosts of alien species occupied
the ground.
— Thomas Macbride, 1895

Judging from the few goods they carried, one might have thought that Iowa's Euroamerican settlers arrived fairly empty-handed. But looks can be deceiving. The livestock straggling behind their wagons and the packets of seeds tucked into their satchels told another story. Settlers crossed the Mississippi River hauling with them an entire portable ecosystem, one detailed by preconceptions and models carried in their memories.

Settlement implied wiping the earth clean of native prairies, oak woodlands, and bottomland forests and installing a more familiar landscape, a comforting quiltwork of villages and farmsteads that had proven successful in Europe and in the eastern states. Predictable domesticated plants and animals were substituted for wild species that had evolved in place. Grains and pasture grasses replaced prairies; cattle, sheep, and hogs replaced bison, elk, and deer; poultry were substituted for prairie-chickens; humans with their guns and domesticated dogs and cats became predators in place of cougars, bears, and wolves. City dwellers brought familiar garden flowers and ornamental shrubs to their new homes and conifers to plant in cemeteries.

Many of these substitutions have proven beneficial. Seemingly overnight, Iowa was transformed into one of the world's richest agricultural regions, a land that appeared destined to provide food, forage, and the functional urban and agricultural landscapes we occupy today. Grains and meat poured out to feed the nation and the world.

But the advancement of human life was offset by the loss of the native sunflowers, waterfowl, butterflies, orchids, hazelnut thickets, passenger pigeons, elk, and myriad other organisms that once flourished here. Their decline was so precipitous that entire communities vanished even before they were identified. Within a generation, the commonplace had become rare.

Few would argue that Iowa's agricultural transformation should not have occurred. But many mourn that it happened so fast and so thoroughly — that before the breaking plows and lumber mills ground to a halt, no one set aside significant tracts of prairie, woodland, and forest for providing commodities other than food. Or to serve as sites for education, research, and pleasure. Or simply because of their beauty and intrigue.

The agricultural conversion of North America's tallgrass prairie has been called the most rapid and complete ecological transformation in Earth's history. This conversion and its impacts, as well as the status of remaining species, must be examined in greater detail if we are to find ways to return health to Iowa's remaining native fragments and repair Iowa's self-regulating natural systems.

Removal of the Old Guard

Before new agricultural communities could be installed, species native to Iowa had to be removed. Traders and trappers had begun the process; immigrant farmers accelerated it. Their most overt targets were predatory animals thought to threaten humans or livestock. Hawks, owls, and reptiles were killed without consideration of their beneficial roles. Gray wolves were shot, trapped, or poisoned whenever possible. The slaughter of both wolves and coyotes was encouraged by a bounty system that extended well into the twentieth century. Bounties also were offered for foxes, cougars, and bobcats.

Reveling in the profusion that lay before them and unhampered by hunting or trapping regulations, settlers harvested meat, hides, fur, and feathers in abundance. Game and fur-bearing animals were sufficient to provide a commercial mainstay. They were killed both for personal use and for shipping to eager eastern markets. Skins became a standard early source of revenue and even were used as legal tender. Nearly any animal was taken: muskrat, weasel, beaver, otter, raccoon, squirrel, deer, mink, wolf, bear, bobcat, coyote, fox — whatever was large enough to yield a worthwhile pelt or dinner.

Weather contributed to animal declines. In the legendary harsh winter of 1856–1857, when a crust of freezing rain covered deep snow, many animals sought food and shelter in forests bordering streams and rivers. There the concentrated deer, elk, and other game were slaughtered by predators and settlers, who could simply walk up to the animals and club or stab them to death.

"THE HUNTING SEASON" AT BELLEVUE IA.

Fig. 14. This early-twentieth-century duck hunt was an extension of the market and sport hunting of many tens of thousands of native birds in the previous century. Courtesy State Historical Society of Iowa, Iowa City.

Wild birds similarly were taken for food, feathers, and eggs, with greater prairie-chickens and quail (northern bobwhite) rapidly becoming staples of the family table and market. Thousands of Iowa's prairie-chickens were shot and trapped annually and shipped to markets in Milwaukee, Chicago, and New York, while farmers slaughtered the birds wholesale as a menace to crops. In eastern Iowa's savannas, mammoth flocks of passenger pigeons presented an easy target. The birds were shot, knocked from roost trees at night, hit from the air with long sticks, and netted. They were sold by the barrel and wagonload. In north-central Iowa's abundant wetlands, waterfowl killed by the tens of thousands became a prime target of market hunters as well as sport hunters (fig. 14). Waterfowl also provided a ready source of eggs.

All of these bird species fed the rapidly growing cities of the eastern United States, their harvest and export encouraged by the arrival of railroads and the development of refrigerated railroad cars. As the passenger pigeon's numbers dwindled around 1880, hunters turned to the more than thirty species of shorebirds that migrated through Iowa. The upland sandpiper, long-billed curlew, American woodcock, and common snipe, among others, were commonly harvested for market. Even sandhill and whooping cranes, which nested in north-central Iowa, were occasionally shot for meat. The gathering of eggs for private and museum collections further diminished populations, exterminating some species. The wholesale slaughter of birds and mammals continued into the twentieth century, when it was countermanded by enforcement of wildlife protection laws, establishment of preserves and wildlife management programs, and habitat restoration efforts that were sometimes coupled with reintroduction of extirpated species.

Overt killing and disruption of animal populations were augmented by the conversion of native plant communities to agricultural land. Vegetation constitutes the matrix that feeds and shelters animals, who depend on specific plant structures if not specific plant species for survival. Iowa's agricultural transformation thus constituted massive habitat loss for dependent animals. Habitat loss implies that a site was lost to future as well as present generations of wildlife. Subsequent waves of habitat loss flowed from the post–World War II intensification of agriculture and more recently from the spread of suburbs and homestead acreages. The continued loss and degradation of native wildlife habitat have resulted in the same dramatic collapses of small animal populations that earlier hunting and trapping caused among Iowa's larger animals.

Habitat loss is considered the major force now depressing wildlife populations around the world. It also is undoubtedly affecting less obvious organisms such as Iowa's estimated 4,000 to 5,000 species of fungi, which are omnipresent in soil and crucially important for decomposing dead plant materials (Lois Tiffany, personal communication). Fungi, like insects, soil microbes, and other inconspicuous organisms, have probably declined or disappeared as their habitats dissolved, perhaps even before their existence was recognized.

With native communities shrinking throughout the 1800s, remaining animals and plants began to feel more insidious pressures from habitat fragmentation, the repeated splitting of natural assemblages into smaller and more isolated chunks. Small prairies, oak woodlands, bottomland forests, and wetlands are in no way miniature replicas of the expansive ecosystems originally found here. Small native communities are constantly subjected to disruptions creeping in along their borders — predators, sedimentation, drifting pesticides, and so forth. And a small community's natural processes — cleansing pulses of fire or flood, water flow patterns — rarely function as they once did. Chance events easily wipe out small populations. Elimination of important species sparks widespread repercussions: loss of pollinating insects interrupts plant reproduction, for example, and loss of native predators disrupts food webs. Small populations reproduce poorly and suffer from genetic drift. If species disappear, nearby stock for repopulating a native community is often absent.

With all these stresses, fragmented native communities commonly exhibit ongoing degradation and steadily shrinking population numbers. In an early-twenty-first-century statewide inventory, a full third of Iowa's vertebrate animals and selected invertebrates demonstrated population declines (Zohrer 2005). The parasitic effects of the brown-headed cowbird provide one example of the causal link. Originally a plains bird that followed bison herds, the cowbird now enters woodlands and forests dissected by roadways and housing sites. Cowbirds then lay eggs in the nests of other birds, which are tricked into raising large, aggressive cowbird hatchlings rather than their own smaller young. Fragmentation and the increasing numbers of brown-headed cowbirds have been implicated in the steady declines of native woodland and forest bird populations.

Today remaining natural pockets become more tenuous and frail as each human generation continues to claim its share of the land's bounty. It is nearly impossible to see the silent incremental losses, the dribbling away of the few last wildflowers from a woodlot or prairie plants from a fencerow. Few note the slow, steady loss of migrating songbirds and salamanders. But by studying Iowa's past native diversity, the cumulative impact of the last 200 years becomes obvious.

The Displacing Horde

The vast majority of Iowa is now inhabited by species of plants and animals from distant lands (fig. 15). The current dominance of these exotic species is so great that most people would be hard-pressed to identify our native species — those that were long-term members of the Midwest's original prairies, oak woodlands, bottomland forests, and wetlands. Exotics are so well assimilated into our environment that we assume they are normal and natural. Consider the chicory, dame's rocket, Queen Anne's lace, daylilies, and oxeye daisies that frequent roadsides and most ornamentals in cities and yards. All are exotics. The Kentucky bluegrass of our lawns (a Eurasian native) is likely Iowa's most common present-day perennial plant. Dandelions, common carp, house mice and Norway rats, night crawlers, and cropland weeds such as quackgrass and foxtails all originated on another continent. The corn in our fields has been bred from Mexican progenitors, and apples in our orchards trace their ancestors to Kazakhstan. All livestock species, excluding the turkey, are exotic to North America. Other exotics—

Fig. 15. Iowa's settlers superimposed an entire new biological regime upon the land, comprised of exotic plants and livestock imported from distant regions. As this transpired, the native communities that remained were fragmented into ever-smaller pieces, and many native animals and plants lost suitable habitat. Source: Andreas 1875: 5.

everything from lilacs, tulips, and petunias to broccoli, tomatoes, and the ever-prolific zucchini squash — grace our flower and vegetable gardens.

Many of these exotics — crops and pasture stock, medicinals, garden plants, and the like — were imported for specific economic or sentimental reasons. However, along with desired species, many unknown and unwanted exotics have charted their course across the continent. They entered surreptitiously as seeds hidden in livestock feeds, in mud on boots or hooves, or in ship ballast water. They traveled the continent as fungal parasites of nursery stock, crept along linear railroad corridors, or hitched rides as contaminants in bags of grain and flax seed. Exotics continue to arrive, brought here faster and more easily than ever before by today's rapid transportation and international trade and encouraged by growing human populations creating ever-larger disturbed areas that welcome weedy species.

Today about a quarter (23 percent) of Iowa's approximately 2,000 vascular plant species are exotics. Some 441 plant species have arrived here since Euroamerican settlement. This includes roughly a third of the members of Iowa's largest plant families — the grasses (many were introduced for grain, forage, or lawn use) and composites (daisies, sunflowers, and so forth) — as well as a third of the members of the legume (pea), mint, buckwheat, and willow families. A startling two-thirds of Iowa's mustard (Brassicaceae), pink (Caryophyllaceae), and goosefoot (Chenopodiaceae) family members are exotics. Over nine-tenths of Iowa's exotic plants originated on another continent. Most are from Europe or the Asian steppes, locales with a climate roughly similar to the Midwest's (Eilers and Roosa 1994: 26).

Exotic plants now overwhelmingly dominate Iowa in terms of amount of ground covered and number of individuals present. The mode of operation of exotics introduced for specific purposes is profoundly different from that of native ecosystems. Iowa's native communities, with their tremendous diversity and finely tuned codependencies, were self-sustaining. The populations of individual species waxed and waned and migrated in tune with a changing climate, but native communities as a whole maintained health and resilience for thousands of years, relying only on falling rain and the rising sun.

Introduced species could never achieve this. Today's simplified systems require continual input of energy and effort to survive. Gardens and croplands remain barren if we don't sow the seed, provide fertilizer and water, and control pests and diseases. Even with human care, agricultural systems remain vulnerable to climatic fluctuations and disease, and they typically lose topsoil rather than build it, as the prairies did. These features produce fears that Iowa's agricultural systems are unsustainable.

AMONG THE UNCOUNTED thousands of nonnative plants, animals, and microorganisms that have entered the United States, the vast majority have behaved as expected and served their intended purpose. Their major impact has been usurping the space previously occupied by native organisms. Plant apple trees and you get what you intended: an apple orchard.

However, problems can arise because introduced species arrive one at a time, without natural pathogens, diseases, or parasites to limit their vigor and reproduction, without the natural controls and community structure that hold them in place. A small percentage of exotic species have taken advantage of this situation and become invasive. Exploding in number and intensifying in vigor, invasives spread like a cancerous growth far beyond the site of introduction. Plant an exotic honeysuckle bush, give it time, and you get an expanding impenetrable thicket.

The early settlers realized that such unwanted spread could occur. Midwestern farmers adopted Hungarian grass (a form of millet) with fervor in the late 1850s because of its hardiness and abundant yields. However, the grain soon lost favor because of its "alarming reluctance to abandon fields to following crops" (Bogue 1963: 142).

Only around 4,500 of the exotic organisms introduced to the United States have established free-living populations, and of these, only 15 percent (approximately 675 species) cause severe harm. These exotic invasives have become our most troublesome weeds, playing havoc with agricultural lands and disturbed sites — in fact, about two-thirds of all U.S. weeds have been introduced from elsewhere (Westbrooks 1998: 5–6). Invasive plants are largely responsible for the unfettered use of agricultural and lawn pesticides that now contaminate our water. The plants cost the U.S. economy tens of billions of dollars each year. When total U.S. economic costs are merged with environmental damages, annual costs have been estimated at $137 billion (Pimental et al. 2000). Invasives are becoming increasingly problematic around the world, threatening the quantity and quality of food, forage, and fiber as well as native communities. Invasive microorganisms (such as the West Nile virus) and insects (such as soybean aphids) pose additional major hazards to human health and crops.

The most aggressive invasives can spread beyond disturbed sites or croplands into intact natural ecosystems. "That our native plants can outdo the sturdiest steppe plants gathered by explorers from all over the world is not so certain," wrote botanist Henry Conard (1952: 143). His statement has proven true. The worst invasives (smooth brome, leafy spurge, reed canarygrass, purple loosestrife, and garlic mustard, among others; see fig. 16) seriously degrade or destroy healthy native prairies, woodlands, forests, and wetlands. Invasive plants form dense colonies that hoard available sunlight, water, soil nutrients, and space. Invasive animals conscript food of their native competitors and steal nest sites. Invasive microorganisms and fungi cause widespread disease. A single invasive species can start a chain of effects that eliminates multiple native species. In fact, some experts state that invasive exotics today are second only to habitat loss in their ability to depress wildlife populations and drive species into extinction (Westbrooks 1998: 5).

The number and impact of invasive species seem to be increasing exponentially. Many of their legacies read like biological horror stories. Multiflora rose

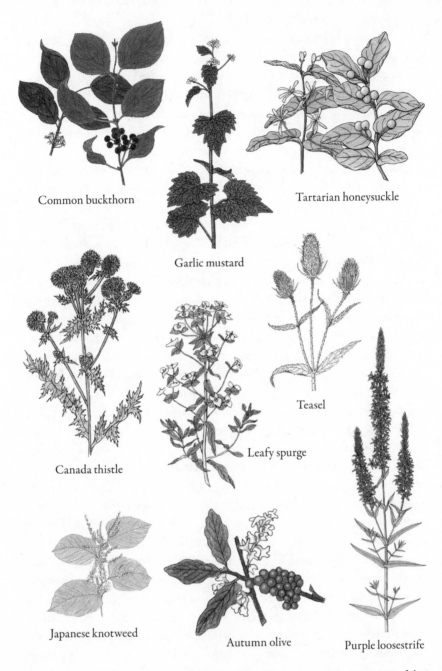

Common buckthorn

Garlic mustard

Tartarian honeysuckle

Canada thistle

Leafy spurge

Teasel

Japanese knotweed

Autumn olive

Purple loosestrife

Fig. 16. These and other invasive plants imported from distant ecosystems pose one of the most profound threats to the integrity of native communities today. Drawing by Mark Müller.

produces thickets impenetrable by humans or cattle. Remaining prairies are lost to leafy spurge, and wetlands become swales of purple loosestrife. Garlic mustard threatens to smother our spring woodland wildflowers, one of Iowa's remaining natural glories. Invasive plants flaunt unbelievable capabilities. A single mature purple loosestrife plant produces 2.5 million seeds annually. Japanese knotweed can spiral its roots sixty feet underneath a highway to send up shoots on the other side. Land managers tell of investing days, weeks, and months of grinding labor to eliminate incoming waves of exotics. Managers employ seemingly absurd techniques — such as bulldozing away topsoil covered by impenetrable mats of reed canarygrass in hopes of installing a healthier, more diverse wetland community.

Invasive plants typically share several characteristics: early maturation, profuse production of seeds that are easily transported long distances (often by attaching to clothes or animal fur), survival under adverse conditions, resistance to local plant diseases, prolonged growing seasons, and high photosynthetic rates. Many possess thorns, spines, biological toxins, or other defenses that repel animals or other plants (Westbrooks 1998: 3).

Table 1 lists the major invasive plants now threatening Iowa's native ecosystems, plants that are actively reshaping our native prairies, wetlands, woodlands, and forests as well as other nonnative areas. The table omits additional serious invasive species that pose major problems in disturbed areas, along roadsides, and in nonnative plant communities but do not necessarily invade native communities. This listing is bound to become dated as new invasive species appear in Iowa.

Considering the stories of invasive species will help explain the challenges they pose. While only ten species of invasive birds now nest in Iowa, they are significant because of their sheer numbers. The house (or English) sparrow was brought to North America in 1852 and to Iowa City in 1881. A few years later, Bohumil Shimek (1883: 564) described it as a "pestiferous, pugnacious little rascal" that would "drive out the bluebird, robin and other common useful birds" from the University of Iowa campus. Such displacement of native birds has proven true of the house sparrow and also of the European starling, which was first successfully introduced in New York City in 1890 and spread to Iowa in the 1920s. These two pest species are today among Iowa's most abundant birds. Here and throughout the United States, they rob natives of nest sites, foul buildings, and feed on stored grain (Dinsmore 2001).

The Asiatic fungus that causes Dutch elm disease (*Ophiostoma ulmi*) entered

Table 1. Major Invasive Exotic Plants Threatening Iowa's Natural Areas

Common Name	Scientific Name	Wetlands (including standing water)	Prairies	Woodlands and Forests
Amur and Tartarian honeysuckle*	*Lonicera maackii, L. tatarica*			x
Autumn olive	*Elaeagnus umbellata*		x	x
Bird's-foot trefoil	*Lotus corniculatus*		x	
Black locust	*Robinia pseudoacacia*		x	x
Brittle waternymph, Brittle naiad	*Najas minor*	x		
Burningbush	*Euonymus alatus*			x
Canada thistle	*Cirsium arvense*		x	
Cattail (hybrid)	*Typha angustifolia* x *T. latifolia*	x	x	
Common buckthorn*	*Rhamnus cathartica*			x
Crownvetch	*Securigera varia*		x	
Curly pondweed	*Potamogeton crispus*	x		
Dame's rocket	*Hesperis matronalis*			x
Eurasian watermilfoil	*Myriophyllum spicatum*	x		
Garlic mustard	*Alliaria petiolata*			x
Japanese barberry	*Berberis thunbergii*			x
Japanese knotweed	*Polygonum cuspidatum*	x		
Leafy spurge	*Euphorbia esula*		x	
Multiflora rose	*Rosa multiflora*		x	x
Norway maple	*Acer platanoides*			x
Oriental bittersweet	*Celastrus orbiculatus*			x
Privet	*Ligustrum* spp.			x
Purple loosestrife	*Lythrum salicaria*	x		

Table 1. *(Continued)*

Common Name	Scientific Name	Wetlands (including standing water)	Prairies	Woodlands and Forests
Reed canarygrass	*Phalaris arundinacea*	x	x	x
Sericea lespedeza	*Lespedeza cuneata*		x	
Siberian elm	*Ulmus pumila*		x	x
Smooth brome	*Bromus inermis*		x	
Spotted knapweed	*Centaurea stoebe* ssp. *Micranthos*		x	
Sweetclover (yellow and white)	*Melilotus officinalis*		x	
Teasel	*Dipsacus sylvestris, D. laciniatus*	x	x	
Tree-of-heaven	*Ailanthus altissima*			x
Wild parsnip	*Pastinaca sativa*		x	

*Exotic bush honeysuckles should not be confused with the native vinelike honeysuckles (which also are *Lonicera*) or with the native *Diervilla* bush honeysuckle that tends to grow in moist woods or rocky sites and is common in northeastern Iowa. Nor should exotic common buckthorns be confused with the smaller native buckthorns.

Sources: This table is adapted from a list of Iowa invasive plants provided in 2006 by John Walkowiak, with personal communications from Kim Bogenschutz, John Pearson, Mark Vitosh, and John Walkowiak, all with the Iowa DNR, and Chris Henze, Johnson County Roadside Vegetation Manager; see also Farrar 2001 and Lewis and Pope 2001.

the United States in the 1930s in a shipment of diseased logs, along with its vector, a European bark beetle. It reached Iowa in 1957, with a more virulent strain (*O. novo-ulmi*) arriving in the 1970s. The disease kills mature specimens of the American elm, formerly a major floodplain and urban tree, and has been dubbed among the most destructive plant diseases of the twentieth century (Tiffany 2001: 114).

State and federal agencies are monitoring the spread of other tree-stressing and killing agents such as the gypsy moth, which by 2000 had spread westward to south-central Wisconsin. Gypsy moths were introduced to the eastern United States in 1869 by a researcher who was trying to develop disease-resistant silkworms when they escaped from his laboratory. Gypsy moth larvae, which prefer oaks, defoliate trees and increase their susceptibility to other diseases. The emerald ash borer, which has killed millions of ashes in Michigan and in 2006 was spreading to surrounding states, would cause major harm to Iowa's forest and woodland communities.

Garlic mustard was hardly known in Iowa before 1990 but then established large populations across the state within a decade. A native of Europe, the plant was introduced to the United States in the 1800s for medicinal and food use. Unlike most invasive herbs, garlic mustard flourishes in shade as well as partial and full sun. Thus rank growth of this rapidly spreading biennial threatens to dramatically alter the character of woodlands and forests by eliminating native understory plants and smothering tree and shrub seedlings.

Reed canarygrass, planted in Iowa since 1900 for forage and erosion control, spreads rapidly and smothers native communities with its coarse sod-forming growth. Although native strains of this grass once occupied Iowa, most current populations are thought to be Eurasian cultivars that are extremely aggressive (Rosburg 2001: 145). While primarily a wetland lover, the ubiquitous grass also creeps into dry uplands and open woodlands. Extensive monocultures of hardy reed canarygrass have robbed Iowa of a high percentage of its native sedge meadows and other moist communities.

The European native purple loosestrife was introduced accidentally in the early 1800s in ship ballast water and then carried westward by pioneers because of loosestrife's medicinal properties and beautiful flowers. A wetland invasive, its dense monocultures impede water's flow and decrease biodiversity of waterfowl, fish, and other native animals and plants. Natural spread, as well as escape from horticultural plantings, form a constant threat.

Multiflora rose has become a notorious pest, with its large dense clusters of thorn-bearing stems that inhibit passage by humans and animals alike. Introduced to the United States from Japan in 1887, it has been planted as rootstock, for living fences, and to curb soil erosion. In addition to prairies and native wooded areas, pastures, abandoned croplands, and disturbed areas are readily invaded by this forbidding shrub, and by black locust (introduced from the southeastern United States) and other spine-bearing woody plants.

Every new plant introduction is an experiment with an unknown outcome. While we know that over half of the more than 300 exotic species invading U.S.

natural areas were introduced as ornamentals, it is difficult to predict whether any given introduced plant will become invasive (Westbrooks 1998: 20). Exotics may behave themselves for decades as they go through a lag period before beginning to reproduce profusely and expand their range. The Norway maple, for example, has long been one of Iowa's most extensively planted trees, prized for its appearance, excellent shade, and hardiness. But in the early twenty-first century, it became a troublesome invader of eastern Iowa native woodlands (Mark Vitosh, personal communication). Constant vigilance is imperative to detect such exotic plants that are becoming invasive. The more quickly invasives are eradicated, the easier the task and the less harm they will do. Once firmly established, invasive species may be nearly impossible to eradicate.

Those That Remain

Considering the many onslaughts endured by Iowa's wildlife and plants, it is amazing that native species have survived at all. Yet a large majority can still be found, albeit in greatly reduced numbers. Many native plants and animals were able to adapt to new niches in the refurbished landscape, competing well even though their competitors had changed overnight. The majority of smaller prairie birds and mammals, for example, transferred their allegiance to hayfields, pastures, and meadows. More recently many of these animals have been aided by the Conservation Reserve Program (CRP), a federally subsidized program that establishes grassland plantings on erodible agricultural land. CRP lands may be providing important new habitat for certain grassland birds that have been exhibiting major declines as well as for the spotted skunk, white-tailed jackrabbit, bobcat, and others that have suffered as former pastures have been converted to cropland or reverted to dense woody growth.

In general, habitat for native plants and animals remains most plentiful where farming has been least intensive. Thus remaining native organisms are distributed unevenly across Iowa, a fact that was clearly reflected by the Gap Analysis Program, which assessed Iowa's overall vertebrate diversity. In the 1990s the habits and geographic patterns of 288 amphibians, reptiles, birds, and mammals were used to create a predictive map of animal species richness (Kane et al. 2003). Figure 17 shows that modern animal diversity is highest on sites with the roughest terrain and poorest soils. These are the areas where agricultural use has been least manipulative, and native or planted grasslands and woody vegetation are most intact.

Fig. 17. The diversity and abundance of terrestrial vertebrate animals are predicted to be highest where this map is darkest. These more rugged landscapes — river corridors, the Loess Hills, south-central Iowa, and northeastern Iowa — are least suitable for intensive agriculture and thus retain more permanent vegetation. Only 4 percent of Iowa's predicted vertebrate animal habitat is publicly owned, and much of this is in small and scattered tracts (Kane et al. 2002: xi). Source: Kane et al. 2002, based on 1992 land-cover types and species habitat needs, courtesy Casey Kohrt, Iowa Geological Survey.

Forested bottomlands throughout the state remain important migration corridors and sanctuaries for birds and mammals. But far fewer natives are now found over most of the fairly flat terrain of north-central and northwestern Iowa, where vast prairies have been replaced by equally vast croplands. Rugged pasturelands of the Little Sioux River valley constitute one exception. North-central Iowa originally was part of the midcontinental prairie pothole region; current wetland restoration efforts are attempting to bring back a fraction of the region's original abundant waterfowl.

To the southwest, the Loess Hills initially were plowed, but the steepest croplands were soon abandoned, and many spontaneously returned to prairie. Now used as pastureland, these constitute Iowa's largest remaining prairie remnants and maintain significant concentrations of smaller prairie wildlife. However, the prairies are challenged by ongoing woody invasion — the spread of shrubs and trees that favors animals of woodlands, forests, and edge habitats at the expense of prairie species.

Woody invasion is also a problem among the rolling grassland expanses that remain abundant in south-central Iowa, with invasion intensifying since the post-1970s decline of Iowa's cattle industry. Here planted pastures mingle with patches of degraded prairie and savanna, which are more numerous in this region than previously realized. The landscape provides suitable habitat for many adaptable animals.

Northeastern Iowa was and is the most heavily wooded area of the state, with many sites too rugged to plow. This corner of the state has remained a haven for birds and other animals dependent on large, intact forests and woodlands. However, logging has cut significant inroads into both wooded tracts and native abundance.

While these rugged areas retain Iowa's greatest diversity, native animals can be found throughout the state. Their presence reflects the animals' adaptability and each region's land-use practices. Agriculture and suburban sprawl have fragmented Iowa into a land of edges inhabited by edge species — opportunistic animals of the shrubby interface between woodland and grassland or of linear brushy or semiwooded corridors alongside roads, streams, and fences. Edge species often move between the cover of woodlands and shrublands and the nearby agricultural lands where they feed. Formerly species of savannas and woodlands, they include the woodchuck, white-footed mouse, red fox, raccoon, white-tailed deer, indigo bunting, and gray catbird (fig. 18). While long, thin woody edges can be tremendously important to wildlife and savanna plants, they also can be harmful. Edge habitats tend to favor common, adaptable animals at the expense of rarer, more discriminating species. And the success of nesting birds in or near edges is typically low because of brown-headed cowbirds and predators (for example, snakes, feral housecats, raccoons, blue jays, rodents) that proliferate in linear woodlands and edge habitats.

Other native animals have remained common because they mesh well with human settlement. Big and little brown bats now roost in houses. Common nighthawks lay their eggs on flat rooftops as well as on bare ground in prairie openings. Eastern moles dig through lawns. Short-tailed shrews, deer mice, and eastern garter snakes abound in both disturbed and native habitats. Eastern cottontails, fox squirrels, eastern chipmunks, and a number of birds are common in treed neighborhoods of cities and suburbs, which substitute for the oak

Fig. 18. Iowa is today a land of edge habitat and edge species, such as the young red foxes shown here. Photograph by Carl Kurtz.

savannas and open oak woodlands of past centuries. And some natives such as coyotes, opossums, and American crows abound simply because they are opportunistic and very adaptable, managing to find food and live well in multiple habitats.

Modern native plant populations, like those of animals, reflect how well certain species have melded with human activity. A number of native plants (such as walnut trees) have been favored by plantings. Natives that benefit from disturbance, such as poison ivy and eastern redcedar, are increasing. Others, such as former bottomland trees (boxelder, hackberry, green ash, and the like) and the fire-intolerant sugar maple, have increased and spread because they are no longer restrained by wildfire. Some woodland and forest birds — for example, the cardinal and tufted titmouse — have followed expanding woody edges into new parts of Iowa.

Native woodland animals and understory plants have survived in aging oak groves. While oaks are extremely long-lived plants, they are reproducing poorly today. The many common animals dependent on their acorns (blue jays, squirrels, and wild turkeys, among others) may be faring well now, but likely will suffer without improved oak regeneration.

In contrast to the abundant generalists that are broadly adaptable to a diversity of sites and conditions, many of Iowa's native plants and animals survive in far fewer numbers. These are the habitat-restricted organisms (also called habitat specialists or obligates) that depend on precise environmental conditions. They cling tenuously to life on small sites that still resemble presettlement Iowa, surviving as refugees in their own homelands. They continue to shrink in number and range.

Specialists restricted to a narrow range of natural habitats include many rarer natives such as our highly prized orchids, trilliums, and other spring wildflowers; skipper butterflies; and many neotropical migrant birds. They are increasingly found in small, disjunct patches where they struggle to maintain healthy breeding populations while becoming ever more vulnerable to disturbance. Because of their sensitivity, they remain crucial indicators of environmental health.

Lacking the resilience they once displayed in large intact ecosystems, our most sensitive habitat specialists are prone to quiet declines. At some point they become rare enough that their survival is questionable. They then may be listed by the Iowa Department of Natural Resources (Iowa DNR) as being of special concern, threatened, or endangered — an action that now encompasses about 13 percent (264 species) of Iowa's higher plants (Iowa Department of Natural Resources 2006a; Lewis 1998). Similar federal delineations list nationally endangered species. Rare and endangered species are found across Iowa, but are especially numerous in the diverse microhabitats of northeastern Iowa and westernmost Iowa's Loess Hills.

In the 1990s the plants in and immediately surrounding Ames, in central Story County, received the most detailed survey ever performed of Iowa's plants. This ten-year study revealed three disturbing trends. The proportion of native species has been declining relative to exotics. Populations of natives are smaller than those of exotic species. And historically uncommon plants are prone to disappear completely (Norris, Widrlechner, et al. 2001: 124).

However, the number of natives found in this one small area was much greater than had been expected: a total of 916 species were found, 71 percent of which were native. These plants comprise an amazing 47 percent of Iowa's total number of plant species (Norris, Lewis, et al. 2001). A plant survey in Johnson County revealed similar wealth: in a single growing season, 426 species (22 percent of Iowa's total flora) were identified along a mere 3.5-mile-long stretch of Clear Creek, 80 percent (338 species) of which were native (Conservation Design Forum 1998).

These studies demonstrate that although their populations may be small and precarious, an amazing proportion of Iowa's native species have clung tenaciously to life. They survive along fencerows, in roadside rights-of-ways, within woodlots and preserves, near watercourses and on rugged lands, and in other small, forgotten nooks and crannies. These clumps and clusters of Iowa's original nature hold quite literally the seeds of the future. They lie at the heart of today's efforts to preserve and restore our state's native biodiversity.

Butterflies and Dragonflies

Invertebrate animals dominate the world's fauna in both species number and biomass. These are the most diverse, least understood, and potentially most endangered animals of Iowa's ecosystems. They also are crucially important to other native organisms' survival, providing a vital food source for many larger animals and pollinating the majority of flowering plants.

Two of Iowa's insect groups have been surveyed in depth in recent years: butterflies, and dragonflies and damselflies. The original numbers of some of these organisms must have been stupendous. Read, for example, this description of Iowa's nineteenth-century monarchs:

> This extremely abundant butterfly seems to prefer open prairie, but is driven to the groves by the winds which sweep furiously over the prairies in the summer months, and especially in September; here the butterflies are collected in such vast numbers, on the lee side of trees, and particularly on the lower branches, as almost to hide the foliage, and give to the trees their own peculiar color. This was not seen in one grove alone, but in all of those which were visited about the middle of September. (Scudder 1869)

While good numbers of monarchs and other adaptable butterflies still grace Iowa's skies, habitat-restricted species dependent on specific plant hosts have declined tremendously. Larvae of the strikingly beautiful regal fritillary, for example, feed on birdfoot violets and perhaps other prairie violets — and only on these plants. Over the past several decades its numbers have declined significantly across the Midwest, especially in Iowa. Between twenty and thirty of Iowa's butterflies, including many of the native grassland-loving skippers, are restricted to prairie habitat. Skippers trace the prairie seasons by their rapid passage, with new species replacing the old every two weeks or so. Feisty skipper males establish and defend territories by clinging to the top of protruding plant stems and darting after intruders. Concern for the survival of habitat-restricted butterflies necessitates extremely careful prairie management, possibly incorporating techniques such as substituting rotational grazing for fire (which, when overused, may depress or eliminate populations of rare butterflies in small preserves).

Today one of Iowa's most abundant butterflies is an exotic introduced to the United States around 1860, the small European cabbage white butterfly whose caterpillars (cabbage worms) plague our vegetable gardens. Native species that remain in abundance are widespread generalists that are typical of a variety of open, disturbed sites. Examples include the painted lady (the most widely distributed butterfly in the world), buckeye, and American lady. These butterflies are, on the whole, larger than native skippers and other prairie butterflies that once dominated Iowa's butterfly fauna, whose small size and relatively large wing muscles allowed them to navigate well among dense waving grasses and to negotiate the prairie's summer winds. This switch from small specialists to larger generalists defines Iowa's butterfly fauna today.

Although many are now uncommon, Iowa still claims 100 species of resident butterflies. Originally about 40 percent of the 100 residents inhabited Iowa's prairies, and an equal number resided in wooded lands, with the remaining species drifting between these communities or inhabiting wetlands. In 2006, 32 of these were included on Iowa's official listing of endangered, threatened, or special concern species. However, researchers who study Iowa's butterflies state that nearly half of our native residents are imperiled. Concerns are expressed not only about declines in total numbers but also about shrinking ranges. Prairie butterflies are more threatened than those of other habitats. The larger remnants of the Loess Hills provide important refuges for skippers and other habitat-restricted organisms (Schlicht and Orwig 1998).

In addition to butterflies, habitat restrictions are exhibited by certain moths, katydids, walking sticks, beetles, jumping spiders, and other invertebrates. Estimates of the number of invertebrates restricted to tallgrass prairies range from around 700 to 1,500 species or possibly even more since small species may remain unnoticed and unknown to the present day (Schlicht and Orwig 1998). Healthy populations of habitat-restricted insects are sensitive indicators of high-quality native habitat.

Iowa's dragonflies and damselflies number 110 species (fig. 19). These insects reflect the profound changes in the state's wetlands and river systems, where they live and reproduce. All species are thought to have declined tremendously in total number, and a few species have disappeared from the state. Losses have been especially marked along the Mississippi River. While about a quarter (30 species) are thought to be secure and are found across the state, an equal number are considered imperiled. Some of these have naturally small populations, but many are declining because of habitat loss. Seven new species have spread into Iowa, and another seven are expanding their range westward to occupy gravel pits, farm ponds, and other constructed water bodies (Cruden and Gode 1998).

Frogs and Toads, Turtles and Snakes

In 1981 a survey predicted that given present trends, less than a third of Iowa's seventy-six amphibians and reptiles were likely to remain in fifty to a hundred years. The other two-thirds were declining or found in populations too small and isolated to be considered viable (Christiansen 1981: 27).

A few years later, this statewide trend was reflected on a larger scale. In 1989 researchers around the world realized that certain frog and toad populations were crashing. These global declines were troubling because of their suddenness and size, and because they were seen as harbingers of undetected imbalances among other types of organisms. (Amphibians serve as sensitive biological indicators because their permeable skin and close association with water make them particularly sensitive to waterborne pollutants.)

Iowa's Blanchard's cricket frog, a tiny dark-colored animal of ponds and streams, has been exhibiting such a crash. The frog was once found throughout most of the state, but it has been disappearing from its northern ranges since the 1970s and now is nearly absent in the northern two tiers of Iowa counties, as well as Minnesota and most of Wisconsin (Christiansen 1998). Cricket frogs remain abundant in central and southern Iowa, where late spring evenings remain filled with their calls — rapid clicks that sound like two marbles rubbing together.

What could explain this southward-moving disappearance and the continued declines in numbers and populations of other Iowa amphibians? Thinning of the atmospheric ozone layer and increases in ultraviolet (UV) exposure, atrazine and other agricultural chemicals, changing climate, acid rain, infections with trematodes (parasitic flatworms), increased predation, and habitat

Fig. 19. The twelve-spotted skimmer remains one of our more common dragonflies. As with other animals, however, Iowa's dragonflies in general have decreased in total number, with the relative abundance of each remaining species shifting with changes in land use. Photograph by Carl Kurtz.

destruction all have been considered. Increasing intensity of row crop agriculture since the 1970s has magnified several of these stressors. Their effects are compounded when several stressors simultaneously affect a single frog or toad. Urban environments with their roadkills, predators, and contaminant runoff from lawns also are known to tax Iowa's amphibians seriously. Trematodes and chemical contaminants, along with increasing UV radiation and habitat alteration (namely the increase in constructed ponds with highly fertile waters), have been implicated in the severe skeletal malformations increasingly found in midwestern toads and frogs (Blaustein and Johnson 2003; Knutson et al. 2000; Lannoo 2000).

Falling amphibian numbers and increasing deformities could be warnings of severe environmental degradation. Perhaps most troubling is a continuing decline of one of Iowa's most abundant and widely distributed species, the American toad. A comparison of pre-1950 and recent records reveals the loss of about a third of these toads by the late 1900s. The only Iowa frog that is increasing greatly, the fiercely competitive and predatory bullfrog, has done so through the post-1930s stocking of farm ponds and native wetlands outside the bullfrog's normal southern Iowa range. Large bullfrogs devour amphibians and other small animals. Their introductions have led to crashes of native frog populations (Christiansen 1998, 2001).

On a positive note, the penetrating late winter peep of the minute spring peeper, once classified as threatened in Iowa, may be more common than previously thought. Populations are most abundant along the Mississippi River and in far eastern Iowa, but peepers are also heard in scattered locations in central Iowa. Iowa retains widespread populations of the gray treefrog and American toad as well as the leopard frog, cricket frog, bullfrog, and chorus frog (Iowa's most frequently recorded frog species).

Tiger and smallmouth salamander populations are thought to be stable, although recent searches for tiger salamanders have been disappointing. Two of Iowa's other three salamanders are rare enough to be state-listed as threatened or endangered.

Reptiles, like amphibians, have exhibited large population declines among all but the most adaptable generalists. Iowa's five lizards have been especially hard hit by land conversion to agricultural use. All are declining, and two are state-listed as threatened or endangered.

Iowa claims thirteen turtle species. Two of these, the snapping turtle and painted turtle, have flourished in farm ponds and increased in abundance. These and the spiny softshell are found statewide; most other Iowa turtles are quite restricted in range. Another two (the ornate box turtle and Blanding's turtle) are state-listed as threatened in Iowa.

Iowa's only fully terrestrial turtle, the ornate box turtle, is an appealing creature with its high yellow-striped upper shell and love of fruit. In season, the turtle's mouth commonly is smeared with strawberry or mulberry remains, but it also eats plants, fungi, and invertebrates. The turtle lays its eggs in sandy or loess soils. Sand deposits along the Iowa and Cedar rivers must have, at one time, been crawling with these reptiles. Today's small populations in Johnson County, the Muscatine area, the Loess Hills, and a few other locations are thought to represent the fractured remains of once-extensive colonies. Fragmentation of habitat concentrates remaining turtles in smaller areas, where their eggs are highly prone to predation by skunks and raccoons. Like all land-dwelling turtles, this turtle has also been harmed by human collecting.

If you spot a snake today, it is likely to be the eastern garter snake, probably Iowa's most abundant snake and a species capable of coexisting with humans in cities, as long as house cats are not too numerous. This is but one of Iowa's twenty-eight snake species. More than a third (ten species) were in 2006 state-listed as endangered, threatened, or special concern species. Many of the others have declined in number, with Iowa's four venomous snakes having been decimated by willful extermination as well as habitat destruction. All venomous snakes except the timber rattler are now endangered in Iowa, and timber rattlesnake range has shrunken to less than half its historic size (Christiansen 1981).

The northern water snake and Iowa's garter snakes, aided by high reproductive rates, seem to be maintaining their earlier distribution patterns. These snakes, along with fox and brown snakes, are widespread and reasonably common. However, examination of bullsnake records reveals that this species has experienced severe decline throughout Iowa, suffering greatly (as have all snakes) from the vehicles on Iowa's dense road network, as well as from continued habitat destruction (Christiansen 1998). Once again, the decline of a common and ubiquitous species bodes poorly for other more discriminating species.

Feathers and Wings

Birds are arguably Iowa's most conspicuous and best-known animals. If invertebrates are excluded, birds dominate our state's wildlife in sheer number and diversity, comprising about 60 percent of all vertebrates known from Iowa. About 150 birds now nest regularly in the state. In all, around 200 species have nested here between 1840 and 2000. Including migrants, over 400 bird species have been observed in Iowa — nearly half of the roughly 900 birds known to North America (Dinsmore 1998). These diverse animals serve many crucial functions. They consistently put pressure on weed seeds, rodents, and insects (whose peak populations correspond with birds' peak breeding season), thus reducing the threat of pest outbreaks. Birds help pollinate flowers, disperse beneficial seeds, eliminate carrion, and become food for others.

Following settlement, the numbers of many abundant birds declined or crashed within a few decades. The most precipitous drops occurred among birds that were intolerant of human disturbance, heavily hunted, or at the edge of their distribution range. By 1900, nine nesting species had disappeared from Iowa, including the common loon, long-billed curlew, and whooping crane. The passenger pigeon (once the most abundant vertebrate in North America) soon thereafter passed into extinction. The Canada goose and wild turkey, both popular game animals, vanished by around 1910, and nine more species disappeared from Iowa in coming decades. Several of these have since been reestablished in Iowa.

Many birds that survived initial settlement continued to exhibit smaller, ongoing declines due to habitat loss and fragmentation and cowbird parasitism, as well as competition with exotic birds; changing agricultural land use; domestic and feral cat predation; collision with human structures, including windows and communications towers; and more recently pesticides and other chemical toxins and pollutants.

With the help of ongoing breeding bird surveys, conducted nationwide since 1966, we now know more about modern population trends of birds than those of any other animal group. We can document, for example, that the house wren, American robin, cliff swallow, great blue heron, and wood duck (nearly extinct around 1900, but now Iowa's most widespread nesting duck) demonstrated significant increases in Iowa as well as North America from the mid 1960s to the mid 1990s, as their populations rose annually between 2 and 17 percent (Dinsmore 1998: 118).

Iowa's most widely distributed species and those that breed here most successfully are edge species that abound in human-created landscapes such as suburban environments and shrubby borders — between woodland and pasture, for example, or road and cornfield. These include many of our best-known birds: the house sparrow, red-winged blackbird, mourning dove, brown-headed cowbird, barn swallow, common grackle, house wren, and American robin, among others. The adaptable red-tailed hawk and great horned owl are among our most common predators. Four of Iowa's introduced exotics — the ring-necked pheasant, house sparrow, European starling, and rock pigeon — represent a large portion of today's total bird population. Several of these broadly adaptable birds now take refuge in human-built structures. Cliff swallows, for example, once nested on bluffs or streamside cliffs. As rivers were channelized in the 1800s, these birds moved under the eaves of farm buildings. Now cliff swallows form colonies under bridges and in culverts, where they maintain healthy populations.

While some birds thrive, others falter. Both nationwide and in Iowa, about a third of all breeding bird species exhibited statistically significant declines between 1966 and 2003 (Sauer et al. 2004; National Audubon Society 2004). Easily half of Iowa's birds are neotropical migrants, which as a group have been experiencing alarming declines in recent decades. These long-distance migrants nest in the United States or Canada and winter in Central or South America. The group includes many of our shorebirds, raptors, and songbirds (warblers, vireos, grosbeaks, thrushes, and others). Neotropical migrants are struggling with habitat destruction and fragmentation in both their summer and winter ranges. Additionally, in their winter ranges, many are killed as agricultural pests or poisoned by pesticides. These stresses are compounded by the birds' habits. Many neotropical migrants are habitat specialists that arrive later in spring, depart earlier, and lay fewer eggs than short-distance migrants or year-round residents. Their difficulties are further increased by the dangers of lengthy migrations. Concerns about the fate of neotropical residents are backed by statistics: only 17 percent of Iowa's neotropical migrants are increasing in number, while 31 percent of short-distance and 41 percent of resident birds are increasing (Ehresman 2003: 10).

Perhaps most troubling is the ongoing long-term decline of sixteen of Iowa's more common and abundant birds, among them the red-headed woodpecker, northern flicker, blue jay, brown thrasher, bobolink, and red-winged blackbird. Between the mid 1960s and mid 1990s, their numbers steadily dropped between 1 and 5 percent each year (Dinsmore 1998: 119). For nearly all, Iowa's declines are significantly higher than North America's as a whole. Iowa also is the heart of the breeding range for some (for example, the red-headed woodpecker and bobolink) and thus should be serving as a stronghold for these species. One thought suggests that today's mowed grasslands and fragmented woodlands and forests are insidiously acting as sinks — ecological traps that attract nesters but do not permit successful rearing of young. Nesting in such areas lowers rather than raises the birds' total numbers.

The ongoing decline of common species suggests that Iowa's bird life as a whole may be in trouble. This is known to be true for the majority of former prairie nesters, whose fate has depended on agricultural practices and policies since the mid 1800s. Consider the greater prairie-chicken. Prior to settlement, these common, prolific birds nested throughout Iowa. Their numbers increased following settlement and peaked around 1880, when the intermixing of small farm fields (which provided food) and prairies (nesting sites) created ideal habitat. However, the continued plowing of Iowa's prairies caused prairie-chicken reproduction to drop. This combined with hunting, trapping, and random slaughter to doom the birds. By 1900, they were rare. Introduced ring-necked pheasants, which interact aggressively with prairie-chickens and lay eggs in their nests, may have been the final cause of their 1950s disappearance and may be hindering prairie-chicken reintroduction efforts. These commenced in the 1980s and were successful in the extensive grasslands of south-central Iowa, where visitors now may watch the prairie-chickens' springtime booming display. The Kellerton Grasslands Bird Conservation Area in Ringgold County (which lies within the

Grand River Grasslands) has a naturally reproducing prairie-chicken population and also provides habitat for several other grassland bird species.

Today grassland birds show the most consistent declines of any type of bird in the nation, with declines prevailing across North America (Sauer et al. 2004; National Audubon Society 2004). Between 1966 and 2003, two-thirds of Iowa's breeding grassland birds showed significant negative trends, a figure comparable to the national decline of 70 percent for grassland breeders. A number of the steepest bird declines nationwide have been among grassland birds: the Henslow's sparrow lost 96 percent of its population between 1966 and 2003, the short-eared owl 80 percent, the grasshopper sparrow 77 percent. Bobolink numbers have been cut in half during this same period.

Habitat loss, predation, and changing agricultural practices have combined to produce these losses. Following the precipitous bird declines of the 1800s, many grassland birds survived in small diversified farms typical of the early 1900s, only to suffer massive declines after World War II as family farms transitioned to large-scale industrialized agriculture and intensified agricultural practices. Consider, for example, nestings in alfalfa plantings and hayfields, farmlands that through the 1950s substituted for prairies as nesting habitat for Iowa species such as the bobolink, dickcissel, meadowlark, and grasshopper sparrow. Since then the birds' reproductive success has declined greatly due to new hay-alfalfa cultivars, which allow earlier and more frequent hay cuttings. Because these cuttings are completed before ground-nested young have fledged, they result in destruction of active nests and death of large fractions of the young from mowing, baling, and subsequent predation. Consider also that the elimination of pasturelands and grass rotations and the expansion of vast homogeneous croplands have shrunk Iowa's grassland bird habitat, as have declines in livestock production and the switch from open grazing to confinement operations for cattle. Grasslands that survived the late-twentieth-century intensification of agriculture still provide significant functional habitat for grassland animals. But many have been invaded by shrubs and trees or fragmented by bands of woody growth, which invite numerous predators that regularly lunch on eggs and nestlings.

The plight of grassland birds points out the crucial importance of CRP plantings, established in 1985, which in 2002, with the Wetlands Reserve Program, covered about 1.7 million acres of Iowa.[1] Some birds find these grasslands to be

1. The amount of land in CRP plantings and the Wetlands Reserve Program is given in National Agricultural Statistics Service 2002: 15 — State Data, Land: 2002 and 1997.

structurally suitable for nesting habitat and have benefited from these plantings, among them the grasshopper sparrow, sedge wren, dickcissel, bobolink, and ring-necked pheasant (Jackson et al. 1996). The intensity of use of CRP lands seems to vary from bird to bird and region to region. Not all species have demonstrated the increases that were anticipated.

Fragmentation-related predation seems to be shrinking populations not only of grassland birds but also of many woodland and forest birds, although the latter are not declining as uniformly as grassland birds. The summer tanager, rose-breasted grosbeak, red-shouldered hawk, ovenbird, red-eyed vireo, and other thrushes, vireos, and warblers require large, unbroken wooded tracts to reproduce successfully. However, formerly large tracts are shrinking. Area-sensitive birds may be attracted to smaller wooded lots, where they face very high rates of predation as well as cowbird parasitism and other problems that dramatically reduce nesting success.

On a more positive note, the number of bird species sighted in Iowa continues to rise. The house finch, great-tailed grackle, Eurasian tree sparrow, and Eurasian collared-dove, for example, all have established nesting populations in Iowa since 1980. And the reservoirs and lakes constructed in Iowa in the twentieth century have attracted birds that were regionally rare or absent in previous years. Most spectacular are the summertime flocks of hundreds of nonbreeding American white pelicans. During migration in April and September, their numbers can increase to thousands. The diversity and abundance of gulls have soared. Most common is the ring-billed gull, first known to nest in Iowa in 1994. This gull thrives in association with humans and is one of the most rapidly increasing birds in North America.

Forested river bottoms serve as crucial migration corridors for songbirds. Lakes, reservoirs, and their associated rivers also attract a diversity and abundance of migrating ducks, geese, loons, grebes, cormorants, herons, and terns that congregate here to feed and rest. In late summer, when water is low, thousands of shorebirds forage on exposed mudflats. The retention of open water in wintertime (a result of warm temperatures, larger water bodies, and aerated ponds) has lengthened the stay of migrating water birds. In mild winters, when lakes and rivers retain open water, bald eagles can be seen across Iowa, even in urban areas. The snow-white heads and tails of soaring adult eagles increasingly shimmer through blue Iowa skies during much of the year. Eagles had disappeared as Iowa nesters in the early 1900s, but populations started to rise across the country in the 1970s, thanks to laws prohibiting the pesticide DDT and controlling human persecution. Nesting eagles returned to the Mississippi River near Lansing in 1977, and since then nestings have spread westward and continued to increase. In 2005 Iowa boasted an estimated 190 active eagle nests, far surpassing the state's recovery goals for this bird (Iowa Department of Natural Resources 2005).

Each species tells its own story. The sandhill crane, originally a common nester in northern Iowa, was extirpated by 1894 because of egg collectors, hunters, and habitat destruction. In recent decades, expanding populations around the Great Lakes pushed cranes to the southwest until, starting in 1992, they were found nesting along the Iowa River in Otter Creek Marsh. Sandhill cranes now nest at a number of wetlands in eastern and northern Iowa, and their numbers are expected to keep rising.

While bald eagles and sandhill cranes have rallied on their own, other birds have been purposefully reintroduced. Trumpeter swans, which nested in northern Iowa until 1883, were reintroduced starting in 1995. Faring well and aided by wetland restoration efforts, the Iowa swans spread and raised more young each year; by 2004 they were hatching 150 cygnets (Iowa Department of Natural Resources 2005).

The peregrine falcon disappeared from Iowa around 1960, largely because of pesticide use. Reintroduction programs began in 1989, using tall buildings in Cedar Rapids and Des Moines as release and hopeful nesting sites. Additional releases have produced nesting populations in several Iowa cities. Peregrine numbers in Iowa continue to rise, and in 2000 wild birds started to recolonize their historic nesting habitat on Mississippi River cliff ledges. Adult ospreys have been increasingly seen summering at Iowa's reservoirs and large lakes. Young ospreys have been released and fed here since 1997, in hopes of establishing a successful breeding population.

Some reintroductions have been wildly successful. Both the giant Canada goose and the wild turkey were common nesters in Iowa until the early 1900s. Both were successfully reintroduced in the mid 1960s. Thanks to controlled hunting, the establishment of wildlife refuges, restored wetlands, the turkey's ability to use fragmented forests and woodlands, and the goose's comfort with artificial nest structures, these birds are now found in the tens of thousands across the state. Such wildly successful resurgences give hope that given the right conditions, populations of additional declining bird species may be sufficiently resilient to rebound and repopulate our landscape.

Four Legs and Fur

In 1800 nearly six dozen mammal species inhabited Iowa. These included herds of the large herbivores elk and bison and the impressive predators cougars, black bears, and gray wolves. Only decades later all these large animals were gone, victims of unrelenting hunting, trapping, and predator eradication efforts. Elk, coveted by hunters because of their fine meat, once roamed most of the United States and were common in Iowa. They disappeared by the 1860s. Less common in Iowa were bison, which probably were scattered across the state in modest numbers. These "large wild cattle" (so named by explorers Marquette and Joliet) were most abundant in northwestern and north-central Iowa, where they used the headwaters of the Iowa, Cedar, and Des Moines rivers as calving grounds. Bison were rapidly killed off by early settlers, disappearing before the elk.

The same pressures by 1900 had decimated or eliminated populations of smaller predators such as badgers, coyotes, bobcats, river otters, fur-bearing beavers, and white-tailed deer. Animals that probably never were common in Iowa — pronghorns, swift foxes, fishers, martens, lynx, wolverines, and porcupines — also faded away with the land's transformation.

What remained were smaller mammals that did not threaten humans: mice and voles scurrying under leaves and grasses; bats nursing their young in bark crevices of trees; tiny insect-eaters such as shrews and moles; slightly larger carnivores such as striped skunks, mink, raccoons, and foxes; muskrats, woodchucks, and eastern cottontails; squirrels clambering through treetops, and eastern chipmunks scurrying about their bases (see fig. 20). The few introduced mammals flourished: the house mice and Norway rats that today plague urban areas, feral cats, and feral dogs (which also may have been here in presettlement times, since Native Americans possessed domestic dogs).

Many smaller native mammals were reduced in number as their native habitats were transformed to farmland. Some grass-dwelling species (for example, the meadow vole) flourished while others (for example, the prairie vole) declined. The thirteen-lined ground squirrel (which abounds in short grasses of managed landscapes) became Iowa's dominant ground squirrel, a position formerly held by Franklin's ground squirrel, an animal of tall grasses. In 1997 thirty-one of Iowa's presettlement mammal species were considered extirpated or survived in greatly reduced numbers (Bowles et al. 1998). The most common mammals remaining are adaptable generalists and opportunistic woodland-edge species

Fox squirrel

Big brown bat

Beaver

Eastern chipmunk

Plains pocket gopher

Opossum

Short-tailed shrew

White-footed mouse

Mink

Raccoon

White-tailed deer

Striped skunk

Eastern cottontail

Red fox

Coyote

Muskrat

Fig. 20. Today's native mammals are on the whole smaller in size and more adaptable than those of past centuries. Drawing by Mark Müller.

with broad ecological tolerances — animals like the white-tailed deer, raccoon, eastern mole, and big brown bat — which may be abundant in town as well as the countryside. Some (for example, the eastern cottontail, woodchuck, and opossum) are probably more numerous now than before Iowa was cleared for agriculture.

Changing agricultural practices have continually reshaped the numbers and distribution of our mammals. For example, as Iowa's tallgrass prairies were reduced to pastures, croplands, and farmsteads, the white-tailed jackrabbit and spotted skunk increased and spread from their presettlement range in western Iowa eastward to the Mississippi River. However, in recent decades their populations have plummeted. Intensification and industrialization of agriculture have robbed the jackrabbit of the necessary short-grass habitat it once found in pasture, hay, and small grain acreages, and the spotted skunk lost the large haystacks and wooden farm outbuildings that furnished den sites and ready prey. The spotted skunk is state-listed as endangered. CRP and other agricultural set-aside programs hopefully are allowing these and other grassland animals the opportunity to increase once again.

Today, thanks to hunting and trapping regulations, wildlife preserves, habitat restorations, and reintroductions, many nearly extirpated mammals have returned. Badger populations, for example, collapsed in the 1800s when burrowing rodents (its favored prey) were poisoned, while coyote populations plummeted by 1870 as bounties intensified hunting pressures. Both now permeate the state.

Other sizable predators have returned in more limited numbers. Cougars, always rare, were eliminated by 1870. However, scattered reports of free-ranging cougars increased in the mid 1990s, with cats probably moving into Iowa from expanding populations to the south and west. The cougars are presumably being drawn eastward across the United States by exploding populations of white-tailed deer, their favored prey. Reports of bobcats, once common but by 1900 almost extirpated, also continue to rise as these small cats increase in number and expand their range.

Although once common and widespread, black bears (Iowa's largest predator) were killed by settlers whenever encountered and thus disappeared early. Bears no longer reside in Iowa, but reports of occasional vagrants increased in the 1990s, the individuals wandering into eastern Iowa from states to the north and south. Some believe that the gray wolf may soon be following.

In 1500 the beaver, with an estimated population of 60 million, was one of

North America's most abundant furbearers. It became the backbone of the fur industry, and by 1900 its continental population had dropped to around 100,000, and it had disappeared from Iowa (Dinsmore 1994: 84). About the same time, trapping pressures and water pollution nearly eliminated river otter from Iowa. By 1930, beaver had reinvaded Iowa from the northwest. In the two subsequent decades, the Iowa Conservation Commission (now the Iowa DNR) restocked central and eastern Iowa with beaver trapped in western Iowa. In 1985 the Iowa DNR started stocking otter in Iowa's streams. Today both have returned to suitable habitats statewide, their numbers increasing enough to generate complaints of flooding and foraging activities from landowners.

Free-roaming bison and elk are unlikely to wander Iowa's farmlands ever again, but captive herds can be seen at the Neal Smith National Wildlife Refuge southeast of Des Moines, and bison are raised commercially for meat by some farmers.

The Question of Deer

Rebounding native species are hopeful reminders of the resilience of nature. Yet self-regulating natural communities are far more than associations of native species. Natural communities possess finely tuned checks and balances that allow them to function as integrated, sustainable units. Soaring populations of any one species usually imply the disappearance of these sensitive checks and balances. A species irruption can lead to a cascading sequence of destructive events. This is nowhere more obvious than with today's herds of white-tailed deer (Gibbon 1999).

Deer were common across Iowa at the time of settlement, wandering both wooded areas and prairies. Because deerskins and deer meat were prized for consumption and trade, unregulated hunting nearly eliminated deer from eastern and central Iowa by the mid 1860s. By the 1880s, deer were essentially eradicated from the state.

Today's Iowa herds are the offspring of wild individuals wandering in from adjacent states and escapees from captive game herds. Returning white-tailed deer have proved extremely adaptable. They thrive in Iowa's heavily farmed landscape, inhabiting woodlands and forests much smaller than those of presettlement times and cornfields that provide a ready source of winter feed. Without starvation, predation, or unregulated hunting to hold numbers in check, Iowa's deer populations have grown rapidly — from several hundred in the 1930s, to several thousand in the 1950s (when deer hunting was reinstituted following a fifty-five-year ban), to an estimated 360,000 in 2004 before the fawning season (Iowa Department of Natural Resources 2005).

Present-day Iowa constitutes ideal deer habitat: a land of abundant food and cover with moderate winter temperatures and snowfall. Deer numbers are especially high in suburban areas where cover (young woody growth) and food (gardens and nearby croplands) abound but houses prevent intense hunting. Well-fed does often breed in their first year of life and subsequently produce two or even three offspring annually for more than a decade. If unchecked by hunting, Iowa's deer herd could increase 20 to 40 percent a year, doubling in size every three years.

So many deer reproducing rapidly on landscapes dedicated to human use can't help but mean trouble — and indeed white-tailed deer are now causing a diversity of problems throughout the eastern United States. Farmers complain about significant crop loss to deer. Christmas tree farmers find their crop browsed beyond use. Urban and suburban residents lose ornamental plantings and fruit trees and need to fence their vegetable gardens to claim a harvest. Iowa's car-deer collisions cost an estimated $25 million to $35 million annually (Stone 2003: 54). And deer are significantly degrading the structure and composition of native communities, as they spread exotic plants and eliminate populations of native plants and birds (fig. 21; see also chapter 5).

Researchers agree that densities should not exceed 20 to 35 deer per square mile, and even at those numbers deer are severely degrading woodlands. Iowa City has recorded numbers exceeding 160 deer per square mile, many times the land's carrying capacity (Stone 2003: 42). Starting in the 1990s, Iowa instituted special hunting seasons, issued extra antlerless deer licenses, and established special zones where hunters or sharpshooters culled the number of does (killing the polygamous bucks does little for population control). Despite these efforts, early in the twenty-first century Iowa's deer population continued to increase, with each year producing historic highs. Hunting kills, which exceeded 100,000 for the first time in 1996, were nearly 200,000 during the 2004–2005 season (Iowa Department of Natural Resources 2005).

Hidden Hopes

Today native plants and animals and their introduced counterparts cover Iowa's landscape with a complex patchwork that sometimes fosters and sometimes

Fig. 21. With their natural predators no longer present, white-tailed deer have increased to the point that they are severely damaging native vegetation, as well as croplands and landscaping plantings. Note the obvious browse line along this woodland edge; deer have eaten all shrubs and tree branches below this line, but cannot reach any higher. Photograph by Carl Kurtz.

smothers native biodiversity, sustainability, and stability. Considering all natives, we can see that adaptable generalists, which flourish in today's mix of fragmented habitats, have maintained relatively large populations. Edge species in particular have thrived. In contrast, habitat-restricted specialists have declined in abundance and diversity, with common species becoming rarer and the rarest species disappearing. These declines, although understandable, are worrisome because specialists are the most sensitive indicators of environmental health and wholeness.

While we might expect declines of the most specialized, habitat-restricted species, another trend has recently become clear: the slow but steady decline of certain common birds and reptiles, the only classes of organisms for which we have time-sequenced data. Steady decreases in abundant year-round Iowa residents, such as the blue jay and American goldfinch and the bullsnake and American toad, are shocking and distressing. Losses of these, our most bullet-proof species, could imply that today's fragmented native communities are imploding. If this is indeed the case, the result could be the termination of nature as we know it in Iowa. Such an event would be very serious indeed for humans as well as native species.

Population declines reflect a given species' daily struggles with multiple stressors: habitat loss and fragmentation, pesticides, domestic predators, roads and cars, and other modern landscape features. Invasive species that hoard space and resources have joined habitat destruction as major causes of decreasing wildlife populations and species extinctions. Carried to the extreme, the spread of invasives threatens to reduce Iowa's remaining native communities to a common ground of the world's most aggressive and unmanageable species. The end result would be the homogenization and gross simplification of Iowa's biological diversity, a dissolution of the bonds between specific organisms and environments that have developed through the ages.

On a more hopeful level, detailed surveys have demonstrated the continued survival of an amazing diversity of native plants. These plants provide us with a glimpse of the Iowa that once existed and serve as harbingers of ecological sustainability and stability. In addition, in recent decades we have witnessed the return of a number of native mammals and birds that had been eliminated by Euroamerican settlement. A century ago, no one would have believed that white-tailed deer and Canada geese would become overly abundant pest species, otters would again play in our rivers, trumpeter swans would nest in grassland swales, and the glistening white heads and tails of mature bald eagles would become common sights over our rivers and fields. If such seeming impossibilities are now reality, then we might boldly ask what else might come to be if we act appropriately.

4 Prairies Today

One can hardly imagine anything more richly beautiful than an
Iowa prairie in full bloom under the summer sun. Only the fertile
pastures of the Alps can show such wealth of color and these by
their scant dimensions hardly offer a comparison.
— Thomas Macbride, 1895

One early Iowan, John Newhall, expressed the sentiments of all: "However our prairies may have added to the beauty of the landscape, they are impediments to the settlements of a country" (1846: 55). Governed by this maxim, with an eye for agricultural productivity, settlers began to convert North America's ancient perennial grasslands into exotic annual croplands and pastures. All midcontinental grasslands were subjected to the human will to some degree, but agriculture ruled supreme in the tallgrass prairies, where rich soils and abundant rainfall provided ideal growing conditions. The greatest quantity was destroyed in Iowa, the tallgrass heartland, the state with the most prairie to lose.

The transformation has been called the most rapid and complete ecological conversion of a major biological system in Earth's history. In any given area, prairies that had dominated Iowa for millennia were reshaped within a decade. The entire state was settled within a single human lifetime. By 1900, 97 percent of the state (34.6 million acres) had been converted to farmland, up from 8 percent just forty years earlier (Jackson and Jackson 2002: 138).

These statistics indicate the dramatic pressures that were rapidly superimposed on the thousands of native species that once occupied Iowa. Within a few decades, commonplace natives became rare. Prairie habitat, which declined precipitously from the 1830s until around 1900, has continued to dwindle ever since. It is commonly said that under 0.1 percent of Iowa's prairies remain today — a percentage translating to 28,000 acres or fewer of the original 28 million prairie acres. However, recent studies of far-western Iowa's Loess Hills, home of Iowa's largest and most extensive prairie remains, identified a heartening 22,250 prairie acres (including many degraded prairies) remaining in this one region in 1980

(National Park Service 2002: 12, D1-8). This figure implies that in the entire state, a bit over 0.1 percent of Iowa's original prairies likely remains. Other small prairie clusters have been identified in southern Iowa's historic pasturelands, northeastern Iowa's blufflands, and the Little Sioux valley. Elsewhere Iowa's remaining prairies are mostly small and scattered and are either neglected or continue to be altered by human use. Their size and rarity explain why the term "remnant" is often used when talking about the surviving traces of the original native tallgrass prairie.

Declining prairie species and communities were not solitary losses. The important functions that prairies had performed also faltered and failed, along with the landscape's stability and sustainability. Indeed, the plowing of the prairies initiated many of the environmental problems Iowans struggle with today: water pollution, soil degradation and erosion, excessive runoff and flooding, loss of prairie animals and wildlife habitat. Cultivation of most of Iowa's soils also contributed significantly to far-reaching environmental problems such as oceanic dead zones and global warming.

Certainly some nineteenth-century Iowans mourned the loss of the prairie, sensing the stilling of the vast integrated system that had produced life and beauty in such abundance. In any case the settlers used prairie products to meet their every need. Food, medicines, and building materials all came from nature. Gamebirds sizzled in stewpots. Cattle munched the prairie grasses. Early settlers slept on mattresses stuffed with prairie hay and laid their heads on pillows plumped with gamebird feathers. Even wildfires provided bounty: settlers roamed newly burned grasslands collecting abundant prairie chicken eggs, eating those cooked by the fire immediately and storing other eggs for later use (Dinsmore 1994: 110).

Yet use of prairie products did not translate to perceived value. The settlers had arrived armed with technological prowess and firm conviction. Value equated with productivity, and productivity depended on crops and livestock imported from eastern states. And so the prairie transformation continued.

The tenacious prairies did not yield without a fight. They spit the settlers' plows from the soil, sometimes breaking their iron blades in the process. Prairie plants continued to pop up as "weeds" in croplands. Indeed, almost a century after the first timid plow had groaned through Iowa's thick-rooted prairies, Bohumil Shimek wrote that "it requires continued cultivation to keep them [prairie plants] out [of cropland]." He went on to theorize that the "various remnants of the prairie flora are widely scattered, and they are amply sufficient to reseed all suitable areas. No native prairie species has entirely disappeared, though all have been much reduced [in number]." At that time, Shimek thought prairie plants, if left to themselves, would slowly reseed disturbed areas and gradually spread. He also wrote that "few introduced plants have been able to establish themselves in belts of unbroken prairie, and most of these in very small numbers" (Shimek 1925: 3, 6). Prairie remnants at that time apparently remained remarkably intact, stable, and competitive — traits we cannot claim for them today (Weaver 1954: 118–122).

Already by Shimek's time, the majority of the state was populated by imported crops. Prairie patches remained as hayed or grazed grasslands or as wetlands too mucky to plow. Small remnants and isolated prairie species also survived on unplowed nooks and crannies. These refuges were not uncommon in diversified farms with smaller fields utilizing traditional crop rotations. During the last half of the twentieth century, these prairie enclaves were greatly reduced as farming was intensified and row crops were extended. As exceedingly fertile tallgrass soils boosted the United States into world agricultural leadership, an entire major ecosystem became functionally, and nearly physically, extinct. Today only a few North American landscapes remain dominated by tallgrass variants. In addition to Iowa's Loess Hills, these include the Flint Hills of Kansas and Nebraska's Sandhills, most of which have been degraded by heavy grazing.

Plow and Furrow

The settlers' drive for productive labor was most readily achieved with the plow, which imposed immediate and complete transformation on the land. Settlers cut and plowed the oak woodlands and floodplain forests first, following patterns they had established in the eastern United States. They avoided the prairies with their fearsome fires, unfamiliar soils, and absence of essential timber. However, by the early 1840s settlers were becoming aware of the prairie's fertility and starting to bring it under cultivation.

Plowing the prairie was an arduous task. The interwoven, tough roots of prairie grasses, forbs, and interspersed shrubs defied conventional plows. Thus prairies were not "plowed" but "broken," a verb that speaks for the loss of the ecosystem as well as the gain of the farmer. Even the most massive of the ponderous, specially constructed breaking plows, which used teams of five to seven yokes of oxen to produce furrows more than thirty inches wide, could break only a few acres a day. Settlers recounted that plows cutting through fibrous prairie roots sounded like cloth ripping or the dull roaring of a distant storm, punctuated by a volley of pistol shots as larger, tougher roots were severed.

Settlers devised tricks that eased their task. They burned off tangles of thatch in spring. They discovered that closely grazed prairies broke more easily and that flax sown in an April plowing competed with native plants and helped decompose prairie sod. However, their largest boon was John Deere's steel moldboard plow, invented in the 1830s and readily available by the 1850s. Unlike its cast-iron and ironclad wooden predecessors, the self-scouring steel moldboard could cut through the prairie's tough roots and shed clinging clumps of mud. This strong, light plow revolutionized plowing of the prairie.

Once the prairie soils had been plowed and planted, their richness was quickly acknowledged. The best of garden products were reportedly raised on a new breaking of the prairie sod. On cropland, "sod corn" was planted by dropping seed directly into the breaking plow's newly formed furrow. "Twenty or thirty bushels to the acre are often gathered, nothing having ever been done to it after planting," bragged one farmer of sod corn plantings. He also claimed that "very fine crops of wheat are raised in this way" (Robinson 1842: 14–16). An alternative was to slash the overturned sod with an ax, drop a few seed kernels into the opening, and stomp down to seal the earth.

Today's agricultural regime is the result of a series of experimental crop introductions. Initially wheat reigned in Iowa's fields. Hemp, rye, oats, barley, buckwheat, and flax were all grown on small diversified farms. Tobacco, cotton, hops, sugar beets, and more were attempted on Iowa's prairie soils but won less acceptance.

The term "Corn Belt" was first used in 1870. By that time farmers had realized that surplus corn, grown initially for personal use and for the market, could instead be fed to hogs and beef cattle. As one flamboyant 1860s writer stated, "Corn thus becomes incarnate; for what is a hog but fifteen or twenty bushels of corn on four legs?" (quoted in Bogue 1963: 105). By then the number of Iowa cattle as well as hogs was increasing rapidly, and corn production was outstripping wheat.

With their fertile soils, rolling uplands were the first to be converted to cropland. Most of Iowa's well-drained mesic prairie was cultivated by the Civil War. Difficult-to-plow moist meadows and seasonal wetlands were hayed or grazed instead, becoming Iowa's last major tallgrass vestiges. In 1896 wild hay was harvested from 1.55 million acres (5.5 percent) of Iowa's original prairie. By that time, however, intense application of drainage technologies was allowing even moist prairies to be plowed. By 1920, wild hay was harvested from only 1.7 percent of Iowa's native prairie, a percentage that fell to 0.3 percent in 1946 (Smith 1998: 98). Additional prairie acres were utilized as pastures. These last prairie refuges awaited the next onslaught: post–World War II technologies that encouraged larger farms and farming machinery, wider roads, and industrialized agriculture. These changes, along with simplified cropping systems, eliminated prairie pastures and other native remnants that had survived on earlier, more diversified farms.

The results of plowing the prairie were dramatic. Millions of native plants disappeared immediately, with prairie-dependent animals following soon thereafter. Never again would they proliferate in their original abundance.

Few people could have guessed that the demise of the visible prairie would be mirrored by an even greater annihilation underground, a crash of an ancient complex living system (Blumberg 1999). This extermination began with the plow's first slice through the living framework of root, rhizome, and fungi. That cut, and those that followed, destroyed the living mesh of pores and tunnels that had provided niches for millions of microorganisms and insects as well as larger burrowing animals. Thus the prairie's teeming underground life began its inexorable slide toward the poorer assemblage characterizing today's agricultural soils. Today's cornfields contain roughly half the belowground biomass they once held as prairie (Michael Thompson, personal communication).

The loss of biological activity led to declining fertility. The earliest settlers believed that prairie soils required little care, and for the first few decades the notion held true: fertilizer did little to improve the newly broken prairie soil's yields. However, by the late 1800s the decline in organic content and fertility induced farmers to apply manure, use crop rotation, and utilize clover plantings to add nitrogen to prairie soils (Bogue 1963: 145).

Fertility declines were accompanied by a breakdown in the prairie soil's defining granular structure. Aggregates of mineral and organic particles held together by bacteria had produced many of the prairie's finer qualities: water and air infiltration, erosion and compaction resistance, storage of organic matter and carbon sequestration, and a slow, steady release of nutrients and water. On cropland, these relatively large aggregates have been pummeled into smaller and smaller sizes by repeated plowing and tilling, along with falling raindrops that batter the now-bare cropland soil.

In today's cornfields, macroaggregates comprise a small fraction of those present in virgin prairie soils. The cornfields' smaller soil aggregates and pores are less able to absorb water and air. The loss of large aggregates and their living matrix causes cropland soils to collapse and become denser. They tend to bake and harden when dry and puddle when wet. These varied soil changes lead many to say that we haven't farmed our prairie soils, we have mined them.

The loss of macroaggregates links to global warming concerns. For thousands of years prairie soils sequestered carbon-based organic matter in these aggregates. Cultivation led to the aggregates' rapid oxidation, resulting in the loss of some 50 to 80 percent of the prairie soil's original organic matter (McKinley and Wolek 2003). The resulting rush of carbon dioxide is thought to have significantly elevated atmospheric levels of this greenhouse gas (Blumberg 1999: 14).

Iowa's loss of soil organic matter and fertility has been aggravated by the absolute loss of soil through water and wind erosion. Thus both the quality and quantity of the prairie soils have decreased dramatically, and these decreases have cut the soil's productivity. Soil erosion accelerated as row crop agriculture expanded, as farming became more mechanized, and as fencerows and buffer strips were plowed to create larger fields. Erosion has cut the average depth of Iowa's prairie-bred topsoils by more than half (Michael T. Sucik, personal communication). Today's virgin prairie remnant may stand like a pillar a foot or more above surrounding cropland (fig. 22). Erosion's effects are evident in spring when dark-colored soils low on plowed slopes stand in stark contrast to adjacent lighter-colored, eroded hilltops and in fall when crops on hilltops turn yellow earlier than lower crops. Eroded soils can be seen as a slimy coating on the bottom of Iowa's streams and lakes, in the chocolate brown color of flowing waters, and along the banks of incised streams. There our original dark topsoils are often covered with several feet of lighter-colored soil deposited by floodwaters and washed down from nearby slopes (Bettis 1992).

Fortunately, since around 1985, thanks to government land set-aside programs and no-till farming practices (which leave crop residues on the soil surface), bare cropland and soil erosion have been declining. No-till also has cut runoff of herbicides, which generally move with the soil. Although lessening, loss of Iowa's "black gold" continues. In the late 1990s the estimated average annual erosion from Iowa's croplands still ranged from 4.9 to 9.6 tons per acre, with streambank, gully, and wind erosion pushing these averages even higher. These rates remained among the highest in the nation (Natural Resources Conservation Service 1996: 39, 2000: table 10).

Given the magnitude and speed of the prairie's conversion, it is worthwhile to compare the prairie with the cornfield. Corn, like big bluestem, is a grass. Both

Fig. 22. The difference between prairie and agricultural soils can sometimes be seen at their juncture, such as this borderline between central Iowa's Doolittle Prairie and adjacent cropland. The ruler shows that the prairie soils (toward the rear of the photo) are nearly a full foot taller than the cropland soils in the foreground. This difference is due to competition and erosion of cropland soils and their collapse due to the loss of organic matter and soil aggregates. Photograph by Carl Kurtz.

corn and prairie grasslands are fostered by Iowa's sunshine, soils, and climate. Both attain lushness beyond compare, flourishing on warm, steamy summer days when one can almost watch the plants grow.

However, there the similarities end. Prairies are diverse assemblages of mostly perennial plants and animals that bloom and breed, build soil, store moisture and organic matter, retain soil nutrients, and suppress outbreaks of pests and diseases, relying only on sunlight, rainfall, and their own complex biotic interactions. Should certain members falter from disease or climatic stress, species with other traits carry the community into the future.

In cornfields and other intensively managed agricultural lands, many of these qualities are diminished or lost (McKinley and Wolek 2003). Because cornfields are monocultures of annuals, a single infectious agent or a single environmental stressor can herald their comprehensive demise. They cannot survive without human input. Modern corn hybrids require nitrogen fertilizer, synthetic pesticides, and fossil fuel energy for the necessary operation of farm equipment. Their dependence on imported energy and raw materials and foreign markets makes the local growth of Iowa's crops dependent on social, political, and environmental conditions elsewhere.

Put another way, modern cornfields are fossil fuel–based systems dependent on imported energy and chemicals. Prairies in contrast are sun-based systems that represent the ultimate in self-reliance and sustainability. Tallgrass prairies produce more than they consume for centuries on end, and store significant amounts of the greenhouse gas carbon dioxide as underground organic matter. If we are to try to recover a sustainable agricultural landscape, we need to mimic the processes and structure of our native tallgrass prairie.

Jaws and Hooves

Iowa's first domestic grazers consisted of oxen that pulled the settlers' wagons and plows and lean, tough, "common cattle" that promised a ready supply of milk, butter, and meat. The livestock found gustatorial wealth upon their arrival: native grasslands stretched for miles beyond the timber-centered farmsteads. Long before the prairies were settled, when they remained in the public domain, livestock were turned out to forage in the lush, unfenced grasslands (fig. 23). The results were exemplary. "The golden age of butter making was while the cow had the native grass for pasturage," Gilbert Irish later wrote, praising the superiority of "the product of the churn of that time for color, flavor and keeping qualities" (quoted in Mansheim 1989: 50). Sheep also thrived in Iowa's prairies, which supported a growing wool industry from the 1840s until the price of wool plummeted after the Civil War.

Large prairies simultaneously served as open range for roving stockmen who, like the cowboys of western states, herded cattle across Iowa's vast commons. Cattle were fattened on tallgrass pastures during the summer and removed to local woods or to feedlots in St. Louis or Chicago in the winter. Range-herding of cattle ended in Illinois in the 1860s and shortly thereafter in Iowa, as expanding settlements eliminated the open range (Bogue 1963: 101).

Tallgrass prairies, from the start, also provided hay. "There was an abundance of wild grass, both on the uplands and in the sloughs, for the covering of sheds and providing of hay for the stock in the winter time," described settler Marion Drury in later years (1931: 12). All one had to do was to scythe and rake the prai-

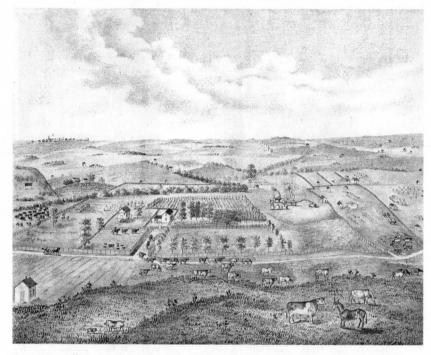

Fig. 23. Initially Iowa's prairies were used as open pasture, as shown in this 1875 sketch of a Dallas County stock farm. The pasturing of the prairie (foreground) and its use as hayfields (center-right) altered the prairie's species composition and abundance, but also preserved many current prairie remnants. Source: Andreas 1875: 258.

rie grass and haul it home. This practice, maintained longest on wet prairies that were not easily plowed, preserved some of today's finest remnants.

The form and impact of grazing evolved as settlement proceeded. In the 1850s grazing pressures intensified when cattle production became a major Iowa industry. Improved transportation and a surplus of feed corn prompted import of purebreds: Durhams, Devons, and Herefords, which sometimes interbred with Texas longhorns, and Jerseys and Holsteins for milk. Purebred cattle could reach weights exceeding 1,300 pounds, 500 pounds more than nondescript prairie steers. However, the expanding herds of "fancy breeds" were too valuable to roam free, as were the thoroughbred horses that in the mid 1800s replaced slower, steadier oxen as work animals.

Thus began the fencing of prairies, frequently accomplished on larger treeless grasslands by the planting of live fences of pruned hawthorn, honeylocust, eastern redcedar, cottonwood, or Osage orange. The last species, introduced from southern states, became the hedge plant of the prairies by the 1850s and maintained that role until the introduction of barbed wire in the 1870s. These hedges stressed prairies in two ways: by introducing some of the first trees into extensive grasslands and by confining cattle so they could no longer move freely and avoid overgrazing.

As settlement intensified, most mesic pastures became too valuable for grazing and were converted to cropland. Prairie pastures that remained were often "improved" by the addition of fertilizers and by farmers harrowing in seeds of aggressive cool-season exotics such as Kentucky bluegrass, smooth brome, timothy, and clover in an effort to extend the prairie's grazing season. These management techniques eliminated prairie plants. In the late 1900s, with the trend toward larger farm fields and machinery, simplified farming systems, more row crops, and declines in Iowa's cattle industry, many pastures (and presumably many prairie pastures) were plowed. Prairie pastures that survived were mostly located on wet soils or dry, steep-sided slopes that resisted plowing. Sparse use and the absence of "improvements" promoted survival of prairie plants. Some of these pastures continue to be grazed and still survive as prairie remnants.

The initial effects of grazing probably were minimal, with cattle replacing elk, bison, deer, and smaller plant-eating animals expelled with settlement. Although free-ranging cattle may have caused shifts in species abundance, they perpetuated the mosaic of patchy disturbance that allowed growth of plants of all types and heights, thus stimulating the diversity and heterogeneity that characterized native prairies.

Increased grazing intensity produced other responses. Carefully grazed prairies can remain in good condition for decades, with the native plants maintaining vigor and replenishing underground food stores. However, overstocked, overgrazed prairies degenerate within a few years. Native plants identified as "decreasers" yield to native "increasers" that are better adapted to grazing pressure. The tall grasses (big bluestem, Indiangrass) give way to shorter prairie species such as sideoats grama and sedges. Tall forbs likewise pass to shorter species. Most legumes decrease; they are preferred by grazers and constitute important forage. Native weedy plants (for example, ragweed, hoary vervain, and thistles) increase, along with introduced cool-season pasture grasses, prostrate plants, and unpalatable species including thorny trees and shrubs. Invading eastern redcedar may become prolific, greatly decreasing the land's value as pasture. Trampled bare spots may be colonized by invasive exotic plants. Eventually the prairie is replaced by an expansive sod of short, shallow-rooted exotics that can survive heavy grazing and trampling, such as Kentucky bluegrass, perhaps interspersed with scattered shoots of grazing-resistant prairie forbs.

Wet prairies are especially prone to trampling, the formation of depressed paths, and the accentuation of natural sedge tussocks. Fens, still commonly grazed today, show an increase of coarse plants such as tussock sedge and sawtooth sunflower. Dry prairies are better able to retain their native prairie character because exotic plants compete poorly with natives on dry sites.

Soil compaction becomes a major problem. Erosion increases as dense native root mats lose integrity and litter dwindles. The prairie soils lose the granular structure that fosters water infiltration and abundant underground life. Soil moisture decreases. As native plants disappear, so do native nesting birds and other animals. Degrading prairie pastures often are tilled, finalizing their passage to nonnative plantings.

Haying typically disrupts prairies less than grazing. Indeed, mowing is sometimes applied to prairie remnants to control woody encroachment and remove plant detritus. However, as with grazing, the haying of prairies induces shifts in plant composition. Cool-season exotics such as smooth brome and Kentucky bluegrass are increased by traditional late-summer hayings, performed during the peak growth and flowering of native species. These and other cool-season species such as timothy and red clover may be present because they were purposefully disked into prairies to supplement the warm-season natives. In addition, frequent mowing removes nutrients held in the hay, decreases native plant heterogeneity, and encourages proliferation of exotic weeds such as sweetclover, which are regularly introduced on haying equipment and via natural spread.

Quenching the Flame

Historic journals tell us that grassland wildfire persisted well beyond Iowa's initial settlement. However, while nomadic Native Americans had utilized fire to tend the prairie landscape, such a release of raw energy was anathema in the newcomers' permanent settlements, with their wooden fences and buildings, confined cattle, and stores of crops. Fire, one of the settlers' most dreaded fears, could rob them of all, including their lives. As an Iowa City historian later described, in the mid 1840s "destructive fires were sweeping over the open prairie, threatening everything on the 'fine farms' with annihilation. Smoke filled the atmosphere and night was made luminous with the glare of the burning grass which was so abundant. Fifty or more men from the town hurried to the assistance of their friends, and to the protection of the stacks of hay and grain, now at the mercy of the flames" (Aurner 1912: 443).

With each passing year, fires became less desirable. So the settlers set out to eliminate wildfire. The task was not easy: fires were started not only by lightning but also by sparks from chimneys, muzzle-loaders, and trains. Settlers combated their destruction by plowing firebreaks around homes and crops. They burned prairies late in spring to reduce fire danger in the coming fall. They threw into the prairie the seeds of cool-season, exotic grasses, which produced less fuel and burned less readily. They organized fire-fighting brigades. And they plowed the prairie itself. Some claim that the removal of the flammable prairie landscape was driven as much by a desire to limit terrifying fires as by a desire for cropland. Fire was still used occasionally as an agricultural tool (for example, to clear roadside ditches or to improve the quality of wild hay), and prairies along railroad tracks were burned to reduce the danger of wildfire. But for the most part, fire suppression became the cultural norm. This trend was aided by the construction of de facto fire breaks: roads, plowed lands, closely grazed pastures. Not until more than a century later would fire be reinstated as a necessary management tool for natural landscapes (McClain and Elzinga 1994).

Eliminating fire immediately and radically reshaped Iowa's native communities. Woody growth proliferated, no longer stunted or killed by fire's heat. Shrub-spattered prairies became thickets; open oak woodlands became dense. Woodlands started to creep onto open prairies, with invading species determined by seed availability.

As woody proliferation reclaimed Iowa's landscape, it threatened prairie species and entire communities. But unburned prairies also suffered in other ways that continue to stress remnants today. The buildup of dead plant material for several years shades and cools the ground surface, constraining both plants and soil organisms, especially in the early spring. The growing season is shortened. Plant vigor, flowering, and seed production decrease. As a prairie becomes choked with detritus, reproduction declines. Plants start to die. Understory plants — in particular small, short, and early-blooming plants — tend to disappear. Unburned prairies eventually lose many plant species. Some of these problems can be lessened by removing excess plant material through mowing, raking, or grazing, but no alternatives have proven to be as effective as fire.

Channeling the Flow

The flow of water through Iowa was, prior to settlement, governed primarily by the tallgrass prairie. However, with the first cut of the settler's plow, the prairie started to lose its remarkable ability to meter water's flow as well as cleanse water and safeguard soil. The logging of streamside forests also played a part, as did increasing concentrations of livestock, whose hooves compacted soils and made them less permeable. In cities, buildings and pavement created impenetrable surfaces. Within a few years, the slow passage of water from prairie foliage into and through the soil gave way to a silt-laden gush streaming into rivers and racing toward the sea. The resulting erosion of the most permeable topsoils then further increased runoff by exposing deeper, less permeable soil layers. The net result was an inadvertent but massive drying of the landscape.

Soon settlers began a more purposeful dewatering of the land. They realized that "useless" wetlands could be dried and transformed into croplands simply by shoveling a water outlet to the nearest stream or, if the land was flat and marshy, digging a new drainage channel. Water's disposal could be accelerated by removing stream meanders or shortcutting river oxbows, reshaping the naturally winding channels into straight, fast-flowing ditches that ate their way into valley floors. As a result, swales once crossed with ease by a horse-drawn wagon soon became impassable gullies. Increasingly rapid runoff intensified flooding, which encouraged settlers to channelize and deepen riverbeds into straight, high-banked, sun-baked ditches to speed runoff even more. All these techniques were applied extensively: stream straightening is estimated to have eliminated as much as 3,000 miles of Iowa's small rivers (Bulkley 1975).

Between 1870 and 1920 and again in the mid-twentieth century, construction of artificial drainage systems was advanced by new technologies, the state's formation of regional drainage districts, and federal drainage incentive programs. These promoted the dredging and leveeing of still deeper, wider, and straighter ditches, which created drop-offs or knick points that rapidly migrated upstream. Development of ever-more-powerful machinery eased ditching efforts. Aboveground drainage systems were supplemented by drainage tiles, buried clay pipes that collected subsurface seeping water and shot it directly into ditches or agricultural drainage wells (fig. 24). Thomas Macbride summarized the results of these multiple efforts, which allowed the settlement of the vast marshlands of northern Iowa: "Prairies of Iowa are everywhere appreciably drier than they were prior to their cultivation. This we may attribute not to any special change

Fig. 24. Tiling the prairie was one step in a many-faceted program to drain and dry the land and convert it to cropland. Over a quarter of Iowa's cropland has been tiled, with the practice continuing today. Courtesy State Historical Society of Iowa, Iowa City.

in climate, but to the simple fact of universal drainage consequent upon the processes of agriculture" (1895: 344). By the late 1900s, about eight million acres, or 25 to 35 percent of all Iowa cropland, had been artificially drained by tiles (Schilling and Libra 2003). New drainage tiles are still installed today, encouraged by computer-aided detection of wet soils.

As infiltration declined and constructed drainage networks reshaped water's flow, the water table began to drop. Shallow wells dried up, as did seeps, springs, and ephemeral ponds. As Scott County pioneer Andrew Hyde wrote, "The rain runs off [the farms now] in a very short time, and [fields] are left as dry as ever. They don't hold the moisture as they used to do. . . . We made a mistake when we went to work and drained them all. It is a hard matter now to find a farm that has a slough on it, at least on our uplands. There were plenty of them forty years ago, and I think we had a better soil and climate then because of them" (1902: 20–21). Remaining wetlands became easier to drain. They also became more susceptible to new forms of woody invasion.

Eroding, deepening creekbeds further dried the land by dropping the water table of the surrounding valley floor. And on hillsides as well as bottomlands, the more rapid and voluminous flows carved finely dissected drainageways that quickly became entrenched. Among the flat boggy swales of north-central Iowa, increased runoff over newly bared soil created well-defined drainages where few had existed before. New drainageways also proliferated in southern Iowa's rougher terrain, counterbalancing that region's simultaneous loss of streams through channelization. Everywhere cycles of drainage, erosion, and lowered water tables fed one another, each exacerbating the dewatering of the land (Andersen 2000).

The twentieth century also saw the reshaping of the vast wetlands along the Mississippi and Missouri rivers, conducted in part to facilitate barge trade. Eleven dams were built along the Mississippi, and the Missouri was intensively channelized. Tremendous reaches of wetland wildlife habitat were lost in the process.

Dewatering of the Iowa landscapes produced a totally new runoff-driven hydrologic regime, one that differs from the infiltration-driven system of past centuries as profoundly as cornfields differ from virgin prairie. This hydrologic revolution has redefined our water's purity, location, flow, and accessibility; topsoil depth and moisture; wetland biodiversity; and extreme events such as flooding and drought. These unintended consequences today comprise some of our most severe environmental problems.

Most obvious is the direct loss of wetlands. Statistics vary because of inconsistencies in defining wetlands and their ephemeral nature, but all agree that the number and size of wetlands have declined dramatically. A generous late-1900s figure lists Iowa's current total vegetated wetland, lake, and river coverage at nearly a million acres, a figure that approaches 11 percent of Iowa's original 8,936,000 wetland acres.[1] Today's remaining native wetlands falter and shrink as they continue to be logged, grazed, and drained for cropland or reshaped for housing developments.

Counterbalancing natural wetland loss has been the widespread construction of farm ponds and other artificial wetlands, which began in the 1930s and 1940s. By 1997, Iowa's created marshes, farm ponds, lakes, and reservoirs covered more than 150,000 acres (Bishop et al. 1998). These relatively deep wetlands are

---

1. Statistics of Iowa wetland loss, which reveal that about one million acres of wetlands remained around 2000 (equaling about 11 percent of presettlement coverage and under 3 percent of the current state), are from the U.S. Fish and Wildlife Service (n.d.), with data compiled in the 1990s. Most other sources give lower coverages for remaining Iowa wetlands: see Bishop 1981: 223; Cooper 1982; and Dahl 1990. In contrast, *The Iowa Gap Analysis Project Final Report* (Kane et al. 2002) assigned a more generous 3.2 percent of the state's modern cover to wetlands — 2.0 percent to herbaceous and woody wetland types, including temporarily flooded lands, and another 1.2 percent to open water coverage.

significant boating, fishing, and hunting areas. While important to certain waterfowl, they lack the natural diversity and complexity of sedge meadows, wet prairies, and other shallow native wetlands that still are being lost to neglect or development.

Protected, restored, and created wetlands have flourished with the North American Waterfowl Management Plan and multiple other governmental and private programs initiated since 1980. Some wetlands have been established for very specific purposes, such as waterfowl breeding grounds or wastewater treatment structures. Other wetland projects are broader in scope. The Iowa River Corridor Project addresses floodplain management along the Iowa River, extending forty-five miles upstream from the Coralville Reservoir. This joint public-private initiative, a response to 1993's tremendous floods, uses easements, land purchase, wetland creation, and the like to prevent future losses on flood-prone lands. Tens of thousands of Iowa acres are currently enrolled in various federal wetland programs (Bishop et al. 1998).

Today's wetlands, be they created or natural, differ greatly from those of past centuries. Once fed by crystalline water seeping through the soil, wetlands are now replenished by polluted surface runoff. Once sites of shallow groundwater discharge, wetlands now recharge groundwater aquifers. Water's flow in Iowa's drainages, once steady and moderate, is now defined by rapid change and extremes. Erratic bursts overflow banks in a matter of hours, then contract to dribbles. Floods are more frequent and severe than in the past, with storm runoff reaching streams faster and peak flows being higher. Once-perennial streams have become flashy and intermittent, their sudden fluctuations a stark contrast to the slow rises and falls of past centuries. At the same time, dewatering of the land has decreased the soil's ability to resist drought. Regional declines in groundwater levels have occurred in the Cambrian-Ordovician aquifer of northeastern Iowa and in the heavily used Silurian aquifer near Cedar Rapids and Iowa City (Prior 2003: 59).

Surviving native wetlands are restricted to discrete locations and lie primarily in lowlands. The flatlands along the lower Cedar and Iowa rivers, with their many oxbows and floodplain forests and swales, comprise one of Iowa's richest remaining wetland regions.

Today we expect the remaining small, degraded wetlands to assist with functions once assumed by the entire landscape, such as flood control, and also to assist with ecological processes, such as water purification. Water pollution was generally unknown prior to row-crop production. When the first plowcuts exposed raw earth to wind and rain, soil started to wash into streams, along with human, livestock, and urban wastes. Deepening drainageways added stream-bed sediments to already turbid waters, as did collapsing banks of downcutting streams. Rapid degradation of Iowa's crystalline waters was colorfully described in 1883:

> Old settlers say the Iowa River used to be a clear stream, except during high water, but now it is always muddy or slimy. . . . The plowing and cultivation of the land causes [sic] more loose soil and vegetable debris to be washed into the river than could be washed in from the native prairie sod; also, nearly every small stream flowing into the river is now utilized as a hog-wallow, or else a hot-day resort for cattle, and the continual filth from these sources passes into the river and contaminates its waters. (Anonymous 1883: 578)

While eroding sediments continue to pollute Iowa's streams, since World War II other highly visible waterborne pollutants such as untreated sewage and packinghouse effluent have been curbed. However, in the mid 1900s a bewildering complex of synthetic agricultural pesticides, inorganic fertilizers, and their breakdown products started to appear. These were mainlined into streams via drainage tiles or were washed in from ever-larger fields plowed to the very edge of drainageways. Agricultural water pollutants have been joined by significant quantities of lawn chemicals, oil and grease from cars, diverse urban and industrial wastes, warmed water from city structures (thermal pollution), and the growing threat of manure from industrial confined animal feeding operations housing tens of thousands of animals.

Many of the more persistent and toxic agricultural pesticides have been banned. However, minute quantities of pesticides and their breakdown products are still found in our water, along with a growing "chemical cocktail" of low levels of new substances — antibiotics, cleaning detergents, hormones, and hormone-disrupting synthetic compounds, among others. Their combined health effects, and those of the ubiquitous small quantities of pesticides and their metabolites, remain largely unknown. In contrast, nitrates are an acknowledged hazard. High levels, correlated with the runoff of nitrogen fertilizers used on midwestern row crops, stimulate algal blooms that jumpstart major die-offs of other stream life. Infants drinking nitrate-contaminated groundwater may suffer a potentially fatal decrease in their blood's oxygen-carrying capacity. Nitrate is Iowa's most common groundwater contaminant. Iowa's stream levels of nitrogen and phosphorus are some of the highest in the nation (Prior 2003: 62; Kalkhoff et al. 2000: 1; Riessen 2002).

While wetlands are extremely efficient water purifiers, sedge meadows and other sensitive native assemblages struggle to handle current sediment and chemical loads. Today's nutrient-rich runoff favors tough, weedy natives and invasive exotics such as purple loosestrife and reed canarygrass. The latter, now our most troublesome and invasive grass, grows vigorously in the nutrient-rich sediments deposited by periodic flooding. Thick, impenetrable mats of reed canarygrass — with its prolific seed production and dense, creeping rhizomes — spread readily into disturbed sites and created wetlands and also threaten natural wetlands where they displace native plants and animals. The same is true of highly competitive natives such as certain bulrushes and sandbar willow. Cattails, which until the 1920s were reported in Iowa only sporadically, now form extensive wetland monocultures.

These plants, in tandem with habitat fragmentation and altered flow patterns, have reshaped wetland biodiversity in Iowa. While much of Iowa's diversity today is still found along stream and river corridors and in their adjacent ravines (where land is less intensively used for agriculture), on the whole the most common wetland animals are adaptable generalists such as the ubiquitous painted and snapping turtles, American toads, muskrat, and mink. Tiger salamanders breed in roadside ditches and farm ponds (as long as they are fish-free). Water snakes still feed on fish and frogs and bask along wetland shores, sites where garter snakes also abound. Bullfrogs as well as leopard, chorus, cricket, and other frog species breed in wetlands and feed on their banks. Certain wetland animals that had nearly disappeared from Iowa have been successfully restored: the river otter, the beaver, and most recently the sandhill crane and trumpeter swan. Geese are doing very well, with both migrating snow geese and nesting Canada geese increasing greatly in recent years.

But finely tuned organisms that require more pristine environments have declined precipitously or disappeared. Take, for example, the sensitive indicators of stream health, the freshwater mussels or unionid bivalves. A century ago they were so abundant that tons of shells were pulled from the Mississippi River to supply the largest pearl button industry in the world. At that time fifty-five mussel species were found in Iowa rivers. By 1985, nearly half of these mussel species had disappeared, and by 1998 average stream species richness had dropped by more than another 50 percent. While 94 percent of Iowa's sites boasted living mussels in 1985, only 53 percent did so in 1998 (Arbuckle 2000).

Iowa's native fish have declined perhaps more than any other state's. They also have shown a decided shift, most pronounced in large rivers, from specialists requiring clear, cool water to less discriminating species tolerant of warmer, silt-laden, polluted water. The latter include exotic rough fish such as the common carp, now abundant throughout Iowa, whose behavior patterns (for example, roiling of bottom sediments) are detrimental to native fish (Sullivan 2000).

Streamside beetles have shifted from diverse presettlement-era complexes typical of high-quality water and undisturbed grasslands or riparian forests to poorer assemblages associated with dung, polluted waters, and cultivated plants (Baker et al. 1993).

Most noticeably, once-abundant water birds, including herons, bitterns, rails, and waterfowl, have dropped greatly in number. About a dozen species of ducks originally nested in Iowa, and millions of waterfowl migrated through in spring and fall. Iowa's generally north-south-running rivers remain important corridors for migrating birds, and the Mississippi and Missouri rivers still constitute major waterfowl flyways. However, the numbers of such birds plummeted starting in the late 1800s as uncontrolled hunting, wetland drainage, and the 1930s drought took their toll. Today Iowa's only commonly nesting ducks are the wood duck, mallard, and blue-winged teal. Ongoing challenges to water birds include agricultural chemicals, nest predation, and inadequate nesting habitat, including lack of upland cover and loss of clustered wetland complexes that meet all stages of the birds' life cycles. Recent programs to restore prairie pothole wetlands have led to increasing numbers of certain waterfowl during years when water conditions are favorable. These may be creating a more hopeful future for Iowa's water birds (James Dinsmore, personal communication).

Iowa's profoundly modified waters have dramatically reshaped aquatic life a thousand miles down the Mississippi River, in the Gulf of Mexico. There high levels of nitrogen, washed in primarily from midwestern field runoff, have stimulated excessive algal growth, which each summer robs the waters of oxygen. The resulting hypoxia kills fish, shellfish, and other organisms, periodically turning the region into a dead zone of increasing duration and frequency, which in 2006 covered about 7,000 square miles (U.S. Geological Survey 2006). This story exemplifies a profound irony: Iowa's rich prairie topsoil, with its agricultural additives, has through displacement become a pollutant. Iowa's formerly crystal clear waters have become health hazards. Our state's life-giving soils and waters have inadvertently become far-reaching messengers of destruction.

Ancient Snippets, Hidden Treasures

A mere 200 years ago the disappearance of North America's midcontinental tall grasslands would have been laughable. Yet today we are left to wonder what it would be like to wander through fields of flowers and shoulder-high grasses or to hunker near a bison wallow and watch clouds of feeding shorebirds. As Aldo Leopold so eloquently expressed, "What a thousand acres of *Silphiums* looked like when they tickled the bellies of the buffalo is a question never again to be answered, and perhaps not even asked" (1949: 45).

If even a single section of Iowa's prairie had been preserved rather than plowed, we could at least ask such questions today. As it was, formal prairie preservation proposals did not commence until 1919, nearly a century after settlement had begun. That year Iowa State University researcher Ada Hayden suggested that small prairie plots be set aside in each county as a heritage for present and future generations (Conard 1997: 182). Variations of this theme were later voiced by others, some of whom suggested locating or rebuilding a very large Iowa prairie preserve. However, none of these suggestions were implemented until 1946, when the Iowa Conservation Commission (today's Iowa Department of Natural Resources) purchased its first prairie preserve, today's Hayden Prairie in Howard County. Prairie preservation efforts gained momentum in the 1960s, with the founding of the Iowa chapter of the Nature Conservancy in 1963 and the Iowa State Preserves System in 1965, the latter established to grant strong permanent protection to Iowa's most pristine remaining natural lands (Smith 1998).

At first Iowa's preserve owners assumed that simply eliminating agricultural use would ensure a prairie's perpetuity. However, they soon observed that following initial recovery from grazing or haying, prairie preserves started to develop a thick smothering thatch, in-fill with woody growth, and lose native species and vigor. To counteract these negative trends, prescribed burns, along with manual clearing of invading trees and shrubs and control of exotic invasives, have been applied since the late 1970s. Today they are routine components of Iowa's management procedures. These management techniques, which mimic the routine disturbances that shaped presettlement prairies, are crucial for restoring the health of degraded remnants and for maintaining a high-quality remnant's integrity (see chapter 6).

County, state, and federal governments now join with private individuals and conservation groups in preserving and restoring Iowa's remaining prairies. How successful have they been? A survey completed in 2000 identified 120 prairies of 10 acres or more scattered across Iowa. Seventy percent of these fell into the smallest category of 10 to 40 acres, and only 15 percent were over 100 acres in size (Rosburg 2001). While there are undoubtedly many additional private and unidentified prairie communities, including a large number that are smaller than 10 acres, this survey gives a sense of the magnitude of the prairie's demise. It starkly illustrates that discussions of Iowa's current prairies are based on a few tattered vestiges of what once was, minuscule snippets cut from the great green cloth that once draped the Midwest.

Four-fifths of the 120 identified prairies were being preserved and presumably managed by the state, a county, or a private conservation organization. These dedicated prairie preserves, native gems on the landscape, represent the best of our remaining prairie heritage. They retain sufficient integrity to be recognizable as prairies even by the novice. One-fifth remained in private hands, where they may be treasured and properly managed but nevertheless remain vulnerable to changes in family sentiment and ownership (Rosburg 2001).

The majority of Iowa's prairie remnants are found along the westernmost edge of the Loess Hills, where they have been redeemed by steep topography necessitating the land's use as pasture rather than cropland. Here dry prairie remnants abound, covering the most rugged, driest sites (see color plate 4). In less extreme sites, most Loess Hills prairies have been transformed to cropland or nonnative pasture or have succumbed to invading shrubs and trees, which present a major ongoing threat. Loess Hills prairies increase in size toward the north; Iowa's largest contiguous native prairie lies within Broken Kettle Grassland, which stretches over more than 7,000 acres of Plymouth County. This managed preserve is protected through easements as well as land ownership. Numerous other managed and unmanaged preserves of varying quality and size dot the Loess Hills, as do private remnants, many of which are still used as pasture. Because of the region's tremendous prairie potential, considerable effort is being focused on restoring large Loess Hills prairies on both preserves and private grazing lands.

The Little Sioux River valley in northwestern Iowa was recognized as a rich source of native prairie remnants in the early 1990s, when the Iowa Department of Natural Resources adopted the Waterman Creek project. Nearly 5,000 acres of O'Brien County's steep riverside blufflands and adjacent lands will eventually constitute an extensive preserve that includes relatively large native prairies, some of which have been grazed only lightly. Efforts are also under way to encourage proper management of privately owned prairie pastures in a longer corridor along the Little Sioux River.

Unknown numbers of additional prairie remnants remain elsewhere in Iowa. The vast majority are in private ownership and are very small (a few acres or less) and isolated from one another. Patches of prairie have long been known to stubbornly persist along railroads and roadways, surviving here because these corridors were carved into virgin prairie or reseeded naturally when prairies still abounded. Pioneer cemeteries often host high-quality remnants, as do isolated corners of land, remote slopes and terraces, and prairie potholes that are difficult to plow. Remnants are most likely to be found on land that is marginally accessible to farm equipment or cattle and on fields far from roads. Like so much of our natural world, these remnants are waiting for a concerned public to discover them, claim ownership, provide the care they need, and afford them a future.

Remnants will always be degraded to some degree. While better remnants might possess a fairly diverse prairie flora, others sport only a few common species. Small associations of adaptable prairie plants may be found along fencerows, in fallow pastures, and even in urban wastelands, having spread there long ago from now-defunct virgin prairies. They are often seen along county roadways, where sporadic clusters of sunflowers, goldenrods, big bluestem, and other hardy species convert road rights-of-way into wildflower gardens during summer and fall months. These clusters will not, however, house more discriminating plants that cannot survive outside a complex prairie assemblage.

The vast majority of today's larger remnants have survived because they were managed as hayfields or pasturelands or because they covered poor soils that were tilled lightly if at all (fig. 25). Both haying and grazing help remove the thick thatch that can suffocate prairie plants. Prairie plants may be obvious in hayed fields, and prairie pastures can sometimes be recognized by the presence of a few plants typical of mature prairies, such as the compassplant, leadplant, or pale purple coneflower, or by clusters of less particular species. But often prairie pastures bear no prairie resemblance. Brush and invading trees have masked their grassland character. Their native plants have survived for decades as stunted, nonflowering individuals that are difficult to identify. Such plants seem to hobble along mostly as root systems, their cropped leaves photosynthesizing barely enough to enable the plant's survival for one more year.

But clear the brush, discontinue grazing, and voilà — prairie plants appear as if by magic. Allow fuel to accumulate for a year or two, burn the area to sup-

Fig. 25. With former prairies now largely converted to cropland, grasslands remain primarily in areas with rugged terrain or on sites that were formerly wooded communities (see fig. 6). Most modern grasslands, mapped here in black, are dominated by introduced pasture grasses and other exotic species. A limited number of sites that were not badly overgrazed or intensively plowed remain a good source of undiscovered prairie remnants. Even lightly tilled, poor-soiled CRP lands may sprout prairie plants. Map by Casey Kohrt, Iowa Geological Survey, from 2002 satellite imagery.

press the cool-season exotics and shrubs, and prairie plants flourish. Regular burns continue to increase native species richness, with new species sometimes appearing over many years. Any pasture that has not been repeatedly plowed or intensively managed has the potential of returning to prairie if cleared of brush and burned. The skills of an experienced botanist may be useful in identifying hopeful prairie restoration sites, as will study of soil maps and land-use history. Given that pastures remain Iowa's most significant source of undiscovered prairie remnants, such actions are well worth the effort.

The quality and diversity of all remnants depend on the character of the original prairie and on the land's disturbance and management history. But any remnant's potential may be high. This has been demonstrated in Iowa County on Indiangrass Hills, a square mile of prior pasture and cropland. Here several private landowners have joined efforts to retire agricultural uses, reintroduce fire, remove woody invaders, and control exotics. Using these tools alone, by

2004, after seven years of effort, the landowners had witnessed the spontane-
ous return of 223 prairie species, which constituted nearly half of the 473 plants
they had identified on their land. They have watched remnant plants spread
and welcomed increasing numbers of prairie birds (R. Sandy Rhodes II, Judy J.
Felder, Mary E. Brown, personal communications).

The search for native remnants can be a hopeful enterprise. For example, a
2003 search for prairie patches in southeastern Ringgold County, where about
a quarter of the land is pastured, revealed 115 remnants ranging in size from
0.04 to 15 acres, totaling 135 acres. These remnants were most numerous along
fence lines and field edges, on sites inaccessible to farm machinery, and on steep
slopes or sites with low fertility. Remnants commonly were associated with
CRP set-aside lands (Rosburg 2003). The study area comprised Iowa's portion
of the Grand River Grasslands, an ambitious project intended to protect and
restore significant functional tallgrass prairies along the Iowa-Missouri state
line. Southern Iowa, with its rolling topography and historic use as pastureland, is known to be richer in prairie remnants than much of Iowa. While the
diversity of some remnants may be low, restoration projects in southern Iowa
could significantly increase the state's amount of healthy prairie and open oak
woodland.

Again, Iowa's prairie fens, identified as seepage-based wetlands that are wet
throughout the growing season and thus accumulate highly degraded plant
materials, were once thought to be very rare and restricted to the northwestern
corner of the state. However, a 1980s inventory revealed over 200 extant prairie
fens, the majority of which were located in Iowa's northeastern quarter. While
only about 25 were truly outstanding because of their high species diversity and
intact vegetation, half of the fens were judged as botanically significant: not only
did they house a large diversity of plant species, they also nurtured about twenty
plants considered rare in Iowa, several of which are typical of more northern
climes (Pearson and Leoschke 1992). Rare fen species include certain orchids,
cottongrasses, grass of Parnassas, and fringed gentian. The very existence of
these previously unrecognized rich communities breathes hope into the search
for remnants of Iowa's presettlement past.

Just as many types of prairies existed in presettlement times, so diverse types
remain today. However, the relative abundance of major prairie types was dramatically altered during the settlement process. Ironically, the upland mesic
prairies that once dominated Iowa are now among the rarest of communities.
They were the first to be plowed and converted to cropland. In contrast, once-

uncommon prairies on dry sites (for example, prairie-covered ridgelines in the Loess Hills and on gravelly moraines) are today disproportionately abundant, having been protected by rugged terrain or unproductive soils.

This turnabout is exemplified in northeastern Iowa's hill (or goat) prairies overlooking the Mississippi River (fig. 26). There dry prairies remain on shallow soils high on steep south- or southwest-facing slopes inaccessible to plowing and haying. Species diversity remains high on these sites. Many have been grazed, however, and heavy grazing has shifted the abundance of certain species — favoring sideoats grama, for example, at the expense of prairie dropseed. With the elimination of wildfire, smooth sumac and gray dogwood have crept upslope in ravines, shading out sun-loving species and providing perches for birds, which carry other woody seeds into the prairies. Both eastern redcedar and common juniper invade hill prairies aggressively, taking advantage of disturbed soils created by cattle. As a result, many of northeastern Iowa's hill prairies are now struggling to survive.

Sand prairies constitute another example of dry remnants. Sand deposited by water or wind is common on the leeward side of the Cedar, Iowa, and other eastern Iowa rivers and is occasionally covered with prairie plants. The Big Sand Mound natural area, south of Muscatine, is Iowa's largest and most spectacular sandy area. It joins Iowa's other extreme sites (algific talus slopes, fens, Loess Hills prairies) as a haven for large numbers of uncommon plants and animals. At Big Sand Mound, shifting dunes with their varied topography and plant cover provide habitat for many state-listed species, including the Illinois mud turtle, plains pocket mouse, ornate box turtle, and several of Iowa's rarest plants.

Modern populations of prairie-remnant animals also became skewed during settlement. Today's postage-stamp preserves maintain sustainable populations of only the smallest animals. Fortunately many prairie mammals are generalists that have been able to substitute other grassy landscapes for native prairie. Plains pocket gophers, western harvest mice, deer mice, meadow voles, meadow jumping mice, thirteen-lined ground squirrels, striped skunks, weasels, and badgers all can be found in pastures, hayfields, and meadows, which remain especially large and abundant in south-central Iowa. The same is true of bobolinks, meadowlarks, dickcissels, and northern harriers; of vesper, Henslow's, and grasshopper sparrows; and of other prairie birds, including the killdeer, the only prairie shorebird that today remains common and widely distributed. Even the state-threatened ornate box turtle, Iowa's only fully terrestrial turtle, can be found in exotic grasslands with sandy soils. These and other rarer, more discriminating

Fig. 26. Dry prairies, such as this goat prairie in northeastern Iowa (Allamakee County), are today disproportionately abundant because the mesic prairies on flatter ground have nearly all been converted to cropland. Photograph by Carl Kurtz.

prairie animals such as prairie voles and plains pocket mice may be present on prairie remnants that are sufficiently large and intact to meet their needs. Oftentimes their presence is linked to land-use history and chance events. Grassland buffers adjacent to prairie remnants may effectively increase a remnant's size and usability for many prairie animals. In contrast, remnants bordered by shrublands or trees may attract wandering woodland animals that prey on prairie residents.

Healthy populations of invertebrates remain crucial to a prairie's long-term survival. Seventy to 80 percent of the plant species in today's prairies are forbs, and nearly all of these depend on pollination by native bees, butterflies, moths, flies, beetles, or other insects or birds. The loss of insect pollinators, which as a group are in serious decline, could lead to the decline of the plants they pollinate (Stephen Hendrix, personal communication).

Conversely, the survival of certain invertebrates is inexorably linked to proper preservation and management of surviving prairie remnants. Ten to 20 percent of prairie insects are habitat restricted, their required food or life-cycles being tied to specific prairie plants (Cochrane and Iltis 2000: 44). Examples are many skippers, hallmark butterflies of the prairie, which are today even more restricted than native prairie remnants. Less-discriminating insects have been able to transfer their allegiance to planted grasslands, garden species, or other introduced plants. The painted lady and black swallowtail — broad generalists whose larvae will feed on certain exotic as well as native plants — are among the most abundant butterflies of Iowa's open areas today.

Well-managed remnants provide a sense of Iowa's original prairie expanse, albeit a truncated sense. As John Madson eloquently wrote, all that we can know today of the prairie is "the setting and the mood — a broad sky of pure and intense light, with a sort of loftiness to the days, and the young prairie-born winds running past us from open horizons" (1972: 19). Many of the landscape's details are gone — earth trembling under the hooves of thundering elk, flickering shadows of hovering shorebirds, infinite varieties of flowered associations extending in all directions as far as the eye can see, and the sense of what it means to belong to a world of grass, sky, wind, and fire.

While much has been lost, much also remains to be admired and enjoyed. In today's higher-quality remnants, which boast between 150 and 300 plant species, new forbs bloom each week throughout the long growing season, just as they did 200 years ago (fig. 27).[2] Flowers glisten in the sun and scent the breeze. They flaunt their hardiness as they greet the rigors of drought and fire. Grasses and forbs promote rainfall's infiltration and pump organic matter into everdeepening soils. Their dense roots host a microscopic life so rich and diverse that we still cannot name all its members. Remnants, dominated by ever-taller species as the season progresses, also display many of the prairie's other defining traits described in chapter 2.

These traits appear most heartily in a minority of our remnants, those that are protected, managed, and highest in quality and diversity. Many more remnants, such as the prairie pastures described above and prairie-covered nooks and crannies, are in various stages of disrepair, often spiraling downward because their owners do not recognize or value them or do not possess the resources needed for proper management. Their native qualities, species, and the prairies themselves are gradually being lost.

As native diversity has declined, exotic plants have become an assumed com-

2. Species numbers are from John Pearson (personal communication) from comprehensive inventories of Iowa's state preserves. Note that these may include a limited number of exotic species or plants more characteristic of nonprairie community types.

New England aster

Prairie coreopsis

Purple prairie clover

Pale purple coneflower

Leadplant

Round-headed bush clover

Prairie blazing star

White wild indigo

Sunshine rose

Gray-headed coneflower

Stiff goldenrod

Prairie violet

Compassplant

Fig. 27. Native forbs such as these add color to the prairie throughout the growing season. Drawing by Mark Müller.

ponent of modern prairie remnants. Remnants that are neither utilized nor managed may look like a sprinkling of natives struggling to compete within a larger matrix of alien forbs and shrubs. Grazing and haying favor introduced pasture grasses. Kentucky bluegrass is ubiquitous even in today's intact, managed remnants. These also may retain timothy, red clover, and other species reminiscent of prior agricultural use. Fortunately most of these pasture plants decrease with fire and are more of a nuisance than a threat. In contrast, the invasion and proliferation of "superinvaders" — smooth brome, leafy spurge, reed canarygrass, purple loosestrife, and woody invasives such as Siberian elm and black locust — bode ill for prairie remnants. These exotics warrant immediate and vigorous suppression. Constant efforts are also needed to eliminate the native woody plants that increase in unmanaged remnants — smooth sumac, roughleaf dogwood, elm, eastern redcedar, box elder, and others.

Both managed preserves and neglected remnants are being reshaped by additional constraints. Perhaps most important, their small size and isolation constrict the resilience, stability, integrity, and diversity that prairies once possessed. Today's remnants are not large enough to sustain viable breeding populations of a number of organisms, larger herbivores and predators being obvious examples. Even when organisms can reproduce successfully, populations on small preserves are vulnerable to genetic drift, inbreeding, and extinction through chance events. In the past, genetic inbreeding was prevented by wide-ranging exchange of pollen and dispersal of animals. Plants or animals lost from one site could be replaced by immigrants from neighboring prairies. Now isolated remnants must carry on alone. Research has shown that this struggle is often unsuccessful, especially in small, unmanaged prairies, which exhibit a steady loss of plant species (Leach and Givnish 1996). Some cite this concern as a reason to supplement a site's genetic diversity by introducing appropriate plants from other preserves.

In coming years, preserves could experience dramatic declines when today's long-lived but aging prairie plants lose their vigor and die. In addition, even a carefully conceived management protocol can alter native species composition. For example, many preserves are experiencing a shift toward taller, coarser grasses (big bluestem, Indiangrass) and forbs typical of mature prairies and a decline of short, early blooming, and more transitory native plants (Rosburg 1996; Christiansen 1996; Dornbush 2004). This shift is thought to stem from the elimination of diverse disturbances and their replacement with uniform management practices — in particular, springtime burns.

The elimination of grazing by large herbivores has compounded prairie management problems. On presettlement prairies, the voracious appetites of roaming ungulates and routine disturbances of smaller animals helped perpetuate a patchwork of low-intensity, small-scale disturbance that was critical to maintaining plant diversity. They produced heterogeneous open sites where shorter forbs and prairie "weeds" could flourish in a matrix of larger patches of ungrazed vegetation. These patches in turn burned with differing intensities. Today's preserve managers typically rely on fire without light grazing, which is not deemed practical on small preserves. Thus modern remnants tend to be grass dominated and lack the sunny, thinly vegetated openings that are crucial to the survival of smaller and more short-lived plants and may also be important for animal diversity (for example, for reptiles that depend on sunlight to heat their bodies). The resulting loss of heterogeneity inevitably leads to continued shifts in species abundance and composition, along with species loss. The trend toward more homogeneous, simplified preserves might be reversed by diversifying fire, light grazing, and other management practices, although doing so is difficult, especially in small preserves (John Pearson, personal communication).

Rebuilding Nature

Restoring prairie remnants is now matched with a second hopeful practice: reconstructing or partially reassembling segments of our native landscape through plantings. Planting prairies has captured the imagination of the lay public and preserve managers alike, who are establishing native plantings for their functionality, beauty, and cultural significance.

The practice began in 1935. That year, researchers at the University of Wisconsin Arboretum took the first steps toward what many feared was impossible: reconstructing, on agricultural ground, a tallgrass prairie (Blewett and Cottam 1984). Great Plains farmers and ranchers were already integrating warm-season native grasses into exotic pastures and using native grass plantings to repair eroding Dust Bowl croplands (Weaver 1954: 309). But Wisconsin's goals and efforts differed. Here a variety of native grasses and forbs would be planted in an attempt to reestablish an entire plant community. These efforts were significant not only to dwindling prairies; they also marked the birth of the discipline now applied around the world: the practice of ecological restoration, or returning native communities to their former health, diversity, and range (Howell and Jordan 1991).

Earlier in that decade, Bohumil Shimek had written that "our experience with the migrant [prairie] flora teaches us that the prairie may be restored . . . [and] enlarged to worthwhile dimensions" (1931b: 16). A few years later, attempts were made to reestablish prairies at Iowa Lakeside Laboratory in Dickinson County (Anderson 1936). However, this site did not receive the continuing care or ongoing research that characterized Wisconsin's Arboretum sites. Few other Iowans concerned themselves with prairie plantings until the 1970s, when the growth of awareness, available information, and environmental concern caused their popularity and abundance to soar.

Today across the Midwest, individual landowners and public and private agencies are using varied techniques to plant prairie species on lands devoid of native growth, thus creating a reconstructed prairie. Plantings cover a small but growing portion of Iowa and stretch from garden-size patches to windswept expanses. They range from switchgrass monocultures (planted in past decades but today scorned by prairie enthusiasts) to the more than 350 species found in a University of Wisconsin Arboretum reconstruction (Howell and Jordan 1991: 396). The number of species commercially available as seeds, as well as the number planted in typical reconstructions, has been steadily increasing. By 2004, higher-quality Iowa plantings included seeds of four to five dozen or more forbs and grasses, although cost frequently pushed this number downward (Daryl Smith, William Johnson, personal communications). The best reconstructions incorporate an abundance of species that were, in presettlement times, native to the specific locale, as well as local ecotype strains that evolved in place and thus have genetically adapted to the particular region's environment.

Although reconstructions can reintroduce plants and perhaps soil microorganisms, no one claims that it is possible to re-create a prairie in all its complexity. However, the oldest, largest, most diverse reconstructions now look and seem to function like actual prairies. Native butterflies, birds, and small mammals establish residence within them, with habitat specialists that are dependent on specific native plants finding crucial refuge here. While not the ecological equivalent of a prairie remnant, high-quality reconstructions present an experience of the presettlement landscape for all but the most sophisticated observer (Allison 2002; Howell and Jordan 1991).

Reconstructions serve multiple purposes. Unlike remnants, reconstructions can be sited in any location. Thus they bring prairie species to the people, in locales long dominated by other human uses: urban parks, school grounds, lawns, government set-aside lands, corporate headquarters, wildlife refuges, housing developments, industrial lands, and roadsides. In these sites, they connect numerous viewers — including many who would never travel to distant remnants — with nature's beauty and their prairie heritage and simultaneously relieve pressure from fragile remnants. Volunteers involved in their planning, planting, and tending learn techniques for healing the land even as they claim ownership of particular projects. School prairies serve as living outdoor laboratories and outdoor classrooms, encourage environmental stewardship, and demonstrate sustainability. Plantings serve as interpretive and research sites. Reconstructions beautify their surroundings. And owners of reconstructions link their plantings to intellectual excitement that blends with feelings of peace and relaxation. Many owners report that during times of stress, reconstructions become sites for retreat and renewal, places where they sense nature's permanence and continuity.

These cultural and personal amenities are crucially important: midwestern prairies have always depended on human influences and must continue to do so if they are to survive. But in addition to nurturing mind and spirit, reconstructions are helping rebuild a diverse, healthy, self-sustaining landscape. The functionality of deep-rooted prairie plantings is often cited as a primary incentive for their creation, especially where hydrologic processes and stormwater management are paramount. Prairie plantings — like the true prairies that preceded them — infiltrate and hold (rather than shed) rain and capture and detoxify (rather than release) agricultural pollutants. Their root masses sequester carbon and decrease erosion. Prairie plants survive severe drought and outcompete (and thus help eliminate) all but the most aggressive weeds. Meanwhile they provide excellent wildlife habitat and, where lightly grazed or carefully hayed, provide income to their owners.

Farmers are coming to see the benefits of reestablishing native prairie vegetation. Prairie plantings of a few dozen species are now encouraged on government set-aside lands (William Johnson, personal communication). Farmers are enhancing pastures and haylands with warm-season grasses, and some have suggested growing prairie plants in rotation with crops (Jackson and Jackson 2002). Prairie plantings restore degraded agricultural soils, for example, by increasing permeability and adding fertility: soil crumb structure has been shown to rebuild more rapidly under prairie plants than under nonprairie plants. Within a few decades, prairie restorations demonstrate significantly greater organic matter, water-holding capacity, and microbial biomass than adjacent croplands (McKinley and Wolek 2003; Miller 2005).

Because of their adaptations to climatic extremes, prairie plantings provide a practical alternative to lawns and other landscaping dominated by exotics. Prairie plantings are low maintenance compared to other forms of landscaping. Occasional burns do the bulk of the work. Hardy prairie natives do not need watering, pruning, or mowing. While saving the gardener or land manager significant effort, resources, and money, prairie plantings eliminate the regular use of gasoline-powered mowers and the typically heavy applications of fertilizers and pesticides that can pollute the air, soil, groundwater, and nearby streams and poison native insects and animals.

Prairie reconstructions offer a means of returning a significant portion of the landscape to native cover. They provide, in a sense, a method for giving the land back to its original inhabitants. They also promise a brighter future for prairie species that may be faltering on current remnants, with their isolation, small size, and declining populations. Reconstructions can countermand inbreeding by increasing local populations of prairie seeds and encouraging diverse strains to mingle and interbreed.

Some prairie enthusiasts express concern that poorly planned prairie reconstructions will further homogenize our landscape, rather than replace distinct native communities. In addition, as remnants become more limited and reconstructions increase, some worry that plants from remnants and reconstructions might interbreed, leading to dilution and loss of local genetic strains. For these reasons, care should be taken to plant species only within their natural geographic range. Purple coneflower, for example, should be planted only in southeastern Iowa, where it grows naturally; elsewhere, one can plant pale purple coneflower, which is native throughout the state. Also, reconstructions should not be located near high-quality remnants. If a buffer is to be planted around a remnant, only seeds collected within that remnant should be used. Pairing planted buffers with remnants effectively increases the size of remnants and protects them from outside influences. Linear or stepping-stone reconstructions also might boost remnant health by linking together dispersed remnants, effectively creating a single unit by providing corridors along which species can migrate and interbreed. Research has shown that corridors connecting remnants are indeed practical tools for enhancing biodiversity without promoting invasion by exotic species (Damschen et al. 2006).

Neither buffers nor stepping-stone reconstructions are now being implemented much in Iowa. However, Iowa has been a pioneer in reestablishing roadside prairies that could serve as future migration corridors. Roadside prairies were first proposed by Iowa State University professor Louis Pammel in 1926. Since the 1960s, roadside prairie assemblages have been planted sporadically in Iowa in attempts to control weeds and beautify rights-of-way. Roadside plantings became abundant after 1989 when the state passed legislation to form an Integrated Roadside Vegetation Management (IRVM) program — a broad-based weed-management program that since has served as a model for surrounding states. This University of Northern Iowa–based program, which works with county-managed roadsides across Iowa, promotes prairie plantings and remnants, managed by fire, to reduce the need for (and cost of) mowing and broadcast herbicide spraying. Roadside plantings, in 2004 composed of seedings of two-to-five-dozen species, also perform the many other prairie functions mentioned above, such as sediment control, water infiltration and cleansing, and the trapping of snow. By 2003, over half of Iowa's counties had established active IRVM programs, and many of these employed IRVM managers experienced in prairie reconstruction and management. The Iowa Department of Transportation has joined ranks, vowing to revegetate all interstate, federal, and state primary highway roadsides in native vegetation. All told, Iowa possesses over 700,000 acres of various roadside rights-of-way. If all of these were revegetated with native plants, the result would be a prairie recovery effort of amazing magnitude (Daryl Smith, personal communication).

Providing seed for these extensive plantings was, until recently, problematic. Here, too, Iowa has provided a model for other states. Since 1990, seed of certain native species has been collected through the Iowa Ecotype Project. Seed is marked according to the region of its collection and propagated and provided to prairie seed dealers. Commercial dealers then further propagate distinct regional seed mixtures and sell them to consumers. Roadside plantings are now seeded almost completely with such source-identified regional ecotype seed (Daryl Smith, personal communication).

Reconstructions should never be seen as substitutes for native remnants. Nor should prairie reconstructions become an excuse for letting remnants slip away or be destroyed; a native prairie, once lost, can never be completely rebuilt. Remnants remain uncommon vestiges of a once-dominant landscape, priceless models that hold within them irreplaceable mysteries. With tallgrass prairies plummeting in status from among the most common to the rarest native communities on Earth, the sane approach is to continue to restore remnants to health, even while using plantings to expand prairie coverage. The prairie's functional benefits then will combine with the joy of working in, and with, natural systems to make prairie reconstruction and restoration a boon to the spirit, community, and environment.

Challenge and Hope

Given their rarity and tremendous value as sources of biodiversity and models of environmental stability, one might think that remaining prairie remnants would be treated as treasures. Unfortunately this is often not the case. Native prairie remnants are still being lost through ignorance and through insufficient concern. Prairie pastures are still being overgrazed, and wet prairies are being drained. Prairie plants and animals continue to fade away because of ongoing homogenization of the rural landscape, encouraged by modern large-scale industrialized agriculture.

Where prairie remnants have been identified, token portions are sometimes preserved while adjacent sections are sacrificed. But often remnants remain unrecognized and unprotected. Sometimes, ironically, they are destroyed in preparation for well-intentioned restoration activities, a problem that arises in part because of the difficulty of identifying a remnant. Where a high-quality remnant might exist, a qualified botanist should inventory the site for at least one full growing season. In fairness for all that the prairie has given Iowa's culture and economy, such an assessment seems only reasonable before a potentially high-quality site is destroyed.

Where remnants survive, they continue to be threatened by disintegration of the presettlement fire and hydrologic regimes and by their small size, fragmentation, and isolation. Small size also means that a remnant has a proportionately large edge, or border, open to influences of surrounding ecosystems (fig. 28). Often prairie preserves and remnants abut intensively used farmland. Agricultural runoff, deposition of water- and wind-borne sediments, and invasion of agricultural weeds are all problematic. Pesticide drift can be devastating, killing highly specialized prairie plants or insects rather than the intended agricultural pests. Remnants adjacent to wooded land face increased challenges from woody invasion and edge-dwelling predators.

Exotic plants continue to challenge prairie remnants and destroy their integrity. Some invasives are limited primarily to disturbed remnants where prairie species have lost their competitive edge and to disturbed sites in healthy managed prairies. These include Canada thistle and sweetclover, which also are frequent problems in reconstructions. A small number of exotics are capable of invading

Fig. 28. Today's prairie remnants, such as this one in Marshall County, face many problems because of their small size and isolation. In addition, invasive species, runoff from surrounding fields, pesticides, and other hazards all enter with ease along such remnants' long borders. This remnant, in the Marietta Sand Prairie Addition, was formerly used as pastureland because of its sandy soils and dissected terrain, but is now being restored and enlarged. Photograph by Carl Kurtz.

intact healthy prairies and crowding out native plants. Chief among these are the deep-rooted perennial leafy spurge, which is now spreading through Iowa, and the grass smooth brome, which is abundant throughout the state and posing management problems in many remnants. Crownvetch, formerly planted along roadsides, aggressively invades prairies. Reed canarygrass invades wet prairies and sedge meadows but also can spread into drier upland sites. Because this plant is now so widespread, control attempts are usually limited to high-quality natural areas. Purple loosestrife is starting to stretch purple-flowered blankets over Iowa's wet prairies, sedge meadows, and shallow-water sites. These very aggressive invasives warrant constant monitoring and extreme efforts at early elimination.

Evidence is growing that nitrogen from agricultural fertilizers and manure poses a hidden but substantial threat to prairie remnants, which are adapted to low-nitrogen environments. This plant nutrient increases the competitive advantage of weedy and exotic invaders, which grow faster when fertilized. Excessive nitrogen is now found in soil, water, and even rainfall, with the nation's deposition of inorganic nitrogen in precipitation being highest in the cultivated Midwest, where it originates primarily from fertilizer and livestock (Porter et al. 2000: 5–6).

Ongoing pressures amply demonstrate that our landscape is now too fractured, the prairies too small, and the foreign interference too aggressive for natural integrity to survive unaided. Comprehensive identification, protection, management, and monitoring efforts are all badly needed. Their absence can kill a remnant or reconstruction just as thoroughly as the bulldozer or plow.

These efforts always depend on funds and people power, which in turn rely on prairie-focused public education. Typically none of these necessities is sufficient for the tasks at hand. Many remnants and prairie plantings are deteriorating for the want of one or two people willing to invest time in their survival. Without greater human concern and attention, Iowa's prairie remnants and species will continue to quietly dwindle.

Given the limitations and stresses of prairie remnants, we may rightly wonder whether tallgrass prairie as concept or reality retains any meaning in Iowa. Can today's small remnants or the tallgrass biological community as a whole survive the indefinite future?

It is true that time and neglect have robbed Iowa of the critical mass that could lead to natural spread and prairie recovery. We no longer can boast about the persistence of the prairie as Bohumil Shimek did in 1925. Nor can we repeat Shimek's claim that "the original prairie flora is practically preserved, and if given an opportunity it would no doubt again spread over a large part of the state" (1925: 4). Yet signs of hope remain: the finding of many more fens than expected, the promise of pastured prairies waiting to be released.

Interest in prairie plantings continues to grow among individuals and institutions. The planting of prairie species should be encouraged everywhere and anywhere, be it in a garden plot, along a roadway, or the back 40 acres. But large areas are also required if we are to ensure perpetuity of the tallgrass prairie and provide habitat for its full complement of plants, large herbivores, nesting birds, and other animals. Fortunately several such efforts are already under way. Massive prairie reconstruction projects are being implemented at Iowa's Neal Smith National Wildlife Refuge, which is slated to reach 8,600 acres; Illinois' 15,400-acre Midewin National Tallgrass Prairie; and the several-hundred-acre

Fermi Laboratory Prairie in Illinois. In western Iowa, Broken Kettle Grassland and the Waterman Creek complex, both covering thousands of acres, are blending reconstructed prairies with native prairie restorations. Even larger remnant restorations in the tens of thousands of acres are possible in the Loess Hills and nearby Little Sioux valley. Very large scale restorations are also possible in south-central Iowa, if current prairie and savanna restoration efforts continue to expand on public and private lands. Beyond Iowa, fire and grazing are being used to restore extensive native prairie remnants in the 10,800-acre Tallgrass Prairie National Preserve in Kansas's Flint Hills and in Oklahoma's Tallgrass Prairie Preserve, which exceeds 37,000 acres. Such landscape-scale efforts should, if properly managed for the long term, produce tallgrass prairies that are indeed self-perpetuating and allow continuing evolution of prairie species and communities.

The continued search for remnants and their subsequent protection require consistent dedication. Their management demands days of physical labor, cutting, and burning. Yet however minuscule, simplified, and degraded many of today's prairie patches may be, they are nevertheless treasures that are thrilling to discover. Each is a conservator of genetic materials specifically adapted to its peculiar locality, a genetic reservoir with enormous potential use. Each small plot is fighting its own battle for survival, a battle that will be lost if the remnant is ignored. But if properly restored, every prairie remnant provides not only the joy and beauty of nature's richness but also the nucleus of larger future prairies and a source of local seed for restoration efforts elsewhere. These remnants are silently calling us to do our part to locate and manage them, and to educate the public so that others across Iowa join in efforts to save what is left.

5 Oak Woodlands and Bottomland Forests Today

There were then still miles upon miles of almost undisturbed timber, fine white oaks predominating on the uplands, the hard maple occasionally dominating the river-bluffs, and the red cedar finding an anchorage on the limestone ledges, while the black walnut and various softwood trees occupied the narrow bottomlands. The upland woods were carpeted in early spring with hepaticas (chiefly on the steeper slopes) and the rue anemone, while the ravines were decked with beautiful ferns, interspersed with pink and yellow ladie's-slippers and many other wild flowers, all in great profusion, while the lowland woods displayed their gorgeous raiment of spring-beauties, *Mertensia*, buttercup, *Phlox* and *Isopyrum*, the whole making a wonderful flower garden.

— Bohumil Shimek, 1948

Perhaps no state has demanded as much of its native communities as has Iowa, where virtually every smidgeon of land has been judged in terms of utility or profit. This judgment was imposed less harshly on woodlands and forests than prairies, but still the majority of wooded communities have been used intensely. In consequence, by 2000 Iowa's timber coverage was only about a third of its original 6.6 million acres: 2.3 million acres of "productive timberland" (covering 6.4 percent of Iowa) remained, a figure that rose to 2.5 million acres when all of Iowa's wooded land was considered.[1]

These coverage statistics tell only a partial story. They reveal nothing about how modern tree-dominated communities differ from their progenitors. Remnants of original oak woodlands and bottomland forests are limited in number. A minority of presettlement communities escaped conversion to cropland. Those that did were located primarily on steeper slopes or poor soils. Among the survivors, light grazing and use as farmstead woodlots have become saviors in disguise, in places preserving relatively high-quality wooded remnants. However, for the most part, the elimination of wildfire, introduction of exotic species, improper logging, and intensive grazing have dramatically reshaped our remaining native wooded lands. Gone are the dry sun-dappled woodlands open enough to drive a cart through with ease, with their lush diverse ground cover, oak canopy uncluttered by other tree species, and little else. In their place are

1. Statistics on modern timber cover are from Smith 1998: 97 and Boykin 2003: 1–2. Data for 2000 are based on partial sampling results and thus should be considered preliminary.

tree and shrub communities that are in many ways new creations on the landscape, communities unlike anything found here prior to settlement.

Alterations in the distribution of Iowa's native woodlands and forests have been equally profound. In presettlement times, trees interrupted Iowa's vast prairies only where moisture increased and fire decreased in intensity or frequency — along waterways, on hilly lands especially on the lee (north and east) sides of rivers, and occasionally on the open prairies.

Today these ancient distribution patterns hold true only in the broadest sense. As before, extensive wooded areas still predominate in northeastern, southeastern, and south-central Iowa, where they define hillier uncultivated terrain, and they string along major river corridors throughout the state (fig. 29). As before, wooded areas generally decrease in number, extent, stature, and plant diversity toward Iowa's northwestern corner, where trees interrupt wide open spaces only occasionally in farmstead plantings, along fencelines, near waterways, along streamside hills, and on topographic breaks. Trees are still least abundant in Iowa's flattest, most intensively cultivated regions. Elsewhere postsettlement clearing, roadways, and more recently housing developments have reduced Iowa's original sweeping oak woodlands and bottomland forests into ever-smaller slivers of multipurpose timbers and clearings. Fragmentation, perhaps as much as internal degradation, has affected the ability of woodlands and forests to maintain healthy populations of certain animals and plants and thus has attacked their sustainability and stability.

The steady division of Iowa's originally wooded areas has been matched by an explosion of trees and shrubs on uncultivated lands that, prior to settlement, were fire-tempered prairies — a process that is starkly obvious in western Iowa's Loess Hills. As a result, across the state, trees and shrubs now cover the land in a random fashion rather than in the more predictable patterns of past centuries.

This chapter describes the multiple causes and broad results of the transformation of Iowa's wooded communities. While all woody communities are covered, native upland oak woodlands — a primary focus of today's conservation efforts — are emphasized at the expense of diverse bottomland forests (which have been little researched) and the thickets that now proliferate on abandoned pastures and wastelands. Comments on oak woodlands apply most comprehensively and specifically to the region that held the vast majority of our presettlement trees and that falls within the range of white oak: the southeastern half to two-thirds of the state, or, more specifically, eastern, central, and southern Iowa excluding the Loess Hills. Native woodlands and forests elsewhere remain both rarer and less well understood.

The Raised Ax

Iowa woodlands and forests were cleared with amazing rapidity and thoroughness. Settlers, arriving from deciduous forests in the eastern United States or their countries of origin, were attracted to trees as if to a magnet. The first log cabins, barns, and homesteads were hewed under the sheltering crowns of oaks that not only offered protection from the storms, winds, and intense fires that raced unfettered across the open grasslands but also provided crucial fuel and building materials.

In truth, wood was as precious to settlers as the soil that grew their crops, for without wood, settlement was impossible. Lumber from locally cut trees processed in local sawmills furnished shelter for humans and their livestock. Rough logs heated those shelters, cooked food, and were shaped into fences. Wood was the raw material of everything from tables, beds, and chairs to kitchen utensils, plows, and farm tools. Tremendous quantities were needed for life's necessities. For example, 6,400 rails were required to construct the traditional worm fence around the first forty acres (Aurner 1912: 429). Woodlands and forests also provided wild fruits, tannin for tanning hides, dyes and honey, sap for maple syrup, and medicines. Thus farm woodlots became treasured and guarded necessities. Anyone settling far from timber was deemed reckless and foolish. Because of lumber's crucial significance, settlement of northwestern Iowa was deferred until railroad lines were available to carry wood into this tree-poor region.

Despite the value of trees as raw materials, many wooded lands were seen as obstacles to be abolished. The first settlers firmly believed that forest-bred soils offered the best cropland. As one Johnson County journal described, "Often the new settler might be seen painfully laboring to clear a field in the woods when thousands of [prairie] acres lay adjoining which might have been prepared with one tenth of the labor" (Anonymous 1883: 589). Thus the cutting and burning of trees to create cropland were approached with religious zeal. New farmsteads fingered their way along Iowa's timbered streams and woodland edges. Settlers ventured into open prairie only after treed lands had been claimed and transformed. However, even these later prairie settlers retained distant woodlots, often purchased at a high price, which were harvested regularly for raw materials.

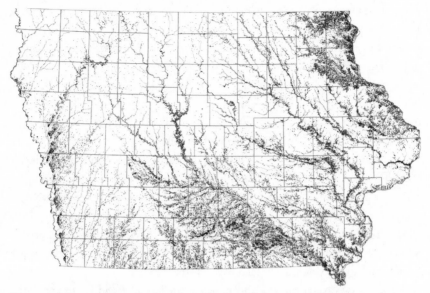

Fig. 29. As was true prior to settlement, modern wooded areas remain most prevalent along watercourses and in eastern and southern Iowa. However, woody plants now also penetrate landscapes across the state that once were extensive prairies. Perhaps more important, the character of woody growth differs vastly from that of Iowa's original native oak woodlands and bottomland forests. Map by Casey Kohrt, Iowa Geological Survey, from 2002 satellite imagery.

In the process of transforming wooded land into cropland and infrastructure, settlers cut virtually every mature tree on the horizon. Researchers dating today's white oaks are hard put to find many that predate 1850; only approximately 300 of such older white oaks have been located in Iowa's public lands. Iowa's oldest trees usually cling to rugged uplands or the sides of cliffs that were inaccessible to loggers. An eastern redcedar dating from around 1550, for example, hangs over a rocky escarpment along the Cedar River in Linn County (Pearson 1989; John Pearson, personal communication).

Closer scrutiny of early logging patterns reveals distinct trends. Trees on flatter lands and better soils were preferentially cleared, while those on rockier and steeper slopes were left to grow. "The groves were the first to suffer," Bohumil Shimek summarized, writing of upland savannas that were wiped from existence immediately upon settlement (1948: 16). In fact, mesic oak savannas, sites highly valued for their timber and soils, disappeared before they could be botanically cataloged. They were not identified as distinct communities until over a century later, when attempts to define and restore them commenced in the late 1900s (Packard 1988, 1993). Today a mere 0.02 percent of estimated presettlement midwestern oak savannas remain intact. Formerly extensive, they are now one of the world's rarest natural communities (Nuzzo 1986).

Certain trees were cut preferentially. White oak, valued for barns, houses, flooring, furniture, and fences, faced intense logging pressure. Black walnut was dragged from Iowa River bottomlands to provide furniture, paneling, and the balustrade for Iowa's first state capitol in Iowa City.

Historic trends have continually influenced woodlands and forests. The arrival of the railroad in the 1860s granted a partial reprieve by allowing importation of pine lumber and bulky wood products. However, the railroad itself exacted tremendous costs from oaklands. White oak ties for a single mile of track gobbled up about six acres of woodland, only to require replacement seven years later. Additional acres of oaks were requisitioned for railroad cars, trestles, stations, telegraph poles, and fuel boxes (Mutel 1996).

Again, a rise in agricultural land values in the late 1870s added fervor to the clearing of trees, even on land poorly suited for row crops. As Thomas Macbride bemoaned, "There are thousands of acres that should never be tilled at all. Nevertheless, there are many men ready to try the experiment, as if to make good the supposedly patriotic boast" (1897: 172). In the late 1800s logging efforts were intensified because of the rising cost of imported pine and were simplified by the arrival of the portable steam sawmill (fig. 30). The steam sawmill, which was hauled from one cutting operation to the next, was described as an "all-devouring monster . . . which has since and in so short a time leveled so much of our majestic forests" (Irish 1868: 325).

In the decades following World War II, a booming farm economy combined with technological advances to shrink Iowa's remaining wooded lands. About that time, larger and more powerful machinery became available to ease the clearing of trees on bottomlands, in ravines, and along waterways and fence-rows. Between 1954 and 1974, U.S. Forest Service inventories registered a drop in Iowa's productive timberland from 2.6 million acres (7.2 percent of the state's land) to an all-time low of 1.5 million acres (4.2 percent). Abandoned wooded pastureland and young scrubby growth subsequently boosted the state's timberland figures so that by 1990, the timberland census had risen to 1.9 million acres (5.8 percent) (Boykin 2003: 1–2). Although selective logging and clear-cutting are still performed today, the steady rise in wooded land is expected to continue,

Fig. 30. The transportable steam-powered sawmill, shown here operating in Johnson County, permitted easier and faster cutting of Iowa's timberlands. Note the log cabin in the background, already an anachronism in this 1890s photograph. Courtesy State Historical Society of Iowa, Iowa City.

supplemented by tree plantings, government-funded conservation initiatives, and the proliferation of hobby farms and suburban lands with wooded outlots.

How did our once-vast oak woodlands respond to intensive cutting and clearing? Initially logging of the nearly pure oak uplands may have been well tolerated. Oaklands evolved with disturbance: they relied on the heat of fire and the browsing of large herbivores to set back competitors, thus maintaining the open status that the sun-loving trees required for regeneration.

Also, the cutting of oaks did not necessarily mean their death. If relatively young when cut, oaks will sprout from the remaining stump, a feature true of all deciduous trees that is lost as they age. One or two sprouts commonly survive to maturity, effectively producing a new tree from an old stump. Oak seedlings also may have replaced cut trees, with reproduction being highest in mast years — those years when acorns are especially prolific, which occur every two to ten years (Van Lear 1991). In the mid 1800s, because there was little competition in oaklands from other tree species, oaks could have filled the gaps produced by logging just as they had filled disease- or wind-produced openings in preceding millennia. Logging may even have given native herbaceous understory a boost by providing a welcome increase in sunlight.

Because today's oak woodlands typically intermingle with numerous competing tree species, the effects of logging are more complex. High-grading a woodland (the preferential cutting of mature oaks) can overnight transform an oakland into a degraded stand of fast-growing competitors with decreased ecological and economic value. In contrast, continuous but moderate disturbance has helped some farm woodlots retain healthy oak communities with a high restoration potential. Today carefully executed logging and other forms of disturbance are incorporated into attempts to restore oak woodlands and their herbaceous understory (see chapter 6).

Jaws and Hooves

Virtually all wooded lands that the settlers did not clear were at some point put to use as pasture. The practice commenced with the arrival of the first pigs and cattle straggling after the settlers' wagons. Cattle were allowed free range in prairies, woodlands, and forests, wintering in the wooded areas to escape the cold winds. Hogs ran wild in unfenced woodlands and forests, reproduced, and periodically were rounded up for slaughter and consumption. Settlement-era's long-nosed, slim-bodied, long-legged swine were legendary for their speed, agility, and leaping abilities, qualities that enabled them to escape predators and snout out acorns and other foods. Such activities earned hogs nicknames like hazel-splitter, stump-sucker, and rail-splitter.

Slim wild hogs were soon replaced by American lard hogs — shorter-legged pigs with cylindrical bodies and longer intestines that could absorb more nutrients and gain more weight. Reaching weights in the hundreds of pounds, these fat-producing breeds met market demands for lard but were less capable than their predecessors of surviving in the wild. And like the later breeds of imported cattle, lard hogs were too valuable to range freely. The introduction of barbed wire in the 1870s promoted the widespread fencing of cattle and swine into wooded lands, which were seen as cheap pasture. This practice surely intensified the impact of these animals on native vegetation.

How did oak woodlands and bottomland forests respond to grazing pressures? Effects of the first cattle and swine may have mimicked the sporadic grazing and browsing of native bison and elk, thus helping keep woodlands open and productive. Unfortunately such positive effects, if ever present, were likely short-lived and confined to lightly grazed sites. Today cattle overgrazing is recognized as one of the most pervasive and significant factors in the decline of Iowa's wooded lands, with few having escaped its touch. More than a century ago, Louis Pammel summarized the degradation process:

> The chief source of danger to forest trees in Iowa is the fact that our woodlands are being used for pastures very extensively. The underbrush is trimmed out and cattle turned in. Sometimes twice as much stock is turned into the forest as it can support. The leaf mould which is needed in a forest rapidly disappears. The forest cannot hold the moisture, and consequently springs and small streams become dry; the forest trees themselves die. I have seen numerous cases where fine half-grown oaks died undoubtedly because of the trampling of cattle and drying up of the surface of the soil. (1896: 78)

We now know that where land is heavily overgrazed, soil compaction, erosion, and reduced organic matter and fertility cause injury to trees, the understory, and the cattle themselves, who suffer from the wooded land's low forage value and potentially from toxic plants. With the animals' browsing and trampling, tree seedlings decrease in number, and eventually tree reproduction ceases. Native wildlife vanishes. The more discriminating wildflowers disappear or decline in abundance, in particular disturbance-intolerant perennials with fleshy roots, including many of our spring wildflowers — Dutchman's breeches, jack-in-the-pulpit, bellwort, and bloodroot, to name a few. In contrast, disturbance-tolerant annuals with fibrous roots become the norm, examples being annual ragweed, burdock, goosefoot, and thistles. Exotic species and thorny shrubs (which are not browsed by cattle), most notably gooseberries, raspberries, common pricklyash, and multiflora rose, increase dramatically. Eventually all native understory cover is lost to these invaders and to a sod of exotic grasses. The original native woodlands and forests are reduced to shells of a few oaks or other large trees, which continue to decline in density and health as they suffer from stress, disease, and injury (fig. 31) (Mabry 2000, 2002).

Today the pasturing of woodlands and forests continues, although with the decline of Iowa's cattle industry, such pasturing occurs less extensively than in the past. While nine-tenths of all Iowa wooded land had been grazed in the 1920s, by the 1980s only two-thirds of wooded land was grazed (Mabry 2002: 53). As a result, many wooded pasturelands, especially in hilly southern Iowa,

Fig. 31. While the grazing of woodlands may preserve open-grown oaks and give a sense of the presettlement-era's early-spring landscape, understory is often reduced to a few introduced pasture grasses. Because the oaks are not reproducing, once the mature trees die, any resemblance to native communities will disappear. Photograph by Carl Kurtz.

were relinquished to other uses or to benign neglect and hence to the proliferation of woody growth. We are now discovering that despite their history, some less degraded pasturelands retain native understory plants that have clung to survival for many decades and thus present high hopes for restoration.

Quenching the Flames

One additional settlement-era practice was destined to initiate profound changes: the elimination of woodland wildfire. Iowa's oak woodlands had been dependent on wildfire for at least 3,000 years. Fire, along with the browsing and rubbing of bison and elk, determined the location and character of presettlement wooded lands, thinning the oaks and confining fire-intolerant trees to forested bottomlands, draws, and other sheltered locations.

Removing fire from oak woodlands was analogous to destroying the plant communities' operating instructions. Their restraints lifted, native shrubs and trees — including the oaks — responded with remarkable speed and vigor. Within a decade, ancient oak grubs and newly germinated acorns, along with upland shrubs, were transposing prairies with shorter brushy patches into thickets of oak saplings and taller shrubs. "The forest area increased by the natural spread of trees over ground protected from fire," wrote Louis Pammel about this postsettlement woodland surge (1896: 77), which expanded Iowa's oaklands even as settlers' logging and clearing efforts worked to shrink them. At the same time, and within a few decades, oak woodlands and savannas throughout the state filled in, becoming denser and losing their fire-pruned open character. Results of these processes remain evident in the Loess Hills, where oak woodlands have expanded greatly since settlement's suppression of fire. The elimination of fire allowed oak grubs that were scattered throughout Loess Hills prairies and savannas to grow into extensive dense bur oak woodlands that remain today.

Across the state, while oaks were busy in-filling the uplands, their eventual competitors started an even greater upheaval. Fast-growing tree species that periodic wildfire had once constrained to bottomland forests and other fire-sheltered sites now started an insidious creep upslope. Their migration into previously forbidden territory was slow at first, especially where soils were poorer or drier — for example, in south-central Iowa. It was more rapid in eastern Iowa where soils were rich and moist. As upland-invading trees increased in range and number and their seeds became more widely available, the invasion accelerated, and Iowa's bottomland forests became homogenized with upland oaks (fig. 32). Within their ranges of distribution, early successional species — the elms, green ash, boxelder, bigtooth aspen — leaped uphill from bottomland forests or small disturbances on lower slopes. Bitternut hickory and hackberry slipped into oak woodlands from streamside terraces. Species that may have already been present in oaklands in low numbers — red oak, black cherry, ironwood, white ash — jumped in number. Formerly fire-suppressed shrubs such as the dogwoods, hazelnut, and chokecherry likely did the same. Sugar and black maples (in eastern and central Iowa) and basswood (throughout the state) crept in from moister, more sheltered slopes and ravines. With time, exotic trees (such as Siberian elm and white mulberry) and shrubs (exotic bush honeysuckles, common buckthorn) joined the throng.

As a group, oakland-invading species included two types of trees: boxelder, elm, green ash, cottonwood, and the like, whose prolific wind-dispersed seeds, fast growth, early-spring leaf-out, and adaptability allowed them to occupy dis-

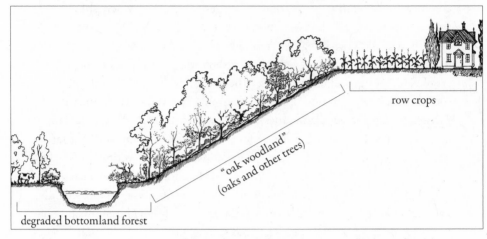

row crops

"oak woodland" (oaks and other trees)

degraded bottomland forest

Fig. 32. Tree growth on the modern landscape differs in character and location from that of presettlement times (see fig. 9). Oak woodlands on hillsides have in-filled through the upslope movement of diverse bottomland trees, and remaining bottomland forests are now degraded. Woody growth (along with row crops) is now also found on flat uplands where fire-tended prairies once swept the landscape. Drawing by Will Thomson.

turbed sites with ease; and shade-tolerant species that could mature in dark, dense timberlands (ironwood, hackberry, and basswood throughout the state, with sugar maple, black maple, bitternut hickory, white ash, and others joining within their ranges). The shade-intolerant oaks, with their heavy acorns and slower growth rates, possessed none of these traits. Thus they started to lose the competitive advantage that had been afforded by their tolerance of fire. Simultaneously, many characteristic oak woodland understory plants either succumbed or were reduced in size, vigor, and bloom.

In this way, settlement's elimination of fire dismembered the patchwork of self-sustaining oak woods and their diverse animal associates and understory plants and spun them in a totally new direction. Thomas Macbride summarized these profound changes: "The woods of to-day are all thickets." He went on to bemoan the loss of "the annual fires which swept all grass-grown regions, forest and prairie alike, keeping down the natural increase of the forest. . . . [Old oaks] are now, owing to the absence of forest fires, wholly surrounded by 'second growth.'" Macbride then invited his readers to walk an overgrown oak woodland and "imagine the smaller trees removed, and the ground beneath the remaining lofty white oaks carpeted with grass" (1895: 344), with these words creating a vision for those who today study our beleaguered oak woodlands and aspire to restore them to their full glory.

Upland Oak Wonderlands

Oaks today still prevail in a goodly proportion of Iowa's wooded lands, where they continue to provide copious recreational pleasures and environmental benefits. In 2000 U.S. Forest Service inventories identified nearly 40 percent of Iowa's timberlands as oak dominated (Boykin 2003: Fig. 3). White oak is the major species throughout eastern, central, and southern Iowa (excluding the Loess Hills), especially on drier uplands and ridgetops. Red oak (on moister sites throughout Iowa, excluding the state's far northwestern corner) and black oak (on drier sites in southern and eastern Iowa) constitute significant associates, with the extremely drought-tolerant bur oak increasing in importance and assuming dominance toward the west.

A portion of these oaklands have resisted severe degradation by dint of their location on steeper unplowed slopes or relatively gentle pasturing or woodlot use. Mature oaklands sometimes retain healthy numbers of native plants and animals, especially species sufficiently adaptable to have survived the many changes of the past 150 years. These woodlands join prairie and wetland remnants in constituting today's wilder Iowa, treasured lands that attract the attention and use of diverse nature lovers. Here birders search the trees for migrating spring warblers, while mushroomers comb the woodland floor for morels and other collectibles. Lucky hikers might stumble upon any of more than a dozen species of orchids (the most common being showy orchis), an all-white stem of parasitic Indian pipe, or other of the natural world's limitless surprises. Wander an oak tract ripe with springtime's freshness, or kick your way through drifts of autumn's newly fallen leaves, and you can imagine yourself lost in a primeval wonderland surrounded by processes and associations as ancient as time.

These woodlands are a joy to wildflower lovers, especially in the spring (fig. 33). Iowa's woodlands, like our prairies, turn green from the bottom up, with a woodland's floor regaining color before its overhanging oak canopy leafs out. Oaklands of eastern Iowa contain an especially rich understory. Many early-blooming perennials overwinter with significant foodstocks stored in fleshy tubers or bulbs so they can burst into flower early, before trees drape them in shade and shadow. This is true of our much-loved spring wildflowers, whose early blossoming has helped them survive the gradual in-filling of our woodlands. The earliest bloomers (for example, bloodroot, hepatica, rue and wood anemone) yield to Jacob's ladder, wild geranium, jack-in-the-pulpit, Pennsylvania sedge, and others that in turn give way to common midsummer flowers such as hog-peanut, ticktrefoils, and the bedstraws, and to patches of woodland grasses. Many summer flowers are opportunistic generalists that thrive in a variety of sites and have clinging seeds that are readily transported by animal fur. Highly shade-tolerant understory plants might also be present, such as blue cohosh, white baneberry, bellwort, and false Solomon's seal. These forbs are usually not common. Easier to find are gardenlike expanses of maidenhair, interrupted, lady, or ostrich ferns sprouting from shady moist slopes. Autumn's understory heralds the blossoms of abundant composites: white snakeroot, goldenrods, asters, and sunflowers. Mature oaklands in western Iowa claim a smaller subset of this rich assortment.

The state's woodland and forest wildlife still abounds, although the animals seen now are far smaller and more docile than the black bears and cougars that once roamed these lands. Many of today's animals are adaptable species we also see in urban "savannas," with their scattered trees and bushes: fox squirrels, chipmunks, moles, bats flitting through warm evening skies, woodchucks, raccoons, and opossums. White-tailed deer are common sights in town and country, often appearing to outnumber the prolific eastern cottontails, the favored prey of wandering coyotes. More abundant but less visible are white-footed mice, which are widespread and abound in areas with shrubs, trees, or other cover. Dense mature timberlands retain elusive bobcats, flying squirrels, and gray squirrels. Red foxes dig dens into wooded hillsides and along creek bottoms and hunt nearby open areas.

Iowa's birds are most diverse in counties with the greatest percentage of woody growth (Jackson et al. 1996: 22). While numbers of many continue to decline — we no longer have the clouds of flitting warblers of even several decades ago — diverse birds are still commonly seen during woodland and forest strolls: thrushes, vireos, woodpeckers, nuthatches, chickadees, the occasional red-tailed hawk or barred owl, and many more. Many birds and mammals remain dependent on the nuts of oaks and hickories. However, the wild turkey, traditionally a bird of oak woodlands, has adapted to Iowa's ecological fragmentation and now feeds on agricultural waste grains and seeds as well as acorns and berries.

American toads still fill spring nights with prolonged chirrings, while treefrogs trill from perches in trees and shrubs. Oak woodlands, bottomland forests,

Bloodroot   Dutchman's breeches   Liverleaf   Rue anemone

Jack-in-the-pulpit   Maidenhair fern   Mayapple

Elmleaf goldenrod   Pennsylvania sedge   White snakeroot   Bottlebrush grass

Fig. 33. Iowa's healthier woodlands boast a diversity of forbs, grasses, sedges, and ferns that add diversity and complexity to these enchanting sites. Drawing by Mark Müller.

and their edges house numerous types of reptiles: brown, milk, fox, rat, bull, and other snake species. Butterflies such as the question mark, mourning cloak, red admirals, and eastern comma still flutter among oaks. Their nighttime counterparts remain impressive in number and include showy species such as the cecropia moth, brilliant green luna moth, and several species of heavy-bodied sphinx or hawk moths. Certain hairstreaks and the great spangled fritillary, butterflies previously found in savannas, now frequent woody edges.

These many animals help define how modern oak woodlands resemble those of presettlement times. Another resemblance relates to the woodland animals: because dispersal of oak and hickory nuts depends on squirrels and birds such as the blue jay, oaklands migrate slowly. Thus today's oak woodlands are usually located within the range of presettlement communities.

But beyond such large-scale similarities, modern oaklands only partially resemble their progenitors. A major divergence lies in today's far greater density of woody plants. The distance between trees is now measured in feet rather than yards, as was true in the past. With the suppression of fire's cleansing pulse, two-layered open-canopy woodlands have given way to multilayered closed-canopy communities of trees and shrubs. Because of their increased density, these communities are shadier, darker, and moister than in presettlement times.

The increased density reflects a second key change — a major shift in the species of trees present (fig. 34). The oaks that overwhelmingly dominated presettlement woodlands are now mixed with a diversity of native trees once typical of bottomland forests and moist sheltered slopes as well as introduced species from other continents. Sites vary in the proportions, ages, and sizes of trees present. Variations are determined by the proximity of tree seed sources, the presence of exotics, and chance events. Land-use history, topography, and other environmental features then combine to shape each site's raw potential into reality.

In eastern, central, and southern Iowa, oaks and shagbark hickory typically remain the largest and most numerous trees of mature woodlands. However, the slow-growing bur and white oaks have declined relative to red oaks, which are faster growing, shorter lived, and less drought and fire tolerant. Red oaks are thought to have increased significantly in abundance (Abrams 2003). Oaks are now interspersed with various mixtures of basswood, elms, hackberry, black cherry, and other native trees, which may be young or mature. The naturalized exotic white mulberry is often present. Ironwood (ubiquitous and extremely abundant) sometimes intermingles with saplings of shade lovers such as sugar or black maple, bitternut hickory, and white ash. Patchy thickets of taller shrubs

White oak

Bur oak

Red oak

Ironwood

Basswood

Sugar maple

Shagbark hickory

Fig. 34. The oaks and scattered shagbark hickory that once dominated Iowa's upland wooded lands are now mixed with a diversity of other tree species, a few of which are pictured here. Drawing by Mark Müller.

(hazelnut, gray and other dogwoods, and chokecherry) may mingle with shorter brambles of raspberry and gooseberry, all of these shrubs increasing in vigor in sunnier patches. Thickets of invasives such as common buckthorn and the exotic bush honeysuckles, if present, may become too dense to penetrate.

Western and northwestern Iowa maintain a far smaller number of relatively mature oak stands, and these are associated with topographic breaks or a history of pasturing. They are often found on sheltered slopes or in ravines, where they can be recognized by their spring wildflowers and other native understory. On lower moister slopes, red oak may be mixed with basswood, ironwood, hackberry, cottonwood climbing slopes from nearby bottomlands, and other trees, with basswood assuming dominance in Iowa's far northwestern corner. Bur oak woodlands dominate on drier higher sites. Open-grown, balloon-topped bur oaks lost in a sea of younger, smaller bur oaks or other tree species are common on upper hillsides and along upper ridgelines in the Loess Hills, as well as on hillsides and in pastures along the Little Sioux River. Western Iowa's mature oaklands, although far more limited in number, size, and plant diversity than those to the east, retain many of the conservation values of more easterly oaklands.

Across the state, groves of savanna-like round-crowned oaks rising from grasslands can still be found in pastures, lawns, and parks. Massive open-grown oaks are also found on less-managed sites, typically surrounded by thickets of younger trees (fig. 35). These sites, which may have a high restoration potential, are especially common in south-central Iowa. Such areas can present a sense of the magnificence of our original savannas and open woodlands, but because they typically lack the diverse flowers, grasses, and sedges of past centuries, picturing past reality requires a goodly share of imagination. Only a handful of remaining oaklands are fully representative of presettlement Iowa. Rochester Cemetery near the Cedar River in Cedar County is one of the finest savanna remnants in Iowa. Restoration efforts are beginning to provide additional semblances of Iowa's original savannas and open woodlands.

A site's land-use history, a factor so important in sculpting today's woodland characteristics, can often be read in the shape and distribution of the remaining oaks. A straight row of massive trees, for example, indicates a bygone fence-line. Trees with multiple trunks near ground level tell of past logging harvests. Oaks standing straight and tall state that they matured in a dense woodland where they needed to stretch upward to the light. Balloon-shaped oaks, with massive trunks bearing stout outstretched branches, in contrast, signify a tree's

Fig. 35. Today many former savannas, recognized by large, open-grown, broad-spanning oaks, are overgrown with younger trees and shrubs. Where native savanna understory remains, even in a suppressed state, these modern thickets have a high restoration potential. Photograph by Carl Kurtz.

maturation in an open setting with abundant sunlight. Sometimes numerous nubs protrude from a massive trunk — a sure sign that a former savanna tree had been shaded in and, over time, lost its lower broad-reaching branches. If a mixture of prairie grasses and native forbs survive in nearby openings, a site may indeed be a remnant savanna with good restoration potential. On the other hand, aggregates of a single understory species, or coverage by only a few highly adaptable natives such as Virginia creeper or woodnettle, are signs of significant past disturbance and degradation or indications that a diverse rich woodland was never present on that site.

Mature, sometimes dying oaks perched atop compacted soils scantly covered by exotic grasses clearly indicate severe overgrazing. Former pastures are also notorious for their dense prickly shrubs and small thorny trees. When mature open-grown trees are hidden among swards of smaller straighter trees, the ages of these younger trees can date the cessation of grazing or whatever other disturbance originally maintained the opening.

The understories of today's oak woodlands also show tremendous divergence from site to site. A smattering of woodland forbs, grasses, and sedges is perhaps most typical, but some oaklands may have no obvious native understory plants, while elsewhere associations of native understory plants may flourish under a non-oak canopy. Anything in between these extremes can also be found.

As a group, how do today's woodland understories resemble those of past centuries? Because of scant understanding of presettlement sun-dappled oaklands, we can only hypothesize answers to this question. Early spring bloomers are still abundant in today's closed woods. But later bloomers, subjected to summertime's greater shade and humidity, are less diverse and abundant. They may be surviving in a vegetative state. The most drought-tolerant, sun-loving summer and fall woodland bloomers may have been lost forever. Even our finest oakland remnants probably maintain an impoverished version of the original understory biodiversity (Wilhelm 1991). Some oakland understory plants are thought to have relocated to the sun-speckled landscapes that remain, such as woodland edges and fencelines. Semishaded roadside rights-of-way may provide especially crucial habitat for remnant woodland species, common examples being Solomon's seal, Culver's root, tall thimbleweed, common spiderwort, American bellflower, and mayapple within their ranges. Once players in a complex interlocking landscape, these types of plants have become displaced survivors of a lost landscape, stragglers struggling to find niches where they can seed out and endure yet one more generation.

Oak Woodlands in Transition

Although oaks have been Iowa's dominant upland trees for thousands of years, their reproductive needs are no longer being met. The postsettlement dispersal of diverse tree species has transformed fire-loving oaks from rulers of the uplands into species whose future is in jeopardy. The decline in oak populations and the shift from oak-dominated to mixed-species woodlands are generating strong concern throughout eastern North America because of the many ecological and economic benefits of oaks.

To understand the alarm, one need only observe today's woodlands and consider their trajectory. In the southeastern half to two-thirds of Iowa, within the range of Iowa's white oaks, today's woodlands are largely united by the common age of their oaks. Many white oaks are growing in even-aged stands that were around 150 years old in 2000, having commenced growth in the mid 1800s (John Pearson, personal communication). These woodlands are the result of

Plate 1. Rochester Cemetery in eastern Iowa, with its massive open-grown white oaks and spectacular native wildflowers, is one of the finest savanna remnants surviving in the Midwest. Photograph by Carl Kurtz.

Plate 2. Mesic tallgrass prairie, once Iowa's dominant plant community, now remains in only a few scattered remnants such as this one, resplendent with its purple prairie clover and compassplant. Photograph by Carl Kurtz.

Plate 3. The dickcissel singing here from a compassplant is a small grassland bird that now nests in old fields and alfalfa as well as prairie habitat. Although its numbers have declined, the dickcissel may be benefiting from agricultural set-aside programs such as CRP. Photograph by Carl Kurtz.

Plate 4. The Loess Hills are home to Iowa's most extensive modern prairie remnants. Photograph by Carl Kurtz.

Plate 5. Elk, once a common Iowa herbivore, had disappeared from the state by the 1860s but in the 1990s were reintroduced to the Neal Smith National Wildlife Refuge. Photograph by Carl Kurtz.

Plate 6. Water's slow course through Iowa's native landscape is still evident at Silver Lake Fen in Dickinson County, here speckled with blossoms of slender false foxglove and other native wildflowers. Photograph by Carl Kurtz.

Plate 7. Yellow marsh marigold, one of many native species limited to wetter soils, lights a central Iowa woodland bog with spring color. Photograph by Carl Kurtz.

Plate 8. The rich multistoried bottomland forests so typical of presettlement times still can be found in select locations, such as this Hardin County forest with its springtime abundance of Virginia bluebells. Photograph by Carl Kurtz.

Plate 9. *(Left)* The red-headed woodpecker, found in wooded areas and nearby grasslands across the state, was formerly a species of Iowa's widespread savannas and open oak woodlands. Photograph by Carl Kurtz.

Plate 10. *(Below)* A decade after restoration efforts commenced, this oak woodland in Poweshiek County was transformed from a thicket of trees and shrubs to a sunny glen displaying numerous grasses, sedges, and about a hundred native wildflowers, such as the wood betony and wild geranium shown here. Photograph by Carl Kurtz.

Plate 11. Fire, so critical to the maintenance of Iowa's prairies and oak woodlands, renews and reinvigorates these native plant communities. Photograph by Carl Kurtz.

Plate 12. Gray-headed coneflowers often dominate young prairie plantings but decrease in abundance after four or five years. In this reconstructed prairie, a sea of these flowers creates a site where people and nature become one. Photograph by Carl Kurtz.

the postsettlement flush of woody growth from fire-released oaks or, possibly, from the stump-sprouting of logged woodlands or seeding in of acorns. Thomas Macbride described the birth of today's oaklands in this way: "Those [oaks] that remained availed to furnish seed, and under the new conditions the forest began to spread, and in the twenty-five years succeeding 1850 became totally changed. What was called 'second-growth' sprang up everywhere. The old trees were soon completely lost in the crowded ranks of their descendants, which, unvexed by fire, and mutually assistant, grew with amazing rapidity" (1897: 171).

Healthy young oaks, in contrast, are hard to locate today, the few exceptions being found in the driest natural woodlands, in plantations, and on sites where light is abundant (for example, woodland edges, roadsides, or along fencerows). Oak seedlings may cover the woodland floor during years of heavy acorn production, but few seedlings survive. Occasional saplings (especially of faster-growing red oak) may reach for the light, often displaying crooked or splayed crowns that signal the difficulty of their search. Because these trees are small they may appear young, but many are stunted older specimens. Lacking adequate light, most appear destined to die. Researchers state that throughout the eastern United States, almost no white oak reproduction has been successful for the past century, and other upland oak species have been similarly failing for at least fifty years (Abrams 2003: 937). Without a steady stream of youthful replacements, our oak woodlands are facing eventual elimination.

Iowans may think that this is not a problem, at least not yet. Under ideal circumstances, exceptional white oaks can live for 400 years, bur oaks for 300 years. Thus early in the twenty-first century, many of our mature woodlands could be considered middle-aged, with decades if not centuries of life remaining.

But too often disease, storms, or random events kill oaks before such ideal longevity is reached, a fact that unfortunately is already being demonstrated in some of Iowa's oak stands. In presettlement times, a supply of younger oaks would have stood ready to replace dying mature trees. Periodic fire would have held back competing trees, cleansed the woodland floor, and opened it to the necessary sunshine. Healthy sapling oaks, perhaps with a small number of shagbark hickory, white ash, black cherry, or other common associates, would have filled in the gap. The cycle of young oaks replacing old would be completed, as it had been for thousands of years.

In contrast, today cut a gap in an oakland or abandon a field near a mature oak woodland and another sequence begins. For whatever reason, be it fire suppression, deep shade, browsing deer, or root or shoot competition, oaks fail to invade, thrive, and reclaim disturbed land. Instead the abundant seeds of the oaks' ubiquitous competitors are readily available to sprout on any site — a standing or logged oakland, a gap created by disease or windthrow, or an abandoned pasture or cropland. Their fast-growing seedlings race toward the sky, overtopping and shading out younger, slower-growing oaks. Given time, they may reach high enough to shade out even mature oaks. Thus disturbances such as disease and selective logging, which once opened and renewed our oaklands, now accelerate their loss: remove the dominant oaks and woodlands are relinquished to mixtures of whatever opportunistic tree seedlings are available.

What will ultimately become of our mature oak-dominated woodlands as the oaks die out? Examine Iowa's woodlands for thriving saplings, and you see that the most abundant young trees, by far, are those of shade-tolerant species such as sugar maple in eastern Iowa (and the less aggressive, less invasive black maple in central Iowa) and basswood, bitternut hickory, white ash, elms, ironwood, and hackberry within their ranges. Barring the reintroduction of fire, mixtures of these maples, basswoods, and their shade-tolerant associates are the likely inheritors of most of eastern and central Iowa's oaklands.

Wander eastern and central Iowa's woodlands today and you will find all stages of the woodland transition process: oaklands still free of invading maples or with a few small saplings, oaklands with a mix of young and old maples and a growing number of their saplings, scattered oaks in a sea of large maples, and even mature maple stands lacking large oaks (fig. 36). Other shade-tolerant trees are also usually abundant and may be quite large. Many oak woodlands are in the midstages of the transition, with mature oaks and shagbark hickory, a scattering of mature opportunistic trees such as elm and black cherry, abundant ironwood, and pockets of maturing maples and basswood. Here the transition to maple-basswood and mixed shade-tolerant hardwoods is occurring slowly and inexorably, tree by tree, as the oaks die. Elsewhere, where logging or disease suddenly removes many oaks, the transition can occur overnight.

This is a simplified version of a complex situation with much potential variation. For example, oak woodland transformation occurs most readily on moist slopes with rich soils, while dry ridgetops and regions with poorer soils tend to resist transformation and remain more open. Transition to maple-basswood is most advanced in the moist rugged uplands of northeastern Iowa. Here, where sugar maple was always more abundant, its saplings are now ubiquitous. These

Fig. 36. Here dense, young sugar maples are invading a stand of mature red oaks. This process, now occurring throughout eastern and southern Iowa's woodlands, signifies the eventual loss of oak — a keystone species for many native animals — as Iowa's dominant tree. Photograph by Carl Kurtz.

heavily invaded northeastern woodlands present a glimpse into the future, allowing us to see the fate of Iowa's rich white oak woodlands everywhere if steps are not taken to halt the transition to maple-basswood. Toward the drier center of the state, where black maple and other shade-tolerant trees replace the far more aggressive sugar maple, basswood assumes greater dominance and continues (with red oak) to govern mesic woodlands farther to the west.

The changing face of Iowa's timberland composition can be traced through U.S. Forest Service inventory data. These data clearly show the steady, proportional decline of Iowa's oak-dominated woodlands of all types — from around 50 percent of Iowa's upland timberlands in 1954 and 1974, to 46 percent in 1990, to 37 percent in 2000. Simultaneously, Iowa's maple-basswood timberlands increased from 3 percent in 1954, to 19 percent in 1974, to 25 percent in 1990, to 34 percent in 2000.[2] Note that these data show only the completed transformation from one timberland type to another; the shift would be even more dramatic if mature oaklands on their way to becoming maple-basswood were included.

Additional U.S. Forest Service data show that in 2003, only 933,000 acres of oak-dominated timber remained in Iowa, down nearly 300,000 acres since 1954. During that half-century, Iowa lost about 5,800 acres of oak annually — a rate of loss that, if continued, would mean that by around 2020, oak will no longer be the predominant timberland type in Iowa, and by 2160 oak woodlands will have disappeared from the Iowa landscape.[3]

Some might consider this transition from open oaklands to mixed woodlands and thence to closed maple-basswood communities to be a natural process. Ecological theory states that plant communities naturally undergo succession, with one plant community giving way to another until a stable and self-sustaining community is established. Maple and basswood, with their associates, are able to reproduce in their own shade and thus might be considered the rightful inheritors of our oaklands, the culmination of the oakland transition that began soon after settlement. However, ecological communities are defined by process as well as species, and for at least 3,000 years Iowa's woodlands have evolved with fire as a close companion. Fire, browsing, and other disturbances fed the oaklands sunshine and eliminated competing seed sources. The many species of oaks were able to reproduce indefinitely, creating the sustainability and maintaining the biodiversity we seek to restore today. Their diverse associates did the same.

Dense maple-basswood communities with intermixed red oak also existed in limited numbers on moist sheltered sites and presumably fostered a rich shade-tolerant understory (Dick-Peddie 1953; John Pearson, personal communication). Such mature maple-basswood timberlands still can be found in northeastern Iowa, with smaller patches present elsewhere. These rich communities are an

2. Statistics on decreases in oak woodlands and increases in maple-basswood timberlands are based on U.S. Forest Service inventory data for "timberlands" only. Data for 2000 are based on partial sampling results and thus should be considered preliminary. Timbered land not included in this table is primarily diverse bottomland forest (elm, cottonwood, ash, silver maple, and so forth). Data for 1954 are from Thornton and Morgan 1959: Table 6. Data for 1974 are from Leatherberry et al. 1992: Table 1. Data for 1990 are from Brand and Walkowiak 1991: Fig. 4. Data for 2000 are from Boykin 2003: Fig. 3.

3. Information on current loss of oak coverage is from a personal communication with Paul Tauke, Iowa Department of Natural Resources (Iowa DNR), and is based on 2003 U.S. Forest Service inventory data.

important component of our ecological history and should be protected as such. However, today's young maple stands, which are expanding onto far drier sites, do not appear to be bringing any such rich understory layer with them. While some sites retain assemblages of early spring wildflowers, the shade of maple leaves often is so dark that it eliminates all later bloomers. The result is a barren woodland floor and an impoverished plant — and hence animal — community. The expanding maple-basswood communities thus do little to maintain Iowa's native biodiversity.

Just as northeastern Iowa's prolific maple-basswood forests give us a glimpse into Iowa's potential future, so do western Iowa's Loess Hills provide a look at Iowa's past. Here, too, oak woodlands are in transition, but in a manner far different from that described above. The Loess Hills bear the distinction of holding the state's largest remaining native prairies — and continuing to lose them to expanding oaklands in a manner similar to that seen throughout the state immediately following settlement. Here and in the nearby Little Sioux valley, where very dry climes nurture bur oak, young bur oaks still directly invade native prairies where permitted to do so. Therefore while the Loess Hills possess rich pockets of mature oak-dominated communities, many of this region's oaklands are relatively young stands of bur oak that lack diverse understory. Likewise, fire-intolerant diverse bottomland trees and shrubs can still be observed moving upslope in the Loess Hills, just as they did elsewhere in Iowa in the mid 1800s. Upslope migration has been paralleled by the movement of trees and shrubs from the more heavily timbered southern Loess Hills into expansive northern prairies. Both forms of migration are accelerating today.

Throughout western Iowa, the transformation of oak woodlands is occurring more slowly than in eastern Iowa, where both moisture and seeds of competitive woody species are more abundant. Thus the future of Iowa's westernmost, relatively species-poor woodlands is not obvious. It is clear that oak woodlands will not give way to dense maple-basswood stands, since maples (along with many other potential competitors) are uncommon in the western third of Iowa. While bur oak appears to be a strong competitor when it comes to reproducing in western Iowa's extreme environments, here, as elsewhere, the species requires sunlight to reproduce. Younger basswood is abundant in some western oak-woods, as are hackberry, elm, and ash. Perhaps they will take over with time. But until western Iowa's woodlands are more thoroughly investigated, the fate of current stands of dense bur oaks, the more range-limited red oaks, and their associates remains unknown.

Diverse Bottomland Forests

Iowa's bottomland forests do not seem to be faring better than their upland counterparts. Many bottomlands, with their rich soils and flat terrain, were considered ideal farmland and were either cleared for cropland or pastured. Grazing pressures remain heavy on some. Elsewhere the original vegetation layer has been buried under several feet of sediment. Some bottomlands now lie at the bottom of reservoirs. Those that remain have been reshaped by altered rivers and floodplains — channelized waterways, increased riverside constructions, deposition of soil eroded from surrounding hillsides, nutrient-laden sediments washed in by modern floods. Hydrologic alterations include the downcutting of streams and the loss of scouring and other natural restorative processes.

How is bottomland vegetation responding to these changes? Because these communities have been little studied in Iowa, only a few broad generalizations can be made. While Kentucky bluegrass sod or other exotic grasses now cover many pastured areas, some bottomland forests retain sedges and other natives such as toothwort, spring beauty, spring cress, white trout lily, and Virginia waterleaf (see color plate 8). However, it is rare to find the abundance of spring wildflowers described for these sites as late as the mid 1950s (Conard 1952: 17). By midsummer, the ground is typically covered by expanses of touch-me-nots, poison ivy, woodnettle and stinging nettle, clearweed, riverbank grape, giant ragweed, and other opportunistic species, in addition to smooth brome and immense expanses of reed canarygrass, an aggressive exotic whose dense growth is stimulated by the nutrient-rich sediments deposited by today's floods.

Willow thickets are ubiquitous alongside rivers and in wet lowlands. Silver maples are faring well under the changed hydrologic regime. Expansive stands often cloak riverside areas; in fact, silver maple now dominates the majority of the Upper Mississippi River floodplain, where river stabilization has eliminated the regular scouring that once created the bare soil sought by cottonwood seedlings (John Pearson, personal communication). In some floodplain locales, however, even silver maple is unable to flourish, its seedlings being smothered by the ubiquitous reed canarygrass. Elsewhere cottonwood and silver maple, along with younger elms and other tree species, cover expanses of riverside bottomlands. Mature elms are absent because of Dutch elm disease. In places mature sycamores and bur oaks protrude from a younger canopy.

Oak savannas on bottomlands have filled in, just as they have on uplands. The diverse, dynamic terrace forests of hackberry, hawthorn, green ash, boxelder, black walnut, and other trees that once abounded on our bottomlands are still found, and species of these forests still wander uphill in ravines and alongside smaller drainages as they did in the past. Many of the trees that originally flourished on terraces have invaded uplands since settlement and thus may be more numerous now than they were a few centuries ago. But precise interpretation of the extent, location, health, and future of bottomland forest vegetation awaits further study.

Regardless of their multiple stresses, remaining riverside forests constitute strings of wildness that thread their way through an otherwise tamed landscape. As such, they remain crucially important sanctuaries for native wildlife. Much of Iowa's native biodiversity still is found along wooded stream and river corridors, with bird diversity, for example, being richest along major river systems and their tributaries (Kane et al. 2003: 51). These corridors also serve as important migration routes and bird flyways, providing food, cover, and water for many animals moving from site to site.

New Woody Growth

Soon after settlement commenced, new tree associations started to reshape both the content and form of Iowa's landscape. The expansion of native and exotic trees segmented Iowa's once-vast grassland complex into progressively smaller parcels. Today woody growth is ubiquitous. Where Native Americans once searched the grassy horizon for groves to guide their way, today's residents would be hard put to find any sites where woody growth is not overwhelmingly obvious, except perhaps on our flattest, most highly cultivated lands and in far northwestern locales that remain least conducive to tree growth.

The homogenization of grassland and woody growth began when the first settlers planted bottomland natives such as silver maple, boxelder, and cottonwood around their upland homesteads. Thomas Macbride was blunt in his assessment of this practice: "There are today in Iowa thousands upon thousands of groves planted by farmers for the protection and shelter of their homesteads. . . . Men who have labored hard to eradicate every native oak, hickory, walnut and maple from their premises have afterwards gone to the trouble to set out about their houses soft maples and box-elders! The people mean well, but they are deplorably in need of sound information" (1897: 172).

Plantings soon expanded to include exotic species brought to Iowa for functional or decorative purposes. Introduced fruit trees formed orchards, Norway spruce graced cemeteries, windbreaks of conifers became common around farmsteads, Osage orange was shaped into living fences, and black locust was cultivated for fenceposts and firewood. Urban lawns and parks became timberlands in their own right, typically displaying the native trees green ash and sugar or silver maple along with introduced Norway maple and other trees and shrubs from around the world. Today's rural tree plantations often utilize native species — for example, walnuts or oaks mixed with other hardwoods — but also include decorative plantings of Scotch pine or Colorado blue spruce, shrubs and trees established as riparian buffer strips, and rows of conifers in Christmas tree farms.

While settlers were purposefully planting trees and shrubs in chosen locations, elsewhere they created disturbed sites that invited invasion of woody species. Recall that many of our original bottomland trees — elms, boxelder, green ash, hackberry, and cottonwood, among others — are fast-growing opportunistic species that spread readily, compete strongly, and thrive in disturbed areas. Once these species had moved onto uplands, their seeds became readily available to populate any noncultivated land. With time, native species were joined by exotic trees such as Siberian elm, white poplar, Osage orange, white mulberry, Russian and autumn olive, exotic willows, and black locust and by exotic bush honeysuckles, common buckthorn, and other shrubs that had escaped from cultivation and likewise are strong competitors.

Today such species are abundant, and some (such as younger elms) seem to be ubiquitous. These trees and shrubs densely populate waste places and former cropland and pastureland, follow fencelines, cover hillsides too steep for row crops, and line upland drainages. They form widely varying patches, corridors, thickets, and larger woods wherever the ground is not cultivated and efforts are not taken to eliminate them (fig. 37). Each woody plot's exact composition is determined by the availability of seeds, the land's history and use, and chance events. Overgrazed pastures may be heavily invaded by eastern redcedars, which proliferate in the Loess Hills and elsewhere. Abandoned pastures commonly are covered by thorny and prickly species — honeylocust (spread by cattle who eagerly eat the trees' sweet seedpods), hawthorns, multiflora rose, pricklyash, gooseberry, and raspberries. They also may be invaded by elms, eastern redcedar, or other species. Woody proliferation is obvious in south-central Iowa's formerly grazed grasslands.

Prairie remnants across the state are plagued by invading trees and shrubs and often require intensive management efforts to retain grass and forb domina-

Fig. 37. The woody growth now proliferating on former disturbed sites across Iowa seems to have little potential of maturing into stately forests or woodlands of large, sturdy trees. Instead, fast-growing trees and shrubs often perpetuate dense, jumbled thickets of short-lived, opportunistic native and exotic species. Photograph by Carl Kurtz.

tion. Woody expansion is pronounced in Loess Hills prairies. Here the process begins when shrubs creep upslope, gaining command of the many moist ravines that cut into hillsides. These initial invaders moderate the local climate, shading the ground, breaking the wind, and increasing moisture sufficiently to ready microsites for tree invasion. Invading woody growth also provides perches for birds that carry in additional tree seeds. Shrubs and then trees thus creep upward, progressively covering prairies and other unburned grasslands with dense, young thickets of fast-growing trees. Except for sites in the northernmost Loess Hills, woody invasion has claimed most north- and east-facing prairie slopes and uncultivated terrain east of the driest, most westerly bluffs.

Across the state, diverse opportunistic trees continue to take over land that has been allowed to "return to nature" and is managed by benign neglect, whether that land be suburban outlot or abandoned agricultural field. Young woody plots account for most of the recent documented increase in tree cover. Woody expansion remains especially profuse in eastern and southern Iowa, the regions that have always been most conducive to tree growth. However, on the whole, woody proliferation has tended to move trees and shrubs westward. Thus a 2002 survey showed that while portions of eastern Iowa had been reduced to between a quarter and a half of their presettlement timber coverage, woody cover in western Iowa had risen significantly. In the vast grasslands of northwestern Iowa, timber cover was nearly three times as great as it was in presettlement times (an amount still much less than that of eastern Iowa).[4] In this way the proliferation of opportunistic woody growth has been one of Iowa's equalizers, a force tending to homogenize the state's landscape.

Expanding urban and rural woods do provide certain ecological services. Urban plantings reduce heating and cooling costs by blocking winds and moderating temperature extremes. They lower noise and air pollution while providing shelter for birds and aesthetic appeal. Riparian buffer strips protect watersheds by filtering water and removing toxins. All woody growth, regardless of type, manufactures oxygen, sequesters the greenhouse gas carbon dioxide, holds soil moisture, reduces runoff and erosion by water and wind, and creates recreational opportunities. Shrublands provide habitat for ground- and bush-nesting birds such as the eastern towhee. Even relatively small natural communities pour out such benefits to surrounding intensively managed lands, thus buffering against sudden and adverse environmental change and helping to stabilize working landscapes.

However, the patches and thickets of woody species that are proliferating throughout Iowa generally cannot claim a high conservation value. Although they may provide certain wildlife habitat, they nearly always lack the understory herbs and shrubs that characterize native communities. These young unidimensional growths, with their biologically simpler associations, rarely promote or protect native biodiversity. On the whole, they are less resistant than native woodlands and forests to exotic invasives, which not infrequently comprise a significant component of their cover. Add other opportunistic species, the standard prickly shrubs, and poison ivy, and young woody outlots quickly become impenetrable thickets that are not considered pleasant or productive by most people.

What is the future of these woody proliferations, especially the more expansive young woods? Although time will eventually answer these questions, present indications are not positive. One would hope that young tumbled thickets

4. Information on the increase in timber cover in northwestern Iowa is from a personal communication with Paul Tauke, Iowa DNR, and is based on data from 2002 LANDSAT satellite imagery and the ISPAID2 soils database.

would naturally succeed to assemblages of slower-growing, more substantial native trees and diverse understory. However, these woody areas will not evolve into oaklands unless they are cleared and replanted. If appropriate seeds are available, some may eventually mature into maple-basswood stands. But many appear to be self-perpetuating thickets, destined to repeat their early successional stages time and time again, a teenager of sorts forever repeating the same mistakes. Because their fast-growing, smallish trees are substantially weaker and shorter lived than oaks and hickory, they soon die back and fall into a tangled jumble of shrubs, vines, and smaller trees. New individuals of the same opportunistic species become established, only to repeat the process. As these thickets cyclically grow and collapse, the density of dead wood increases and makes passage difficult, and any ground-layer flowering plants that may be present suffocate in the dense overlay of woody life and death.

Expanding woody areas have amplified the problematic fragmentation of our landscape. The strings of woody growth crisscrossing our state have helped transform what remains of Iowa's intergraded native communities into a land of sharp-lined edges that encourage our most common weeds and wildlife at the expense of increasingly rare, more discriminating species.

Challenge and Hope

Euroamerican settlement lifted the cap off the steady state that once characterized Iowa's oak woodlands and bottomland forests, the dynamic mosaic of intergrading but distinctive communities that perpetuated the diverse species living therein. As a result, what we see now differs in location and character from what we would have seen fifty years ago and what we will see fifty years hence.

In general, future changes are likely to include ongoing loss of some native species and communities and continued homogenization of those that remain. The land-use pressures imposed since the 1830s — grazing, clearing, timber harvest, and insufficient management, including the lack of fire — will probably continue.

In addition, housing construction has been increasingly affecting upland woods, especially high-quality oak woodlands near rivers. Housing developments and their roadways overtly destroy woodlands. They then confront remaining oak trees with multiple construction-related challenges. Large construction machinery injures the very sensitive root systems of oaks, killing them slowly over several years even when aboveground damage is not obvious. The same can happen because of soil compaction, digging, and placement of additional soil around the bases of oaks (van der Linden and Farrar 1993: 58). Construction damage can be minimized by fencing off oaks at the outer drip line of a tree's canopy and allowing absolutely no parking, trenching, grade changes, materials storage, or any other activities within this zone.

Spreading suburbs magnify woodland fragmentation, today recognized as a major wildlife stress that favors common generalist species at the expense of rarer, more discriminating species requiring larger timberlands (see chapter 3). In addition, fragmented woodlands and forests with abundant intrusions (roads, recreational trails) or linear edge habitats are less able to resist threats such as invasive species, pesticide drift, insect outbreaks, and predation on nesting birds. As a timberland's size decreases and the relative amount of edge habitat increases, the adverse effects become more pronounced, and the community's sustainability decreases.

Rural housing developments can foster benign neglect of wooded outlots and common lands, an approach very different from the active woodlot management once typical of farmers. Allowing nature to follow its own course submits the land's remaining natives to all the problems described in this chapter. Suburban outlots are prime sites for proliferation of the unwanted — be they exotic invasives, badly eroding creekbeds, or wildlife out of balance. With 92 percent of wooded land privately owned and these wooded lands increasingly shifting out of the hands of Iowa farmers, the need for landowners who are willing to commit to active management and restoration is starkly evident (Jungst et al. 1998).

In coming years, Iowa's wooded lands are likely to be spun in unexpected directions by the continuing proliferation of exotic invasives and diseases. Without careful management, these influences can become overwhelming. By 2000, a quarter (seventy species) of Iowa's woody plants were nonnative, the majority being intentional horticultural introductions. About half of these seventy species have become invasive in Iowa, their seeds often spread as edible berries carried in the guts of birds (Farrar 2001: 154). Some, such as multiflora rose, Japanese barberry, and the very invasive exotic bush honeysuckles and common buckthorn, have become serious understory pests in native woodlands and forests. Invasive shrubs, many of which were originally planted as ornamentals, hedges, or wildlife habitat, are shade tolerant, commonly leaf out early, and can eliminate native understory species, including our native spring wildflowers.

Garlic mustard threatens to become the most invasive and destructive timberland exotic. This plant dramatically alters woodlands and forests of all types by eliminating native herbs (including spring wildflowers) and smothering young trees and shrubs. Its prolific, tiny seeds are easily transported by animal fur, human shoes and clothing, and running water. Constant monitoring and eradication of all new populations are critically important to halt this devastating plant's spread.

Wooded areas that escape invasive plants remain vulnerable to destructive insects and diseases. Healthy mature butternuts, formerly a common component of bottomland forests and moist slopes, have been reduced to a rarity by butternut canker, a fungal disease with unknown origins (Lewis 1998: 51). Young elms remain common in Iowa, but Dutch elm disease pulses through our wooded areas in a thirty-to-forty-year infection cycle, killing the larger trees (Walkowiak and Haanstad 2001: 183).

Now considered Iowa's most important tree disease, the oak wilt fungus, which some believe is native, has been infecting several thousand acres of Iowa's oaklands annually (Walkowiak and Haanstad 2001: 182). This fungus, spread belowground through root grafts and aboveground by beetles, clogs trees' water-conducting tissues and wilts their foliage. Red and black oaks die the fastest, often within weeks of infection. White and bur oaks, which produce cellular blocks (tyloses) that compartmentalize injuries and infections, are more resistant to oak wilt and other diseases and thus die slowly over several years. Because infections are scattered and spotty, control is very difficult.

In the first few years of the twenty-first century, foresters in east-central and northeastern Iowa started to notice greater-than-normal numbers of unexplained deaths of scattered mature white oaks. They also noted an increasing incidence of tatters, a springtime shredding and loss of leaves possibly caused by herbicide drift (Mark Vitosh, personal communication). Such incidences may be warnings that our oaks are becoming stressed beyond their limits.

Disease threats require constant vigilance. Land managers are attempting to prevent importation of the disease sudden oak death (caused by a funguslike pathogen) from California nursery stock into Iowa and of the emerald ash borer, an Asian beetle that by 2005 had killed millions of southern Michigan ashes. Either could dramatically and rapidly alter our native woodlands and forests. The predicted increase of tree diseases and stressors argues for maintaining some diversity in native oaklands (Mark Vitosh, personal communication).

One more major problem demands attention — white-tailed deer, now so numerous that they are producing major transformations of Iowa's woodlands and forests. Deer impact is progressive. At first, before effects become obvious, deer feed selectively on certain plant species, including some of our rarest flowers, such as members of the lily (Liliaceae) and orchid (Orchidaceae) families. Ferns and other unpalatable species may multiply. Once the most palatable species have been eliminated, deer become less selective and eat leaves from low tree branches and anything else within reach, creating a visible browse line a few yards above the ground (Gibbon 1999).

Preferential browsing produces declines in wildflower diversity when deer reach nine or ten per square mile. As densities increase, deer eliminate understory herbs and most shrubs, leaving open wooded lands inhabited by unpalatable species (often invasives and briars) and trees tall enough to avoid browsing. These biologically simplified, fragile plant communities cannot support birds and other wildlife as they once did. Researchers in Pennsylvania have found that when deer exceed twenty per square mile, birds that nested or fed in the midlevel tree canopy (such as the eastern wood-pewee, yellow-billed cuckoo, indigo bunting, and wood thrush) disappear (Gibbon 1999). In addition, tree reproduction and forest regeneration are constrained, with our already-besieged oaklands being particularly threatened: acorns are a favored deer food, and oak seedlings and young oaks are highly preferred browse. Thus high deer numbers confound efforts to restore oak woodlands.

Deer are closely linked to the spread of exotic invasive plants. A study at the Coralville Reservoir in Johnson County demonstrated deer's selective browsing of native plants and the consequent increase of exotic weeds (Rosburg 2004). Deer also create trampled areas that are prime for exotic invasion. They disperse the small seeds of garlic mustard on their hooves and hair, seeding ribbons of this exotic along deer trails. They browse honeysuckle and other invasives and spread their seeds in droppings.

Major deer-induced degradation is now becoming evident in Iowa's wooded areas, causing significant changes in plant distribution and diversity. To reverse these changes, we need to either bring back natural predators or cull deer herds ourselves. Doing the latter involves welcoming hunters as valued members of the conservation community who are helping return our woodlands to balance and health. While reducing deer populations is painful to some animal rights activists, the effort can be seen as a push for "ecosystem rights" — that is, a way of giving life to multiple native plants, birds, and woodlands on the decline, all of which have equal worth and the right to survive. Limiting deer numbers also helps keep deer populations strong and healthy. Fully embracing this vision implies that the Iowa Department of Natural Resources would manage Iowa's deer herd to maintain the health of native species and communities, even if this meant decreasing the abundance of deer available to hunters. Deer-hunting quotas would be set accordingly and would be adjusted locally from year to year. Education regarding the negative effects of deer can bring people of all walks of life together to work for the health of the entire ecosystem.

Take these many ongoing challenges, add concerns about declining oaks and degrading wooded lands in general, and one is tempted to forget about efforts to retain Iowa's oak woodlands, bottomland forests, and their distinctive native species. Ignoring the slow but steady degradation of these communities has obvious appeal, especially when considering the resources that can go into managing wooded lands and controlling invasives. Time, labor, and money never seem to be sufficient either on public or on private lands.

Despite the obstacles, in the last decade of the twentieth century certain of Iowa's public land managers started to deal proactively with the ongoing loss of oaks, oak woodlands, and oak woodlands' many species. Realizing that the once-expansive oak woodlands still held an important key to Iowa's ecological integrity and acknowledging that modern oak woodlands differed greatly from those of past centuries, land managers started to welcome disturbance and sunshine back into these woodlands. In 1990 they started to impose prescribed fire and hands-on management techniques to woodlands, just as such techniques had first been applied to Iowa's prairie remnants a few decades earlier.

By 1990, Iowa's neighbors had been burning oak woodlands for many years — Minnesota's Nature Conservancy since 1961, Wisconsin and Missouri's public agencies since around 1980 (Colin McGuigan, Rich Henderson, Paul Nelson, personal communications). At first, many had questioned this reimposition of disturbance into seemingly intact natural areas. Communities of native trees, organisms that typically exceed the human life span, were considered entities that could care for themselves and thus should not be manipulated.

But then woodlands undergoing restoration spoke for themselves. They began to respond in spectacular fashion, their dense canopies opening and allowing suppressed native understory plants to reappear, flower, and flourish. The potential for excellent success has now been demonstrated in several Iowa locations, one being the privately owned 200-acre preserve Timberhill in Decatur County. Here, by 2005, after ten years of burning and clearing, more than

350 plant species had been identified, with new woodland natives continuing to appear as restoration provided increasingly appropriate habitat (Sibylla Brown, personal communication).

Woodland restorations are now being attempted across the state on private and public lands. The growing number of sites are living signs of hope and rebirth. So, too, is the increasing involvement of private citizens and public agencies, along with their excitement, determination, dedication, and application of creative techniques. Fortunately Iowa's oak woodland remnants remain in relative abundance, waiting to be discovered and nursed back to health.

This is not to say that widespread efforts to return health to our oak woodlands will be easy. More landowners need to recognize the ancient treasures and potential held within woodland and forest remnants. And education is needed to demonstrate the efficacy of restoration efforts and to engage more volunteers.

Oak woodland restoration is now undergoing the same experimentation that characterized prairie restoration efforts several decades ago. While restoration techniques, approaches, and desired endpoints are being refined, we need to try to save our diminishing oaks in any way possible, in particular the white oaks that were so prevalent in presettlement woodlands. Young oaks should be preferentially planted, encouraged, and protected wherever they are found, be it in fencerows, along woodland edges, in lawns and parks, or any other place where adequate sunshine allows them life.

In the meantime, restorations will be rising in extent, number, and maturity. Where they succeed, the rewards will be tremendous. For generations to come, restored oak woodlands, managed for sustainability, will provide homes not only for currently displaced savanna and open woodland understory plants but also for the many native mammals, birds, insects, and other animals that once helped define nature in Iowa.

6 Restoring Nature's Systems

[If restoration succeeds,] we can have hope that children . . . for millennia to come . . . will be able to lie quietly in the grass on a sunny prairie hillside filled with flowers, watch bumblebees visit shooting-stars and pasqueflowers, hear dickcissels and meadowlarks call in the sky, and be ever enchanted and empowered by that great symphony we call life.
— Hugh Iltis, 2000

 Restoration ecology is the art and science of healing nature by reinstituting the native biodiversity and ecological processes that once defined a given region. As ecologist Don Falk writes, "Restoration uses the past not as a goal but as a reference point for the future . . . not to turn back the evolutionary clock but to set it ticking again" (1990: 71). Restoration thus aims to reassemble our fractured native communities so they can once again function as diverse, self-sustaining units.

In the last few decades of the twentieth century, restoration ecology took hold as a scientific discipline that countermanded previous preservationist sentiments emphasizing that nature could take care of itself. With the elimination of fire and other natural processes, such attempts at self-care had often allowed native remnants to degrade into simplified assemblages of the most aggressive alien species. Many of the finest native qualities and species were being lost. Restoration ecology accepts that even in remote areas, humans may need to take a knowledgeable and considered hands-on approach in ensuring nature's integrity. People need to encourage native species and processes, as indeed fire-setting Native Americans had done for thousands of years. Today restoration efforts are undertaken by professionals and amateurs alike, on everything from garden-size plots to far-flung landscapes.

Restoration Primer

Restoration often refers to rehabilitating remnants, areas where some natural elements and species remain, albeit in a degraded state. However, one can also reconstruct a native community on bare ground. (Reconstructed wetlands are referred to as "created wetlands.") All these efforts must be followed by ongoing management that enhances native diversity.

This book uses the term "restoration" to embrace all these activities: working with remnants, reconstructing (or creating) communities from scratch, and managing natural communities in perpetuity. All restoration efforts follow the same general principles, which are broadly outlined below.

First, determine your goals. Many restorationists attempt to return natural areas to their presettlement condition, that is, to a semblance of what existed just before the cataclysmic changes invoked by Euroamericans. Others may want to maximize bird diversity, encourage game, or even consider economic gains through timber harvest. Goals come in many forms; all are to be applauded if they encourage appropriate natural biodiversity and, conversely, do no harm to existing native systems and species.

Second, evaluate your site. Get to know your land, its inhabitants, its fire history, and its previous use, so that restoration techniques and species can be properly matched to the site. Historic features can be deciphered in many ways, including the examination of early land surveys, photographs, maps, and other historic records and interpretation of environmental features (see Egan and Howell 2005). You also should observe a site for at least one growing season, noting variations in soils, topography, growth patterns, seeps and moisture, and so on, and identifying native and invasive plants. This will allow realistic evaluation of your site's needs and potential. Longer-term observations will continue to deepen your understanding of your land and teach simple truths — for example, that common dandelions die out naturally in prairie restorations but sweetclover does not.

Next, create a restoration and management plan appropriate to your site. For example, if new plants are to be introduced, place moisture-loving species lower on slopes and drought-tolerant ones higher up. Your plan should clearly identify your goals. It should consider the timing of efforts and your dedication to the project, as well as your personal capabilities. Badly degraded sites will require considerably more effort; you may want to work on less-disturbed or smaller sections of such a site first. Any level of restoration activity should be seen as positive. Incorporating a diversity of management techniques will help create heterogeneity and maximize diversity.

Several sources of information can be tapped when developing and implementing a restoration plan. Organizations such as the Iowa Natural Heritage

Foundation, the Nature Conservancy's Iowa chapter, county conservation boards, nature centers, and local land trusts can provide connections or recommend sites to visit. Groups such as the Iowa Native Plant Society and Iowa Prairie Network discuss restoration at their meetings and provide helpful field trips where one can meet other landowners likely to share practical experiences. The Iowa Department of Natural Resources (Iowa DNR) and others sponsor occasional field days that can be extremely informative. Information can also be found in restoration-oriented journals such as *Ecological Restoration*, on Web sites, and in technical guides and books. Private and governmental restoration consultants are increasing; the latter are listed in the following paragraph. Additional prairie information sources include the biennial North American Prairie Conference and its proceedings, and the Iowa Prairie Conference. Basic planting procedures for prairie reconstructions are outlined in native seed catalogs, booklets published by county conservation boards and others, and a growing body of literature. Restoration handbooks invaluable for Iowans include Kurtz 2001, a straightforward guide for planting prairie reconstructions on bare ground, and Packard and Mutel 2005, a comprehensive manual that includes information on restoring wooded lands, interseeding, soils, and other topics not typically covered.

Technical and financial assistance regarding restorations is available through the Soil and Water Conservation District (SWCD)/Natural Resources Conservation Service (NRCS) field offices, the U.S. Fish and Wildlife Service's (USFWS) Partners for Fish and Wildlife Program, and the Iowa DNR's district foresters and private land wildlife biologists. Representatives from each of these agencies can assist private landowners by making site visits and assessing the land's restoration potential, drawing up simple restoration/management plans adapted to the owner's goals, and connecting landowners with the proper administrator for cost-sharing programs. Occasionally some may even provide hands-on restoration labor: in south-central Iowa, for example, the USFWS in 2005 hired staff to assist with wildland fire-training efforts and execution.

Connecting landowners with appropriate cost-sharing programs is complex and often confusing because of such programs' varied and changing stipulations. Many governmental programs focus on planting native assemblages; a smaller number work with existing remnants. In 2005 some of the major governmental programs addressing restoration included the state-funded Resource Enhancement and Protection (REAP) program, for soil- and water-conservation-related projects that establish native plantings or restore and manage woodlands and forests, administered by the SWCD; the Landowner Incentive Program (LIP), for protecting or enhancing habitats used by endangered species, administered by Iowa DNR private land wildlife biologists; the federal Wildlife Habitat Incentive Program (WHIP), for planting or enhancing native vegetation as wildlife habitat; and the Wetlands Reserve Program, for restoring wetlands altered by agricultural use, especially in the prairie pothole region. Many of the federal programs are administered by the NRCS. The WHIP and LIP programs are exemplary for addressing biodiversity issues and funding ongoing management efforts.

Private conservation organizations such as Pheasants Forever and the National Wild Turkey Federation may also provide planning and management consultations, site assessments, seed, assistance with prairie and tree plantings and wetland construction, and financial incentives. And private consultants and land managers can be hired to assess a site, provide information on restoration and management techniques, and perform hands-on restoration work. Because the background, opinions, and mandates of each government office, conservation group, and private consultant will vary, landowners will do best to gather restoration information from multiple sources. Unintended consequences can be avoided by explaining goals and intentions clearly to everyone who is executing restoration plans.

Restoration efforts include constant attention to invasive plants. These are most easily eliminated when their populations are small. Control methods must be carefully adjusted for each species and situation. They may include prescribed fire, repeated cutting or mowing, covering with plastic, hand pulling and digging, and biological controls. These plants often require the prudent application of herbicides, with care given to human safety and the effects on surrounding vegetation. Trees are eliminated through cutting, girdling (severing conductive tissues just under the bark), or applying herbicides to bark and cut stumps. Aggressive efforts invested immediately, when an invasive species is first identified, will save effort in the long run. Iowans should take heart in our state's midcontinental location: many invasives are more extensive closer to their points of entry, in states to the east or west. Once established, invasives may be extremely difficult or impossible to eradicate. Abundant information about controlling invasives can be found on the Internet, through your local county conservation board, and in a growing number of publications, including Czarapata 2005.

Restoration also involves reinstituting stresses that once governed our native communities. Prescribed fire is almost always used. Its effects vary greatly with fire frequency and intensity; burn programs should thus be matched to specific goals. Carrying out burns is exciting as well as enjoyable, but fire is a dangerous force that demands caution and respect. Guidance from trained personnel should be sought when attempting burns, and proper precautions should be scrupulously followed.

Tiny native plants may become obvious for the first time following fire, as fire-adapted species respond by growing, blooming, and spreading. Remnants should therefore be burned and assessed for a few years before additional species are introduced in an attempt to increase native biodiversity.

Care should be taken to limit restoration plantings to appropriate species. Gardening stores may sell "native" plants that are actually imported species or varieties. Garden cultivars and nonnative species should be avoided.

In addition, attempts should be made to limit seedings to species that were present in the county or region in question during presettlement times. Such attempts will be aided by using only local ecotype seeds, nuts, and plants. These are genetic strains that originated close enough to the restoration site to be genetically adapted to the region's particular environment. Thus these plants should grow better than individuals of the same species that evolved, for example, where the growing season was significantly longer or shorter. Use of local ecotypes also helps prevent the gene dilution that results when planted individuals interbreed with nearby remnant populations, a significant conservation concern. Local ecotype seed is now commercially available from multiple sources.

Planting site-appropriate species, using local ecotypes, and working to maintain each native species' geographic range will help maintain Iowa's distinctive, locally adapted native communities. Fighting the homogenization of our landscape in this way will help make our restored natural world a more resilient as well as a more interesting place.

Restorations change with time. They may not look like much for the first few years; patience and faith are necessary during this period. As the years pass, monitoring the restoration will allow goals and plans to be reevaluated and adjusted. Actions as simple as keeping a dated list of newly observed plant species or taking photographs each year from the same vantage point can allow one to assess changes. Sharing successes and failures with others will help assess restoration attempts.

Restoring plant communities necessarily precedes restoration of native animals, which may spontaneously colonize restored sites as their preferred food and habitat are re-created. Summer bird diversity, for example, increased from eight to over forty species in eight years in one pasture site that was transformed to a riparian buffer community with trees, shrubs, and native grasses and forbs (Ehresman 2003: 21). The type of restoration, and the manner in which it is performed, will determine the animal species likely to repopulate an area. Thinning a woodland and removing the shrub layer, for example, will alter the types of birds nesting therein. In general, larger restorations will be more conducive to healthy animal populations than will smaller restorations. We have a great deal to learn about purposefully returning key animals to restored sites. Initial steps are being taken with the introductions of regal fritillary butterflies, bison, and elk at the Neal Smith National Wildlife Refuge.

The physical labor needed to establish and manage a restoration can be lessened by bringing in local volunteers. Children, neighbors, and nature enthusiasts may welcome the opportunity to work on the land, close to nature, especially if the work is accompanied by food and camaraderie. Conversely, volunteering on someone else's restoration teaches invaluable skills.

Much is demanded of persons attempting restorations: patience, flexibility, persistence, hard physical labor, cash. New problems such as the arrival of invasives or diseases are likely to present themselves midstream. Starting a restoration is like bringing home a new pet or child: it needs you and your long-term commitment. The restoration effort is deeply satisfying, however. The restorationist is constantly learning more about the site and, in the process, is presented with delightful surprises — the first appearance of a new bird, the chance flowering of an unexpected plant. Restorationists have the privilege of seeing the phoenix rise from the fire — of watching long-depleted species and communities quite literally rise from the ashes. Restoring native communities is a joyful, hopeful effort, one in which the overwhelming aspects of environmental degradation are reversed and the natural complexity of the ages once again takes hold.

Restoring Oak Woodlands: Focus and Rationale

In 1925 Thomas Macbride decried the ongoing logging and grazing of Iowa's wooded areas: "Taken altogether, the prospect for our Iowa woods is discouraging in the extreme. The only hope of preserving any of our primitive forest area lies in the possibility of stirring the intelligent sentiment of our people" (1925: 172).

How are we to respond to these somber words today? Our search for answers points us first toward the progeny of the species-rich oak-dominated uplands that once characterized the southeastern half to two-thirds of Iowa, within the distributional ranges of white oak and hard maples. Across the eastern United States, wherever white oaks are found, aging woodlands are a major conservation concern because of the slow, steady loss of oaks, understory diversity, and integrity — losses that in Iowa are most advanced in our moist easternmost counties. While natural processes seem determined to push oak woodlands toward extermination, Iowans are working hard to return diversity and sustainability to the land by reversing this trend.

Some might wonder if this is a needless exercise. Wouldn't a landscape dominated by dense groves of basswood, black cherry, sugar maple, and multiple species of ash and hickory or any of our other flourishing native trees serve just as well? Why, one might ask, is so much emphasis being placed on oak-dominated communities?

There are many answers to these questions. Not only were the majority of Iowa's presettlement wooded lands dominated by oaks, oak woodlands still comprise Iowa's most extensive and abundant natural areas. These communities support many understory plants that once were common in Iowa but today are limited to shrinking patches. What's more, oak trees are critical midwestern keystone species — that is, they are crucial to the existence of a large number of other woodland species. Put another way, the disappearance of oaks would produce major shifts in the structure, function, and species composition of Iowa's remaining wooded lands. Many insect species depend on oaks, and no other Iowa tree is as important to wildlife. Acorns and their common associates, hickory nuts, function as the staff of life for many more birds (blue jays, wild turkeys, grouses, woodpeckers, and nuthatches, among others) and mammals (squirrels, raccoons, deer, and so forth) than any other tree seeds. Nationally nearly 100 different animals eat acorns, many of them deriving a significant amount of their nutrition from these fat- and protein-rich seeds. In contrast, only 33 animal species utilize maple seeds, 20 utilize elm, and 10 utilize basswood. Acorns are especially critical in winter when other foods are scarce. The disappearance of acorns would not only stress dependent animals but also increase crop damage as animals sought alternative food sources (Martin et al. 1951).

Oak woodlands have also evolved valuable functional benefits. For example, a lush oakland understory, greening up early in spring, absorbs rainfall, holds soil, and captures the springtime flush of nutrients that otherwise would run rapidly into water bodies.

Economically significant as a source of hard, durable lumber with multiple uses, the tall, slow-growing, long-lived oaks possess an uncanny emotional and aesthetic appeal that remains unduplicated by other regional trees (which as a group are weaker, smaller, and shorter lived than oaks). People seem to be naturally drawn to massive, stately oaks as symbols of continuity and quality.

This perhaps explains not only why the oak is Iowa's state tree and why oaks are highly regarded nationally but also why they have been prized by past civilizations. The oak tree and oak gods (Zeus, Jupiter, and others) were worshipped throughout ancient Europe. Oaks kindled and fed ceremonial fires. Yule logs traditionally were oak. Oak leaves were incorporated into sacred rituals, and voices of the gods were heard in their rustle. Oaks, hallowed by the gods, constituted holy trees and sacred groves, sites of rituals and sanctified services. Thus oaks formed an inescapable part of Europe's natural and cultural landscape, just as they do ours today (Frazer 1922).

These many factors single out the perpetuation of oaklands as one of our most important conservation priorities. Their existence seems to be crucial both to the physical survival of an abundance of native species and, at some level, to the human spirit itself.

How then should we attempt to rebuild healthy, diverse, attractive oak woodlands and ensure their continuity in coming centuries? What sites and locations do we choose for restoration, what practices do we apply, and how should we envision our end product? The following pages pose tentative answers that address the full gamut of oaklands and their understories, from those with canopy cover of 80 percent or more (still open enough ideally to allow white oak regeneration; Curtis 1959: 146) to the very open savannas that once intermingled with prairies. While techniques are most applicable to the southeastern two-thirds of Iowa, they may also be applied to mature oaklands farther west and north. There restoration activities would be limited to the small number of settlement-era oaklands that remain. These include mature red and bur oak stands in sheltered sites and overgrown bur oak savannas that are especially abundant in the Loess Hills. Specifics of Iowa's northwesterly oak communities differ from those of woodlands farther east and south, but the same types of restoration efforts could bring back a diversity of understory plants.

In the Loess Hills, restored oaklands need to be integrated into the prairie matrix — the community type that rightfully captures most current conservation attention. Here, where bur oak and other woods are invading the best and largest of Iowa's remaining prairies, our present calling should be to prevent further tree encroachment of prairies rather than to encourage oak reproduction or restore young oak woodlands.

Site evaluations and other planning procedures outlined earlier in this chapter should be carefully followed. Landowners are encouraged to make additional inquiries and to proceed with care, so that attempts to restore diversity do not backfire and further degrade our oak remnants. (Readers should note that when forest or woodland restoration is described in other publications, the term often refers to the establishment of tree plantations, not to the encouragement of diverse sustainable communities.)

The following oak woodland restoration techniques section is more detailed than that allotted prairies, for woodland restoration is little discussed in other publications. That said, it is clear that we currently lack the research and experience to guide oakland management with certainty; this discussion is not intended as a manual that can be applied successfully to any site. Much of the following information is anecdotal, gathered from discussions with those working in the field who admit that their results are not totally predictable. While the need to restore oaks and their understory is widely accepted, woodland restoration is a science in its infancy. Long-term research and observations pegged to Iowa, which describe restoration failures as well as successes, are badly needed.

To date nearly all of Iowa's woodland and forest restoration efforts have dealt with oaklands. Techniques described here are not intended for maple-basswood communities on north-facing slopes or for other moist mature forests that probably burned infrequently in presettlement times. Maple-basswood communities are expanding without the aid of restoration. Nor would the following techniques apply to Iowa's diverse bottomland forests. While intact floodplain forests are among our most endangered native communities, which also will need restoration if they are once again to house diverse native plant associations, bottomland restorations have rarely been attempted in Iowa. One of the few exceptions involves the Nature Conservancy's Swamp White Oak Preserve along the Cedar River, where fire and clearing are now being applied to restore oak savannas. Restoration of these other types of communities is sure to increase in coming years, as our knowledge base and experience expand.

Restoring Oak Woodlands: Techniques

Upland woodlands with a canopy of oaks still are common in Iowa. Here, on sites that often were grazed or logged, the essential oak matrix remains, although typically hidden within a dense, dark, multistoried growth of shrubs and other tree species. Efforts to return these oak woodland communities to full health and diversity entail many activities: restoring their two-tiered structure, controlling exotic invasive plants, opening the woodlands to light to encourage growth of native groundcover, restoring that groundcover where necessary, and devising schemes that encourage oak propagation.

Restorationists find that the first three goals can be accomplished to some degree through a single activity: reintroducing prescribed fire. Woodland burns, often lit in late autumn when newly fallen dry oak leaves invite fire (although also performed in winter or spring), are characteristically low, slow-going affairs. Flames flicker upward inches instead of feet, as they do in prairies (fig. 38). Hotter fires, potentially fueled by abundant dead wood, could damage soils but are uncommon. As long as strong or shifting winds do not whirl fires out of control or dead trees do not form chimneys that shoot flames skyward, keeping a woodland fire burning may be more challenging than controlling its spread. Indeed if fuel is insufficient or if the litter is dominated by leaves other than oak, it may be impossible to perform a woodland burn.

Slow, creeping oakleaf fires can have astounding effects. A single fire will kill back small shrubs and young trees, immediately allowing both woodland canopy and understory plants more access to sunlight. Fire sets back many destructive invasives. However, care must be taken, especially with very aggressive invasives such as garlic mustard, to supplement fire with other year-round control techniques. Many landowners repeat woodland burns annually to restrict renewed growth of young trees and shrubs and to stimulate understory renewal, even though annual burns also restrain young oaks, a problem discussed more thoroughly below.

Because larger fire-sensitive trees may survive burns, prescribed fire is often combined with selective thinning to achieve the desired tree density. But how is ideal density to be determined? Remember that presettlement oaklands were characterized by a range of densities. Today's restorations should aim at re-creating that variation, not creating very open savannas everywhere. Restorations should be adapted to the site. For example, it is logical to restore savannas and very open oak woodlands on dry ridgetops and southwest-facing slopes and to restore less open, moister oak woodlands on lower slopes and north- and east-facing hillsides. As for selecting species to cut, trees that were rare in presettlement oak woodlands (for example, elm, green ash, boxelder) and midstory trees and larger shrubs (for example, ironwood, hackberry, dogwood) are typically targeted, with elimination of maple and sometimes basswood (high shade producers, with a great potential for replacing oaks) being major objectives. Some-

Fig. 38. Prescribed woodland fires typically burn with much less vigor than prairie fires. However, they can produce amazing results by opening oak woodlands to greater light and stimulating the growth and flowering of native understory plants. Photograph by the author.

times even oaks are cut if they are very dense. Manual thinning of small trees and shrubs is far more labor intensive than prescribed fire.

Using these techniques to restore the two-tiered, open structure typical of presettlement woodlands is relatively straightforward and simple. Ensuring a positive understory response is more difficult. Much depends on a site's capabilities. Where fire-tolerant understory plants remain, even in reduced size and vigor, they respond to increased light — and decreased competition and leaf litter — by becoming more robust and blooming profusely. Spring wildflowers are often spectacular after a burn, and the fire-bared soil enhances germination of their small seeds. Taller stalks of woodland grasses often survive, ready to drop their seeds on the bared soil. The understory diversity of a high-quality area appears to increase with each burn, as obscure forbs, grasses, and sedges gain strength and stature, start to bloom, and provide fuel for subsequent burns (see color plate 10).

Composition of the understory varies from region to region and even within a given site, depending on multiple factors, including soils and the amount of entering sunlight, with prairie and savanna species increasing where sunlight abounds. Thus the quality and diversity of a restoration are likely to be patchy and to change with time, with eastern Iowa's moister oaklands presenting the greatest challenges. Weedy natives such as clearweed and white snakeroot often come in thick at first. They may give way as other forbs and grasses become established. Plants whose seeds are transported on animal fur, such as stickseed, sweet cicely, and enchanter's nightshade, may become abundant. Aggressive native forbs such as Joepyeweed and hogpeanut also may proliferate for the first few years. On the most successful sites, the increasing frequency, size, diversity, and flowers of less-common native forbs, grasses, and sedges produce a wondrous and inspiring display.

On the other hand, opening sites that lack remnant seeds or plants or that abound in aggressive natives such as woodnettle can result in a flush of unpleasant growth. The increased light often boosts growth of small trees and shrubs. Raspberry species are often particularly obnoxious. Such plants can be partially controlled with fire but may also need intensive manual control. Undesirable growth is most prolific when cutting opens oak woodlands to sunshine rapidly and is less dramatic when fire opens woodlands more gradually. Worst of all, increased sunlight and reduction of competition can stimulate multiflora rose and other exotic invasives that seriously degrade woodlands.

Active efforts to restore the understory may be necessary if restorations do not regain diversity with repeated fire. If rich oak woodlands lie nearby, restorations might be naturally recolonized by woodland natives with fleshy berries dispersed by birds or mammals, or by tufted seeds carried on the wind. However, the natural spread of woodland understory plants typically is slow and is unlikely to include spring wildflowers. Many spring wildflower seeds — for example, those of spring beauty, wild ginger, Dutchman's breeches, bloodroot, and the trilliums — are laboriously transported to new locales by ants. Others, such as those of rue anemone, wood anemone, and hepatica, fall and remain at the base of parent plants. Thus interseeding or overseeding of native plants (that is, sowing seed into existing cover, so that tree roots are not disturbed) is sometimes undertaken (fig. 39). Interseeded species should be appropriate to the site. For example, very open savannas can be seeded with prairie grasses and forbs. As tree density increases, interseeded species adapted to partial shade should gradually give way to what we consider forest species. Restorations would do well to increase summer and fall bloomers that appear to have migrated out of

Fig. 39. Bloodroot, one of the signature spring wild-flowers of Iowa's wood-lands, responds well to res-toration efforts. Its seeds, normally transported and buried by ants, can also be collected in moderation and hand planted. Photo-graph by Carl Kurtz.

today's denser woodlands. Ideas for seed mixes for oak woodland sites are given in Delong and Hooper 1996 and Packard and Mutel 2005.

In areas with rich woodlands nearby, seeds can be hand collected in modera-tion. Commercial dealers are increasingly likely to provide appropriate seed as woodland restoration evolves. Salvaging tubers, bulbs, fibrous roots, and plants from rich oaklands facing imminent destruction and even simply moving top-soil from those sites to open woodlands have also worked well. Dividing and replanting roots and tubers may be a more efficacious method of reintroducing spring wildflowers than planting seeds. Techniques and ease of successful un-derstory reestablishment will vary from species to species and from site to site (Mottl 2000, 2001).

Very occasionally rich assemblages of understory plants, especially spring wildflowers, are found in non-oak woods. These remnant communities imply that former oak canopies have been removed from the site. These understory plants should be fostered by thinning trees and shrubs to admit sunlight.

Restoration is costly in time and effort, requiring commitment as well as goodly amounts of sweat-equity. Given the tremendous variation in understory response, what is a would-be restorationist to do? Where can the least amount of effort yield the best results?

Selecting sites with the best restoration potential is important. Restoration potential decreases on sites that have been heavily overused or deeply shaded for a prolonged period. The domination of dense exotic invasives, weedy natives, or abundant young sugar maples implies continuing management problems. Conversely, the presence of diverse residual native woodland grasses, sedges, and forbs, even if tiny, suggests a more positive restoration response. A rich mixture of spring woodland wildflowers indicates a high-quality site worthy of restoration. However, a site's potential cannot always be estimated. Sites seeming to lack understory plants occasionally respond to fire in unexpectedly positive ways.

Eastern Iowa's rich, moist soils have encouraged weeds, shrubs, and invasive trees to proliferate with such vigor that they have severely degraded many open oaklands. In these dense stands, where loss of integrity is most advanced, restoration is extremely difficult. In contrast, drier sites with thin sandy or rocky soil (for example, Mississippi River bluffs, dry ridgetops, or rocky south-facing hillsides) often retain more savanna characteristics and species and respond better to restoration efforts. The same could be true of oaklands on western Iowa's dry sites.

Many pasturelands in south-central Iowa retain large oaks in abundance. Even after cattle are removed, invasion of woody shrubs and trees is slowed by the area's poorer soils and growth conditions. In this region, where cultivation has not been as ubiquitous as elsewhere in Iowa, the existence of thousands of acres of restorable oak savanna may allow abundant large-scale restorations that would be impossible elsewhere. Advancing such restorations through public-private partnerships is the purpose of the Southern Iowa Oak Savanna Alliance, formed in 2005.

Beginning restorationists are advised to commit themselves only to what they can maintain. It's wise to go slow and easy at first — for example, to burn a small section each year and encourage the natural return of understory species, or to open an area slowly and judge the response. (Cutting more trees is always possible; replacing large trees is not.) Burning an entire large woodland may bring faster results, but ensuring the necessary continuing management may require more time, labor, and commitment than can be provided.

FIRE AND THINNING are capable of re-creating open woodlands with oaks towering majestically above a diverse carpet of flowers, grasses, and sedges. Savannas and open woodlands in the making can be seen at the Neal Smith National Wildlife Refuge near Des Moines, the Indian Creek Nature Center in Cedar Rapids, the Nature Conservancy's Swamp White Oak Preserve in Muscatine County, and other public and private lands across Iowa.

But to guarantee a woodland's perpetuity, young oaks need to follow the old. And getting oaks to reproduce in any number remains an elusive feat. This is especially true of the white oaks that have ruled eastern U.S. woodlands for thousands of years. White oaks seem to be more threatened than red or bur oaks, which inhabit respectively moister or drier sites.

Not all oak reproduction fails. White oak woodlands returned en masse following the initial 1800s loggings. Today plantations of white and other oaks succeed on denuded land (such as abandoned cropland) if competing plants and deer are controlled. White oaks are now reproducing in some very dry woodlands (Johnson-Groh 1985), as are bur oaks in the Loess Hills. Young black oaks, which occupy dry sites with sandy or rocky soils, survive because of few woody competitors on those sites. Individual trees planted on sunny lawns or seeded naturally in open settings reach successfully toward the sky. But on the whole, attempts to nudge large numbers of oaks in woodland complexes to maturity have claimed limited success on all but the very driest sites.

Land managers agree that young oaks require ample sunlight and that faster-growing woody competitors need to be suppressed. But do oaks need more than this? Growth conditions today, shaped by altered soils and hydrologies, abundant competitors, exotic plants and diseases, large numbers of deer, and the absence of the passenger pigeon and other potentially crucial species, differ starkly from those of past centuries. Some researchers hypothesize that root competition, soil fungal associations, or other unrecognized factors are hampering young oaks. All agree that while theories abound, no single theory holds the key for unlocking the complex problem of successful oak reproduction.

Midwestern oak woodlands managed and thinned by routine fire for one or two decades display hopeful signs, especially those on dry sites with poorer soils. Oak seedlings often abound on newly burned sites, pouring energy into roots for their first three or four years. Seedlings might easily be shaded out by fast-growing competitors, but continued fire holds these at bay. Once established, oaks are tenacious and grow steadily as long as they have adequate sunlight. Annual burns kill back aboveground shoots, but the root masses continue to enlarge and produce new sprouts that become increasingly robust. These fire-managed woodlands resemble our image of presettlement woodlands, with scrubby oaks thriving in dappled sunshine, ready to shoot upward whenever a gap in the canopy appears. But if regular burns continue, will any of today's oak youngsters mature into saplings? Or if fire is halted for a few years to allow oak shoots to mature into saplings, will they possess a sufficient competitive advantage to outrace surrounding fast-growing trees? While today's routinely burned woodlands seem to be setting the stage for successful oakland propagation, longer-term observations are needed.

Restoration ecologists and foresters differ somewhat in their goals and approaches, but the two are united in their dedication to perpetuating oaks. Foresters have been seeking methods to harvest oaks while ensuring future oak crops. Realizing that the common practice of selectively logging mature oaks does not encourage oak regeneration, they have sought alternative techniques that produce the disturbance and sunlight young oaks crave. One such technique is the carefully planned, executed, and subsequently managed clear-cut. Clear-cuts, completed at the peak of the oaks' productive lives, are performed during years when acorn production is heavy or are followed by the planting of large numbers of acorns. In either case, roughing the soil to bury the acorns appears to be critical. Once the oaks have been logged, other shade-producing trees and shrubs are cleared. This is done with further cutting and application of herbicides (which essentially mimic fire by clearing the ground surface) or with small bulldozers that remove the understory plants' shallow root systems. Alternatively, if the site is to remain partially vegetated, oak seedlings at least two feet tall are planted. These seedlings are better able to compete with remaining shrubs and trees.

Clear-cuts may cover substantial areas or be limited to small patches within larger woodlands. Some foresters state that at least a five-acre clear-cut is required for oak seedlings to receive the necessary sunlight. Others claim that oak regeneration will transpire in smaller holes, down to a few acres or possibly even less, especially when these are oriented to maximize sunlight penetration.

Clear-cuts do indeed provide the sunshine craved by oaks, but the increased light also stimulates seedlings and stump sprouts of fast-growing competitors.

The result often is a thicket of extremely dense saplings, only a few of which are oaks. Thus foresters must return at regular intervals to remove shrubs or trees that surround oak saplings.

Clear-cuts usually result in stands of mixed trees, with oak stocking often less than the forester's goal of 30 percent. Thus, on the downside, clear-cuts convert oak canopies to mixed timberlands facing all the problems of today's mixed woodlands. In addition, clear-cuts favor faster-growing red oaks rather than slow-growing white oaks that are less tolerant of shade. And the high density of saplings and routine management practices typical of clear-cuts may destroy native woodland understory, a feature not usually considered in forestry management plans. On the positive side, with clear-cuts, at least some oaks are retained. This is a major triumph when the alternatives are considered: the gradual loss of all large oaks to natural causes or their sudden loss through selective logging.

Various renditions of the shelterwood technique — basically a two-step clear-cut — claim to increase the probability of good oakland regeneration. A stand is thinned to allow partial sunlight penetration, leaving large oaks to produce acorns. The growth of competing trees is then suppressed (via cutting or herbicides) until three- or four-foot-tall oak seedlings are established, a process that may require one to two decades. During this intermediate period, native understory may flourish, and the semiopen woodland can come to resemble the fire-managed woodland restorations discussed earlier. Once young oaks seem to be sufficiently established, economic goals dictate the cutting of the larger oaks. Although successful implementation of shelterwood techniques can be challenging, this practice shows promise for sustainable oak harvest and regeneration. On the downside, restorationists point out that while shelterwood activities may be less harsh and extreme than those of one-step clear-cutting, the same problems result: damaged understory, the favoring of red oaks, and resulting mixed-tree stands.

A few other approaches to oak regeneration should be mentioned. Plantings of oaks, now usually mixed with other trees in hopes that mixed stands will better resist disease outbreaks, are becoming increasingly common on abandoned cropland and pastures. One might consider these plantings the correlates of oaklands that invaded prairies in past centuries. However, today's plantations lack native understory and thus are mere shells of our original diverse oaklands. Perhaps in future decades some of these tree plantations will become sites for restoring native understory plants. Sculpturing them into diverse native communities would demand a long-term commitment.

The young diverse woods and thickets now proliferating across Iowa have minimum restoration potential. Their conversion to oaklands would require removing the current mixed stands and starting over with oak plantations. Alternatively, good-size holes could be cut in the dense thickets and planted with young oaks. Either approach would entail considerable effort over many years.

Prescribed fire could be incorporated into all forestry techniques. Fire could be used to stimulate oak reproduction, suppress competition, and favor native understory plants. However, foresters traditionally avoid fire because of fear of scarring mature trees.

Regardless of technique, everyone agrees that today's large deer herds are making oak reproduction all but impossible. Deer eat acorns (as do wild turkeys) and browse oak seedlings, preferring white oaks, which have less tannin than red oaks and thus are more palatable. Even large, dense oak plantations may have few survivors. Stark new measures such as protecting individual seedlings from deer may now be required.

Given the many questions and problems involved, no one dares to say that full restoration of our oaklands will be easy or indeed even possible. Until the problem of oak reproduction is solved, the long-term fate of oak woodlands remains undetermined. Future research and field trials will enable us to better describe innovative management techniques. However, neither will come fast: time is required both to apply restoration techniques and to wait for slow-growing plants to mature. Variations among sites, within sites, and among oak and understory species will present many challenges, as will the arrival of new invasives and diseases.

While time will define the best oakland management techniques, the fear of misstepping should not be used as an excuse to do nothing. Considering the multiple challenges and lack of explicit guidelines, the community of restorationists will do well to practice flexibility and adopt multiple goals, restoration approaches, and desired endpoints. Doing so will require that public land managers and private landowners communicate and work together, respect each other's approaches, and share one another's techniques, adopting those that appear to be most successful. Restoration ecologists and foresters must do the same. Applied with care and consideration, various mixtures of burning, cutting, mechanical clearing, considered use of herbicides, soil scarification, understory reseeding, planting of oaks, and perhaps other techniques are all likely to have their place in Iowa's future oaklands. Some landowners may balk because they fear imposing some of these disturbances is too harsh, artificial, and problematic. Perhaps such sentiments would shift if skeptics considered the ongoing loss of oak woodlands and then pictured today's manipulations as replacements for past wildfires and the trampling of bison and elk — that is, as forces that renew rather than destroy.

Because of oak's importance, our preservation and restoration efforts should attempt to maintain a goodly portion of oak-dominated woodlands of various densities, underlain by the diverse forbs, grasses, and sedges that we believe bloomed here in presettlement times. Nonetheless, because of the hard physical labor required and inherent difficulties, a considerable number of today's oak woodlands will continue their inexorable shift toward mixed-species timberlands or maple and basswood forests. Some researchers believe that given our limited resources and people-power, intensive restoration efforts could maintain perhaps 10 percent of Iowa's timberland as high-quality, oak-dominated woodlands (John Pearson, personal communication).

While we should continue to propagate oak woodlands to the maximum degree possible, other types of wooded lands may claim certain benefits. A greater diversity of trees may, for example, be less vulnerable to plant diseases. Perhaps non-oak woody growth can, in future centuries, become part of a mosaic of distinct native communities, each fostering its own unique assemblage of native species. Our goal for the landscape as a whole should always be to encourage functional communities that support a diversity of native species. This goal will work against the current trend toward homogenization of the botanical landscape, the blending of all woody species into a single community type, as well as the loss of many plants and animals dependent on ancient oak-dominated woodlands.

Prairie Restoration

In 1925 Thomas Macbride wrote, "How shall one bring back the upland with its velvet grasses in rippling changing shades, an ever varying background for alternating light of sun and storm, or picture in the lowlands the wide mantle of the sedges, swarthy green with lustrous sheer waving in the breath of summer like the rolling of some darkling water, where cloud-shadows are wont to move, softly, like floating islands!" (1925: 18).

How indeed? At that time botanists knew next to nothing about caring for prairie remnants. And when efforts to reconstruct prairies through plantings commenced a decade later, pioneering restorationists lacked information about

Fig. 40. Reconstructed prairies (such as this spectacular display of spiderwort and fox-glove penstemon along Highway 30 in Story County) are increasingly common along Iowa roadsides and in other locations, where they hold soil and water, beautify the land-scape, and provide numerous other benefits. Photograph by Carl Kurtz.

basic procedures involving seed treatment, soil preparation, and the necessity of fire.

Since then, trial-and-error efforts have demonstrated multiple successful procedures both for restoring native remnants and for reconstructing prairies on bare soil (fig. 40). New procedures appear regularly. Because of the abundance of techniques and their ready description elsewhere, this section summarizes only the most basic considerations. Anyone conducting a reconstruction or remnant restoration should peruse additional information sources. Points described at the beginning of this chapter are crucial to the success of prairie-centered efforts. Site considerations are also important, as is size: in general, the larger the remnant restoration or reconstruction, the greater its potential diversity, functionality, and authenticity.

Today restorationists wanting to reconstruct a prairie from scratch have easy access to high-quality seeds and plants, sold by reputable dealers. These allow people to customize planting mixtures, designing them for specific environments and purposes. Nursery seeds are often cleaned and certified as to their viability and number. However, the cost of certified seeds can limit the size and diversity of plantings. An alternative is provided by bulk seeds harvested from diverse prairie plantings, which are sold without further treatment. Bulk seeds typically result in a lush growth of dozens of species over large areas at a fraction of the cost of certified seeds. Because of their expense, nursery-raised plants are generally used only for gardens or small plantings.

Purchasers should ensure that seeds are local ecotypes that are appropriate to their locale — that is, regionally present in presettlement prairies. "Meadow-in-a-can" and similar "prairie" mixes commonly sold by nonspecialized seed dealers are notorious for including exotic and inappropriate species. Some seed mixes promoted for wildlife habitat do the same. Both should be avoided. Purchasers should also ensure that seeds have been legally obtained and that plants have been grown from seed rather than dug from the wild. Persons hand-collecting seeds should gather only small quantities from any one site. Most prairie seeds need to be conditioned by cold temperature and moisture before they will germinate (see Rock 1977).

Occasionally, when a remnant is about to be destroyed, last-minute efforts are made to rescue the remnant's unique genetic resources by collecting seeds, digging plants, or removing soil along with its seeds and roots, and then relocating these in a suitable location. However, an absolute rule is to never remove plants or sod from existing remnants unless their destruction is imminent.

Matching species to a site's environment greatly increases the success of a planting. Sometimes additional considerations factor in. For example, small or highly visible prairie plantings (such as those replacing lawns around homes or schools) might selectively emphasize the neater-looking shorter native grasses and forbs. If taller, coarser species are included, they can be placed near the back of the planting. A mowed edge framing the planting boosts viewers' acceptance. A landscape architect or other knowledgeable person might help plan such native plantings.

Because it is difficult (although not impossible) to add diversity to an established prairie sod, the greatest number of species possible should be included in the initial seeding. Forbs should be emphasized at the expense of grasses, which are more aggressive. A high forb diversity will increase the stability, functionality, and longevity of a planting; provide flowers throughout the growing season; feed more insects and animals; and ensure the competitive exclusion of weeds. Before planting, be certain that a reconstruction site is not a remnant in disguise: burning and waiting to see if suppressed natives return are appropriate on all uncultivated land.

Prairie species respond to any number of proven planting techniques. Seed can be sown into tilled soils, soils with the surface barely scratched, or existing stubble. In general a firm seedbed helps. Fertilizers should be avoided: they only encourage exotic weeds. Seed can be sown by hand, with a broadcast spreader or hydroseeder, or planted by a drill. Plantings, once traditionally completed in June, are now undertaken in other seasons, particularly late October and early November. These late-fall plantings are thought to give an equal start to a wider variety of species, and sown seed is conditioned naturally by winter's cold and moisture.

Regardless of technique, consideration of weed cover and dormant weed seed is crucial. When sowing onto bare ground, eliminate weeds by tilling the soil several times prior to planting or by applying herbicide. Intensive weed treatment is recommended when dealing with very aggressive exotics such as smooth brome, reed canarygrass, or Canada thistle.

An alternative to bare-ground planting is interseeding prairie seed into established plant cover, which is then gradually eliminated by the introduced natives. This technique is favored on erosion-prone sites and on old fields or pastured sites where limited numbers of native plants may already be present. Interseeding is also used when spreading seed from prairie remnants into surrounding buffer lands covered primarily with exotic grasses. Burning or mowing a site before sowing helps establish seed-soil contact. Interseeding, which preserves native species already present, capitalizes on the structure of established vegetation and bypasses the first flush of weedy growth. However, interseedings require more time for establishment than do plantings on bare ground.

Postplanting weed control is essential. Mowing several times the first (and when necessary the second) year is crucially important. It suppresses weeds and grants tiny prairie seedlings the sun and moisture they require. Mowing new plantings also promotes root development, which decreases winter kill. Burning, which stimulates seedling growth, should begin as soon as fuel is sufficient, usually the third year. By then plantings are starting to look more like prairies than weed patches. Patience is crucial to prairie reconstruction efforts: prairie plants establish root systems first, and time is required for them to reach upward. Diverse plantings will continue to mature and exhibit new species for many years.

ONLY A FORTUNATE FEW have the privilege of restoring one of Iowa's native prairie remnants. Doing so involves the same activities as managing an established prairie planting: periodic fire, removal of invading woody vegetation (and stump treatment to prevent resprouting), and combating aggressive invasive plants at their first appearance (fig. 41). This triumvirate also constitutes the core of long-term remnant management. Additional activities might address erosion concerns and the reinstitution of prior water-flow patterns. With such management efforts, inconspicuous prairie species often reappear and return to their prior vigor, forming amazingly self-sufficient entities. Once again patience is called for, especially if working with pastures or other badly degraded remnants: keep burning, keep waiting, and species may return several years following initial restoration efforts.

While fire is the key to restoring remnants, burns may stimulate woody proliferation in sites with abundant shrubby growth. Or shrubby sites may lack sufficient fuel to carry a fire. In such cases, removal of weeds and shrubs through cutting, weeding, and careful spraying should precede prescribed burns.

Prescribed burns are often applied on average every three years to invigorate native plants, increase their leaf and seed production, and suppress the growth of woody and invasive plants. Moist sites require more frequent burning than dry sites. Removing the suffocating layer of thatch by fire produces maximum benefits. In areas where burns are impossible, mowing and raking and even light grazing are sometimes used to accomplish similar ends. In 2005 trial programs to link cattle ranchers with owners of prairie remnants were under way in the Loess Hills, and discussions were commencing about doing the same in the Little Sioux valley's and south-central Iowa's relatively abundant remnants. Stocking rates would be carefully managed. Ranchers would enhance native grasslands while obtaining long-term high-quality forage, and landowners would profit economically. These win-win linkages could bring ranchers higher profit margins with fewer cattle and also create an economic incentive for land-

Fig. 41. Constant effort is typically required to keep native prairie remnants free of invading shrubs and trees. While fire helps this cause, it often must be accompanied by cutting woody growth and treating newly cut stumps with appropriate herbicide to prevent resprouting. Photograph by Carl Kurtz.

owners to control woody invasion on prairie pastures (Kathy Koskovich, personal communication).

Because patchy disturbances of differing intensities and types are crucial to retaining a remnant's full complement of species, many land managers are attempting to vary the frequency and season of their burns. For example, they apply fire in spring one year but in fall or even summer the next. This avoids favoring any one plant type over another — for example, the proliferation of cool-season native and exotic plants following summer burns or warm-season grasses following late-spring burns. While late-spring burns do set back Kentucky bluegrass and other cool-season exotics, frequent spring burns tend to discourage overall species richness and favor the dominance of warm-season prairie grasses, traits also magnified by the absence of native herbivore grazing.

Care must be taken to consider the impacts of fire on all native residents. In particular, certain butterflies and other insects may be killed by fire. Thus burning half or less than half of a remnant in any given year is recommended, along with ignoring (rather than refiring) interspersed unburned patches and avoiding the burning of contiguous units in consecutive years. Surviving insects will then remain to repopulate burned areas. Fire undoubtedly also influences larger species. For example, the grasshopper sparrow shows a strong preference for nesting in low and thus recently burned grasslands, while the Henslow's sparrow nests in the opposite: rank unburned prairies and grasslands with thick litter.

One question remains, that of attempting to introduce new natives into existing reconstructions and remnants. Increasing the diversity of existing species-poor reconstructions through interseeding or planting seedlings is always desirable. Such additions are most easily made early, before highly competitive prairie grasses become established. Seed added to mature plantings will survive primarily in disturbed openings.

Some Iowa prairie enthusiasts reject efforts to increase the diversity of existing remnants through interseeding or importing sod. They point out that each remnant is a repository of genetic material and species adapted specifically to that site, and state that this unique genetic content must be protected to the greatest extent possible. These views certainly are important, especially in our best preserves.

However, some private landowners are introducing species into their lower-quality remnants. They argue that in today's fragmented landscape, a site's future diversity is often constrained because additional species cannot migrate freely, as they did in the past. Thus new species must be brought into degraded remnants, an act that both increases the range and future security of that species and augments the biodiversity of the remnant. Extreme care is required to add only site-appropriate and locally collected seed or plants.

Researchers in surrounding states have taken a more liberal view of the careful reintroduction of native plants, including endangered species, into selected remnants. They also are interseeding remnants in order to restore diverse plants typical of mature prairies and to establish a more complex vegetation structure. This practice is likely to attract consideration in Iowa in the future.

Rewatering the Land and Restoring Wetlands

Two of Iowa's most serious problems — loss of the topsoil that supports our agricultural economy and the declining quality of surface water and groundwater — are intimately tied to the post-1800 drainage and drying of Iowa's landscape. Efforts to reverse these losses rely on rewatering the land — enticing water to slow down, enter the soil, and trickle through it rather than letting water slip rapidly away over the ground surface. Encouraging water's infiltration into the soil provides many benefits. Water is purified as it flows through the ground. Slowly seeping water does not erode topsoil. Soil holds and stores water, releasing it gradually and thus minimizing floods and drought. Infiltrated waters recharge deep aquifers and also feed wetlands that create critical habitat for birds, amphibians, and many other wetland species. In short, rewatering the land is like harnessing a workhorse: it commands the land once again to express its potential, to become fully functional and work as it was meant to.

The myriad techniques for rewatering the land extend from rebuilding soil to remeandering ditched streams, from reflooding prairie potholes to revegetating wetlands. The following pages are not a handbook for building a wetland or rechanneling water's flow. Instead they present a sampling of the diverse efforts now under way, trusting that interested readers will obtain specific implementation techniques from governmental agencies, private consultants, or any of numerous publications. Excellent ecologically oriented wetland restoration guides include Galatowitsch and van der Valk 1994 and Jacobsen 2005.

Agriculturalists have, for many years, adopted structures and techniques that manage runoff: terraced slopes, grassed waterways, grass or woody buffer strips between croplands and streams, decreased grazing of streamside habitats. All these simultaneously slow soil erosion, limit runoff of agricultural chemicals, decrease streambank erosion, and provide wildlife habitat. No-till agriculture adds critical organic matter and porosity to the soil, increasing its permeability and infiltration while rebuilding soil structure and sequestering the greenhouse gas carbon dioxide. Planting permanent vegetation, especially prairie plants, does the same thing — only better. Prairie plants, with their dense foliage and deep roots, far surpass shallow-rooted exotics in slowing surface flows and pulling water downward.

Programs that encourage infiltration in urban and suburban areas have lagged behind those for farms but are equally if not more important. Runoff from construction sites often exceeds that from cropland. Soil compaction by heavy equipment greatly decreases soil porosity and magnifies future runoff, as do a city's many roads, parking lots, and other impermeable surfaces. These changes become significant when considering the amount of water falling on Iowa's land: with thirty-six inches of annual precipitation (a figure representative of eastern Iowa), a single acre receives nearly a million gallons of precipitation a year. In intensely developed areas, the majority is shed into storm sewers.

New green developments seek alternatives that minimize runoff by allowing water to infiltrate the soil or evaporate. The effort starts with maximizing green space and protecting existing tree cover and wetlands. Road networks and compacted surfaces are minimized and are drained into shallow depressions rather than underground sewer pipes. Drainage channels may be transformed into stormwater greenways, where creeks that overflow their banks flood grassy swales rather than housing sites. Drainage channels are often reshaped into shallow creekbeds that follow a meandering course. This slows water's flow and allows for water filtration and purification. The greenways commonly hold recreational trails and are appreciated as wildlife habitat, open space, alternative transportation corridors, and sites for exercise and nature appreciation (Girling et al. 2000).

Alternative housing developments are discussed in greater depth in chapter 7. These developments work to restore water quality and a healthier hydrology over the entire landscape. Wetlands constitute focal points for accomplishing the same goals. They are now routinely created or restored for their environmental benefits, recreational uses, and aesthetic appeal as well as in response to governmental regulations. Wetlands are also constructed for specialty purposes such as alternative wastewater treatment plants. The basic techniques are straightforward: in areas devoid of historic wetlands, a carefully selected site is excavated or dammed to form a basin that naturally fills with water. Increasingly, wetland projects are located on historic wetland sites where such artificial constructs are unnecessary. North-central Iowa's historic prairie potholes are restored by breaking the tiles or plugging and filling the ditches that once drained them. In river corridors, restoring historic wetlands might involve tearing down levees or reflooding oxbows.

Multiple public and private incentives encourage the voluntary creation and restoration of wetlands. Another major inducement stems from the U.S. Clean Water Act. This legislation stipulates that if construction damage to certain natural wetlands cannot be minimized or avoided, a wetland must be restored or created as a replacement, a process called mitigation. The regulation is tied to the governmental goal of no net loss of wetland area or ecological function in the United States, an annual goal that by 2004 had not yet been achieved. Professionals involved with mitigation programs are increasingly realizing that without demanding standards, careful planning, and long-term management, created and restored wetlands frequently fail to become healthy, diverse ecosystems (Zedler and Shabman 2001).

All wetland creations and restorations are praiseworthy because of their determination to reintegrate wetlands, along with their ecological functions, into Iowa's landscape. But bringing back water is merely the beginning of a lengthy effort. Nearly all created wetlands demonstrate a fatal flaw: they are defined by the presence of a few generalist species (fig. 42). Today's generic wetland is a cattail marsh or goose pond surrounded by reed canarygrass or other exotics. These easy-to-construct ponds and marshes, which are increasing in number, are often the result of wetland mitigation projects designed to replace shallower, species-rich sedge meadows, wet prairies, and ephemeral native wetlands that are being destroyed. Because wetland projects rarely encourage the sedges or more discriminating native species or the biological diversity that once heralded Iowa's many types of wetlands, our common understanding of wetlands and their species and traits is becoming more limited (Zedler 2003).

What can be done to address this shift? Most obviously, attempts should be made to restore and create wetland meadows with saturated soils, not just inundated marshes. And created wetlands should be actively revegetated with diverse native species, especially when they are isolated from other native wetlands. The assumption that once water is present, wetlands will appropriately revegetate themselves should be abandoned. This works well for weedy plants whose seed is readily transported by wind or waterfowl (such as cattails, common reed, and the ubiquitous reed canarygrass). But other species, including many sedges and wet-prairie forbs, have less mobile seeds and spread poorly, especially in today's fragmented landscape (Galatowitsch and van der Valk 1996).

Reflooded prairie potholes are often promoted as instant wetlands because wetland seeds from long ago sometimes remain in the soil. Native seeds are most likely to sprout on potholes that were drained fewer than twenty years ago and on sites that were poorly drained or pastured. But other reflooded sites need the rapid introduction of native seeds, plants, or soils containing fresh wetland seeds to avoid domination by a few weedy plants.

Iowa's public agencies and wetland consultants are increasingly aware of the need to create, restore, and revegetate a broad spectrum of wetlands and are trying to replace lost wetlands with constructs of a similar water and vegetation regime. But the task is not easy. Successful models are rare. Seeds and plants, even when available, are costly. Planting them is labor intensive. And the results are not necessarily successful or predictable. Even revegetated sites may convert to monocultures of cattails or other aggressive plants, which are stimulated by agricultural nutrients remaining in soils or washed in from surrounding slopes.

Fig. 42. Wetland restoration often results in the creation of ponds with the most common and aggressive species, such as the cattails bordering this water body. While ponds provide habitat for nondiscriminating species such as Canada geese, restoration efforts would do well to nurture less-common wetland types and species — for example, sedge meadows and their animal associates. Photograph by Carl Kurtz.

Today's landscapes, with their great variety of sites and disturbances, do not lend themselves to simple formulas. More research, field experimentation, and model projects are needed to determine what techniques will bring success, under what circumstances. Nevertheless, a few general principles can be suggested. Restoration projects will profit when multidisciplinary teams work together, so that the expertise of botanists, hydraulicans, and geologists supplements that of engineers. Wetlands that are restored or created should be characterized by diversity of both species and community types. They will flourish best if built as large, interconnected complexes, close to native wetlands from which native plants and animals can spread. Substantial buffers are recommended to shield the wetlands from nutrient drainage and other harmful intrusions. Created wetlands should mimic natural conditions as much as possible using the simplest constructions available. All projects should receive long-term monitoring and stewardship. Recommended management procedures include the cessation of heavy grazing, rerouting of cropland drainage, and control of invading woody and exotic species.

Restorative management efforts should also be applied to degraded native wetlands. However, care should be taken to prevent opening the soil of native communities to sunlight. Reed canarygrass seeds are ubiquitous and are light activated; the aggressive grass can be suppressed by healthy, diverse native growth, but give this invasive's seeds bare soil, and they assume dominance (Lindig-Cisnerso and Zedler 2002). In addition, high-quality native wetlands should not be used in ways that might destroy their biodiversity. Stormwater surges should under no circumstances be shunted into sedge meadows or wet prairies, which are certain to be damaged by the runoff's sediments, dissolved nutrients and pesticides, and widely fluctuating water levels. Created shallow marshlands that lack diverse native vegetation are better suited to catch stormwater surges and serve other demanding functions. Their tough cattails flourish in fluctuating waters laden with pesticides and nutrients.

Assigning functions to specific wetlands makes sense in today's fractured landscape. No single wetland can serve all needs. High-quality wetlands should be protected as providers of native biodiversity. Unfortunately, sensitive wetlands such as fens can never be re-created. Mitigation efforts that substitute common marshlands for fens or for sedge meadows, wet prairies, or wet woods rob us of the diversity that enriched Iowa's original wetland complexes. Any loss or degradation of specialized native wetlands furthers the decline of wetland sedges and orchids, frogs and salamanders, and the many other species that once inhabited Iowa's wetter lands.

No single action will restore the presettlement-era's infiltration hydrology or maintain our diverse wetlands and their inhabitants. But the combined actions of public and private landowners can slowly transform the land. Given time, knowledgeable action can entice soils and wetlands to mimic the hydrology of the historic landscape. This vision presents hope for a sustainable future, one whose benefits will reach from Iowa's slopes and swales all the way downriver to the Gulf of Mexico.

The Benefits of Restoration

Today growing numbers of citizens and land managers are applying restoration techniques to repair long-term damage to the land. While enjoying time spent outside and taking pride in their results, they are enhancing their knowledge of the land and deepening their bond to nature.

For most restorationists, these satisfactions are sufficient motivations. However, restoration efforts are working toward a far greater good. Returning integrity to Iowa's native communities is, in a sense, a way of immunizing our natural landscape against the disturbances that are sure to come. Consider global warming, for example. Computer models predict that Iowa's climate is likely to grow considerably warmer and probably drier in summertime. By the end of the twenty-first century, Iowa's climate may be generally like that of today's northwestern Mississippi (Union of Concerned Scientists 2004). Climate change is also expected to cause more frequent and more intense extreme weather events. A diversity of superbly drought-adapted prairie plants may be crucial in such a drought-prone future.

In coming years we are likely to face an environment that is less predictable and more degraded and a planet that is less responsive to our needs, where our options become ever more constrained. Restoration countermands these pressures. Restored, healthy native communities provide models and species for solving knotty environmental problems and for creating more sustainable agricultural systems. They also operate as sensitive early-warning systems for environmental health issues. Serving as buffers of environmental perturbations, they fight the functional unraveling of our physical world.

Restored communities with a full range of native diversity are innately healthier, more productive, and more capable of providing the free ecological services described throughout this book. These communities have a built-in resilience and stability that are lacking in simpler plant associations. Their many species and varied genetic strains express a broad amplitude of responses and abilities that guarantee their long-term sustainability. Prairies, for example, contain both drought-resistant and moisture-demanding plants, the first flourishing and flowering during dry periods and the second assuming dominance when precipitation increases. Biologically diverse, healthy communities can better handle future environmental intrusions such as invading exotic species. Conversely, plant productivity, resource utilization, community predictability, and ecosystem resilience and stability can falter as communities lose species. These qualities are especially low in species-poor communities such as agricultural croplands (Naeem et al. 1999).

Restoration is also helping combat one of the most significant losses of our time: declining global biodiversity. Earth's varied species and community types hold within them the genetic raw material for an environmentally healthy future. This biodiversity is society's most elementary natural resource, a form of biological capital that is crucial economically as well as environmentally. Biodiversity has always supplied genes for new products and processes, such as more productive crops and novel pharmaceuticals. As the environment morphs, input from our native germplasm is likely to become even more crucial for new technologies, foods, medicines, organic chemicals, fibers, industrial products, and other commodities. However, these benefits are threatened by today's extinction rates, which are now 1,000 to 10,000 times greater than the average throughout our planet's geological history and are rising (Pimm 2001: 7). With these rates, half or more of Earth's 10 million or more species could be lost by 2100 (Naeem et al. 1999: 2). This loss is being combated in Iowa — and around the globe — with every prescribed burn, interseeding of native plants, and attempt to restore nature's balance and health.

Diverse restored communities sustain humans in other ways. Each life-form teaches a different way of perceiving and knowing. Conversely, each animal or plant extinction is also an extinction of human experience. Once gone, that species' beauty and unique attributes will no longer be available to delight and engage the human spirit.

Finally, restoration can be seen as a way of coming home to Iowa, of building connectivity and community with nature, of enhancing our daily contact with the mysteries of life that surround us. The velvet blackness of Iowa's nights, the evening song of whip-poor-wills, wildflowers popping from hidden corners, indigo bunting nests curled against a low shrub, a mother badger waddling through the grass as she growls away threats to her young — these types of gifts are commonplace to those who work with nature in Iowa. With the granting of each such gift, we find that even as we work to restore Iowa's land, nature's creatures and nature's landscapes are restoring us.

7 Present Quandaries, Future Quests

The people would act today if the situation were clearly understood. The question is whether we do the right thing now or wait until the expense shall have increased a hundredfold. The preservation of springs and streams and forests will one day be undertaken as freely as the building of fences or bridges or barns. When that day comes, Iowa . . . shall yield to wisdom's guidance; forest and meadow shall receive each in turn intelligent and appropriate recognition; beauty will become an object of universal popular concern, and once again across the prairie state the clarified waters of a hundred streams will move in perennial freshness toward the great river and the sea.

— Thomas Macbride, 1898

We have seen how Iowa's natural world was transformed into a working landscape. Understanding the speed and magnitude of this transformation cannot help but direct our gaze toward the future. What will Iowa be like for tomorrow's citizens? How can managing the land's productivity blend with maintaining the quality of life through fostering native species and nature's ecological goods and services?

The following pages outline four major ways of doing this: preserving native remnants, restoring the land's health through properly managing remnants and reconstructing additional native communities, extending nature's benefits through establishing functional subsets of native species and natural processes, and building and maintaining an infrastructure for achieving these ends.

With its diversity of suggestions, this chapter acknowledges that there is no single method for achieving the desired end. Concerned citizens with differing abilities and inclinations can all find some effort that appeals to them. Each action, from planting a native garden to restoring dozens of acres, from talking to one's neighbors to changing governmental policies, will contribute to the final goal — as will many other actions not voiced here. There is plenty of room for creativity and exploration and plenty of need for picturing solutions outside the box. We need to think big.

This listing is not intended to ignore the magnitude of Iowa's environmental problems or the amount of effort required to reverse them. Anyone could rightly claim that funding and education will never be sufficient, that economic and personal gain will always supersede nature's needs, or that society's values will never encompass the worth of other species. These claims may indeed be true.

But dreams can be powerful, and ideas planted and given time to grow have a strange way of becoming reality. Some of this chapter's suggestions are already maturing. Note, for example, the growing interest in combating invasives, the increasing use of prescribed woodland fire, and the expanding number of prairies and savannas that are being resurrected from grazed stubble and brushy overgrowth. All were unimaginable a few decades earlier. With time, small actions have the potential to transform our state in a big way.

Thus the following pages, presented as a highway map with numerous alternative routes, all point toward a single endpoint: an Iowa that fosters life for its native plants and animals and by doing so creates a healthful, sustainable, and increasingly beautiful natural environment for its human residents.

Goal 1: Preserve Remaining Remnants

Preserving remaining native remnants must be the core of any program to save nature in Iowa. Distinct remnant communities with unique coherence to site ensure the long-term survival of Iowa's diverse native species and genetic material. Remnants constitute crucial sources of locally adapted seeds. They serve as models for reconstructing native communities elsewhere and for reintegrating ecological functions into intensively managed landscapes. Considering the small percentage of Iowa they now cover, native remnants play a disproportionately large role in retaining the integrity of Iowa's landscape and maintaining our quality of life.

Yet even today remnants are being plowed under, used as fill dirt, logged improperly, covered with roadways, converted to housing sites, drained, filled in, and generally ignored — activities that have been ongoing since settlement. While these travesties are sometimes committed knowingly, often they are done in ignorance, without knowledge that anything special is being lost. So the questions arise: How can remnants be recognized? Which ones should be preserved, and how?

SEARCHING OUT REMNANTS

Preservation efforts should attempt to locate and perpetuate the full spectrum of Iowa's native biological and community diversity: varied prairies, oak woodlands, and bottomland forests as well as sedge meadows, fens, and native marshlands. These communities will provide habitat not only for now-common plants and animals that may be declining but also for rare species that are sensitive indicators of environmental quality. Because adequate habitat for adaptable generalists remains abundant, preservation preferences should be slanted toward species with very specific habitat requirements. A widespread spectrum of protected sites will ensure the future of genetic varieties adapted to specific environments. (To state the obvious, remnant preservation does not extend to wildlands dominated by nonnative species or highly degraded plant associations, even though such areas may provide valuable open space and recreational lands.)

Ideal nature preserves are large enough to ensure perpetuity of their inhabitants and to carry out expected ecological functions. They are sited near other remnants that effectively multiply their size and integrity. They hold a full spectrum of appropriate native species and are sufficiently intact so that management is not overwhelming.

This ideal is rare. In reality, we must work with what we have: small native patches, incomplete communities, inappropriate associations of species, and native communities infiltrated by exotic species. Native plants commonly are suppressed and shrouded by woody growth that requires clearing and fire before a site's potential can be assessed. In such degraded sites, one might wonder just how many native species or how much native coverage constitutes a remnant worth saving.

The answer depends in part on one's location: an isolated, degraded prairie in the Loess Hills might be ignored in favor of one more intact, while any such remnant punctuating north-central Iowa's vast croplands is to be treasured. However, as a broad generalization, any natural component in Iowa, even a patch of a few species, is worthy of consideration. Small preserves are often crucial for saving rare plants or animals or uncommon associations. Even if they are not restored, incomplete patches can provide seed for nearby, more complete remnants.

In an ideal world, a statewide inventory would identify, map, and track all of Iowa's quality native remnants. The Iowa Department of Natural Resources (Iowa DNR) initiated such an inventory in 1981 and continues to map and describe the best of our remnants. A few Iowa counties are producing more detailed natural areas inventories. Because of insufficient funding, all Iowa inventories are far from complete.

In spite of this lack, there are firm guidelines for searching out Iowa's remaining native communities, summarized here from previous chapters. The bulk of Iowa's remnants remain where agricultural use has been least intensive, that is, where slopes are steepest and soils are poorest. Thus most remnants are found in five locales: northeastern Iowa's rugged hills and blufflands, southern (and especially south-central) Iowa's rolling hills, western Iowa's Loess Hills, northwestern Iowa's Little Sioux valley, and river valleys and adjacent hills throughout the state. All these regions contain both prairies and remnant oak woodlands. Remnant wetlands are mostly limited to lowlands and river valleys, with some sites in north-central Iowa's cropland now undergoing prairie pothole restoration.

Other regions of the state are not devoid of remnants. Pastured lands anywhere, where not intensively plowed, constitute potential remnant prairie. Small plots far from roads, in settlement-era cemeteries, along fences or railroad tracks, or on other "wastelands" often contain patches of native plants. Semi-shaded roadside rights-of-way are significant refuges for savanna species, plants that once were common but today have very few sanctuaries. In urban settings, blufflands and ravines are often badly degraded but may offer safe havens for natives and also be geologically interesting. Even formerly cultivated agricultural lands occasionally sparkle with lady's tresses orchids or other wonders. Finding Iowa's remnant species and communities requires constant vigilance, a good eye, and openness to illogical possibilities. Assistance in the process can be received from the governmental offices listed in chapter 6, private consultants, and knowledgeable botanists.

METHODS OF LAND PROTECTION

The surest means of permanent protection may be transfer of title or permanent conservation easement to a public agency or private land conservation organization. Because of funding limitations, preservation through purchase will always be limited to a small number of Iowa's highest-quality sites. With 98 percent of Iowa's land lying in private ownership, the fate of most natural areas depends on the intentions of private citizens and local residents and on their willingness to invest energy as well as funds in a remnant's future.

A growing number of individuals and groups of individuals with pooled resources are buying former agricultural land in south-central Iowa and elsewhere for recreational or conservation purposes. The purchasers enjoy hunting, fishing, nature study, and weekend retreats, and some owners work to rebuild the native character of their land — an activity that should be encouraged. Some profit financially from their land (for example, by leasing hunting rights, careful harvesting of timber, or allowing well-managed grazing) and channel the money back into land management and restoration. Sometimes conservation

buyers, realizing the scarcity of public funding, purchase choice parcels specifically to preserve the land's natural features.

All types of owners often come to treasure their land's natural features, only
to risk having the features destroyed when ownership changes hands. To prevent
such losses, conservation-minded landowners can consider diverse means of voluntary permanent land protection. With a conservation easement, for example,
a person retains ownership and control of the land but permanently restricts certain forms of use. A conservation agency or organization, designated as holder
of the easement, helps monitor land usage. Some governmental cost-sharing
programs can help purchase easements for land with native communities. Or
sometimes a conservation organization or a local individual purchases a parcel's
development rights to ward off future development. A landowner might retain
ownership of a remnant during the owner's lifetime but bequeath the land to a
conservation agency or organization, or perhaps donate the land while alive but
retain full use until death. Conservation groups increasingly request financial
donations to help manage land that they are protecting. Many voluntary protection arrangements have tax benefits, as does bargain sale of land — selling a
remnant to a conservation group at less than fair-market value. The Iowa Natural Heritage Foundation offers free and private consultations regarding these
and many other voluntary preservation techniques and can help ensure that the
owner's desires are legally binding to future owners. Local land trusts, county
conservation boards, and private conservation groups can also assist with preservation efforts.

Unprotected remnants commonly are purchased by land developers, with
local residents then attempting to come to the remnant's defense. Noble as their
efforts may be, attempts to stave off the rumble of approaching bulldozers are
rarely satisfying. Proactive efforts to preserve known native lands are usually far
easier, less expensive, and more successful than reactive efforts.

Remnants on publicly owned land are held in the public trust and should
be treated as such. They should receive absolute and unquestioned protection,
regardless of the land's primary use. This implies performing an inventory to
evaluate each public parcel's natural features and then managing remnants
appropriately.

The fate of rural remnants remains inexorably linked to agricultural policies
and row-crop subsidies that can promote the plowing of remnants and their
conversion into cropland. Massive restructuring would be required to trans-

form federal incentive programs into true green-payment programs that would instead recognize and protect native lands and their environmental services.

Loss of remnants and wildlife habitat is especially high near Iowa's larger cities, where suburban sprawl is pushing into hilly land bordering rivers. While seen as prime development land because of its natural beauty and poor agricultural performance, rougher land often contains abundant native remnants, in particular mature oak woodlands (or, in the Loess Hills, intact prairie). Sprawl can be combated by policies that revitalize city centers, promote in-filling of existing city lots, and prohibit development of open-space areas outside urban growth boundaries.

Where sprawl is inevitable, forward-thinking developers are trying to preserve their land's natural characteristics and native remnants by nontraditional placement of structures. Sometimes housing sites are popped into small holes cut into intact woodlands; other times houses are strung along roads that wind through a remnant, leaving large common areas as outlots. These or other attempts to preserve large undeveloped outlots within subdivisions are certainly preferable to scattering houses throughout a remnant. However, even developments with large undeveloped outlots often cut large intact remnants into small pieces. In addition to resulting fragmentation-related problems, many species are lost and native diversity drops, even in the best-designed woodland subdivisions (Gerken 2005). Ideally, large mature oak remnants and all prairie sites would be spared intensive use; younger degraded woody associations and exotic grasslands are abundant enough to meet development needs. If development of remnant land is unavoidable, the best option is to cluster houses on small lots next to or just inside the remnant, leaving the largest possible uninterrupted common area as intact natural land to be enjoyed by all residents. When outlots are created, it is critically important to stipulate their protection in the property's title to prevent their subdivision in future years.

Whenever any form of development penetrates a remnant, fragmentation should be controlled by keeping structures and nonnative plantings to an absolute minimum. Roads or other transportation routes should be as short and narrow as possible, with one corridor used to fill multiple uses. Trails should be recognized as routes whereby invasives and other disruptive elements enter remnants and should be monitored as such.

Efforts to reduce the impact of construction on native remnants — for example, through clustering development — can be encouraged by zoning regulations. Sensitive-areas ordinances restrict development on the most environmentally fragile lands and remnants. They require a habitat assessment and predevelopment inventory of a tract's natural features. Even without sensitive-areas ordinances, cities and counties could require a predevelopment inventory for all large developments, with guidance then given on how best to manage a site's natural features.

Comprehensive land-use plans, backed up by responsible zoning and ordinances, are urgently needed to guide growth in manners that are advantageous for society and for natural systems. New approaches might include considerations such as the following. Rezoning decisions commonly are made on the basis of a site's Corn Suitability Rating, with housing developments prohibited on agricultural land with a high rating. Perhaps Iowa now needs a parallel "Nature Suitability Rating" system, which prohibits development of lands with high natural or biodiversity values. Or consider Johnson County's Native Plant Community Policy (Johnson County Secondary Roads Department 2006). This stipulates that the county will protect the best remnants found in roadside rights-of-way. These types of forward thinking can help tip the land-use balance back toward favoring native communities and ecological health.

Goal 2: Restore the Land

Once native remnants have been identified and preserved, these communities will benefit from restoration and appropriate management. Restoration allows native remnants to express their best characteristics. Reinstituting natural processes such as regular burns increases the native diversity and coverage of native understory, even in the healthiest oak woodlands and prairie remnants. Proper management also safeguards remnants from pressures creeping in from surrounding lands — everything from sediment runoff and pesticide drift to invasive plants and exploding deer populations.

The restoration techniques outlined in chapter 6 should become routine components of remnant-preservation efforts. Restoration techniques are now implemented on public lands and private preserves, although efforts often fall short of the remnants' needs. The increasing numbers of Iowans moving into rural and semiwild settings should assume that restoring remnants on their land and eliminating invasives are some of the costs and responsibilities of living in these beautiful settings. Otherwise residents are likely to realize, often too late, that "leaving native remnants to nature" means watching their transformation to thickets of the most aggressive exotic plants.

Goal 2 includes a second important component: restoring the land by reconstructing native communities from scratch on cleared or weedy land. Reconstruction is the only way to expand native communities in Iowa — for example, to increase significantly the amount of functional prairie. Well-established techniques now produce prairie plantings that, if carried out correctly, commonly bring satisfying results within a few years. In contrast, techniques for creating diverse native wetlands (wet meadows, ephemeral ponds, and the like) are still in their infancy. And reconstructing diverse oak woodlands from scratch requires an extremely long-term vision. With time, however, woodland reconstruction may become more common. Even now, the encouragement of scattered young bur or white oaks in prairie reconstructions would bring pleasing variety.

SHAPING THE RESTORED LANDSCAPE

Intensive restoration is best invested in the highest-quality remnants available, which have the best probability of success. Restored communities should be as large as possible and should be shaped to minimize contact with nonrestored sites and outside influences. Those approximating a circle or square will have the least amount of edge. Efforts should focus on restoring the full range of appropriate communities and considering the integrated needs of all native inhabitants, maximizing habitat for diverse types of animals as well as plants.

These are the ideals. The reality of any remnant restoration will depend not only on local interest and energy but also on location. Even tiny prairie restorations may be significant where remnants are rare, while greater expectations will be held for remnants in south-central Iowa's extensive pasturelands and the Loess Hills.

Unlike native remnants, reconstructed communities allow considerable latitude in vision and design. Prairie plantings are now common on corporate and industrial lands, with plantings also popping up — and rooting down — across Iowa. Each isolated native planting adds to the health of the whole, regardless of location or size.

But why not think even more creatively about maximizing the results of remnant restoration and reconstruction efforts? What about, for example, establishing urban nature preserves by encouraging strings of prairie plantings and native shrubs that loop through backyards and parks, along creeks, and through urban ravines and other unbuildable sites? Such narrow integrated reconstructions would create habitat for animals such as birds and butterflies, bringing native animals as well as plants into close proximity with the broadest number of people. Or why not aim for a prairie planting in every town in Iowa or an "All Iowa Garden" of native plants at every grade school? Even small plantings would cultivate children's sense of place, tying them to Iowa's history, heritage, and culture as well as natural history. A single dedicated parent or teacher and a supportive school board could implement this activity.

In rural areas, an expansive meshwork of diverse native grasslands, woodlands, forests, and wetlands would service surrounding agricultural land. What if Iowa's public agencies were to adopt seriously the goal of restoring and maximizing biodiversity on all native remnants on lands they now own? They might then surround and supplement the restored remnants with reconstructions that effectively enlarge the core remnants and also act as protective buffers. Farm programs could encourage diverse native plantings on interspersed agricultural lands, and other organizations and landowners could supplement the public meshwork with private projects. Connectivity would be important: tying the restorations together with corridors of natural habitat would allow members of different communities to migrate and interbreed. These effectively larger natural areas might allow rarer native species to once again become functional members of Iowa's landscape.

Restoring remnants and reconstructing natural habitat along Iowa's rivers could provide multiuse areas to meet people's recreational needs, stimulate the local economy, and simultaneously create superb habitat for diverse nesting and migrating animals (fig. 43). Consider the possibility of a lacework of restored river bottoms providing recreational trails, boating access, primitive campgrounds, and sites for fishing and nature observation, with wooded, wetland, and prairie buffer strips that catch and filter surface waters.

Intergrading meshworks of healthy remnants and native plantings would take a big step toward reestablishing the full spectrum of nature in Iowa. The resulting large units could ensure long-term community sustainability and allow species to adapt to ongoing climate change and other challenges. Interconnected preserves, acting in consort, would comprise a larger functional role than the sum of their parts. Spanning the state on lands that were least fit for intensive agriculture, this meshwork would not decrease Iowa's working landscape. Instead it would support and increase the productivity of interspersed agricultural lands. In a win-win situation for both agriculture and nature, a

Fig. 43. Many of Iowa's rivers and their adjacent lands still provide interconnected corridors of wildness that could be restored and developed for multiple uses, to the benefit of people, native animals and plants, and the working landscape. Photograph by Carl Kurtz.

well-executed meshwork could provide the many supportive ecological services described throughout this book, while providing a safe harbor where Iowa's declining and aging natives could once again reproduce, repopulate the land, and carry out their innate functions.

GETTING THE JOB DONE

Sources of restoration information and assistance have been listed in chapter 6. Important as these are, they do not answer a crucial question: how does one supply the necessary physical labor? This single resource always constricts the number, size, and intensity of remnant restoration and reconstruction efforts, which can consume unlimited time and physical energy. While work decreases once a community is in good health, the need to manage native lands never ends. Who then will provide the necessary energy to get the job done?

Successful remnant restorations and reconstructions are frequently under-taken by individuals or single families, who consider their efforts recreational as well as productive. But creative thinking can swell the number of much-needed hands. Friends, family members, and neighbors can be solicited as volunteers. So can teenagers from multiple groups (church, 4-H, Scouts, Future Farmers of America, and other community and service groups). Doing so taps the energy of youth while exposing our next generation to the land and its needs. County conservation boards, nature centers, local parks, land trusts, and other nature-based organizations are increasingly holding work days on nature preserves and also soliciting and training local residents for jobs such as seed collecting and planting. Iowa's minimum security prisoners have been used to manage public restorations. Many learn valuable skills in the process. In addition, prisoners have harvested and processed large quantities of native prairie seeds, providing previously unimagined quantities of seeds and seedlings for public plantings and wildlife habitat across the state. Similarly, labor for private restorations might be solicited from minor offenders who are legally required to perform public-service jobs.

The trick is to tap into the energy of any local group willing to donate out-of-doors volunteer time. Why couldn't corporations and service groups, for example, consider a variation of the "adopt a roadside" program and "adopt a prairie" instead? Creative approaches will bring out the crowds. A work day can be positioned as a community event accompanied by snacks or a picnic or drawings for nature guidebooks. In Iowa City, a late-fall prairie seeding on public property was promoted as a holiday gift that participants were giving to Earth. Such activities invariably become celebrations of the land, much enjoyed by attendees.

Remnants and reconstructions located in or near population centers benefit from an abundance of potential volunteers. This is also true in subdivisions with common lands, where homeowners' associations can share information and or-ganize work days. These associations can provide a tremendous service by devel-oping and showcasing restoration demonstration projects that stimulate similar restorations by other groups. Both management and restoration efforts within subdivisions produce many benefits, including a sense of shared endeavor that increases community cohesiveness, the beauty of the resulting natural areas, and the tremendous pride that comes from watching the rebirth of degraded land.

These advantages might also be felt in cities and suburbs where neighborhood associations organize restoration activities in city parks or plant and maintain prairies on city grounds. Neighborhoods can also unite in attacking invasive plants, which is easier if done in a group led by someone who understands successful eradication. Neighbors unable to participate in physical labor can be involved in other ways. For example, everyone can be invited to a restoration's burning of brush piles, with the event pegged as a marshmallow roast. All such events foster neighborliness and involvement in the natural world and help create the sense of caretaking that our natural world so desperately needs.

Some landowners choose to hire restoration services. Luckily teenagers needing summer or weekend work remain abundant, and the number of knowledgeable consultants and land management professionals is increasing in Iowa. In addition, some landscaping and lawn management companies are emphasizing the use of native species and becoming involved in controlling invasives, interests that should be encouraged among all such businesses.

Perhaps the most important, and the most feared, aspect of restoration is the application of prescribed fire. Efforts are badly needed to reintegrate fire onto the landscape. Training courses and the creation of well-qualified burn crews would help fill the need, and fortunately the availability of both is increasing in Iowa. In 2005 the Iowa DNR hired a cooperative fire specialist to initiate and coordinate fire training statewide and form a well-qualified Iowa fire crew, which will work to increase prescribed fire and provide emergency firefighting. Similar prescribed fire specialists have been hired in the Loess Hills and south-central Iowa. Encouraging landowners' acceptance of prescribed fire is also important, as are local regulations. Cities, for example, need to allow certified fire crews to carry out prescribed burns. Proactive efforts such as integrating smoke permits into subdivision covenants would also move restoration forward. The formation of the Iowa Fire Council in 2006, created to promote public understanding and to enhance training and the exchange of information among prescribed fire practitioners, should increase the safe use of prescribed fire (Inger Lamb, personal communication).

A related item is ensuring the availability of necessary restoration equipment through the creation of regional loan centers. Equipment banks of items such as flappers, backpack sprayers, loppers, and mowers could be established and managed by county conservation boards, local land trusts, prairie clubs, or similar groups.

All restoration activities will be eased by the creation of regional coalitions to share information and implement necessary action. In 2005 Iowa claimed two excellent partnerships that envisioned landscape-scale restorations spanning thousands of acres and multiple ownerships. The Stewardship Committee of the Loess Hills Alliance, created in 1999, has brought together private landowners, organizations, and public agencies to plan regional restoration goals and work on achieving them. Its management plan and hired staff have pushed land managers to envision prescribed burns covering tens of thousands of acres per year, carried out across ownership boundaries. The alliance has worked to educate private landowners, hold fire ecology and training workshops, tap cost-sharing monies, and create a mobile fire crew that executes prescribed burns in the Loess Hills each fall and spring. The energetic activities and private-public partnerships demonstrated by this group provide a positive example for the rest of Iowa. Because of the size and significance of Loess Hills prairies and their rare species, there are many programs to ensure their permanent protection and to work with private landowners who are holding prairies.

The Southern Iowa Oak Savanna Alliance, formed in 2005 and modeled after the Loess Hills Alliance, is dedicated to protecting, restoring, and maintaining oak woodlands in south-central Iowa and adjacent Missouri. Similar partnerships of any size would be an excellent means of restoring Iowa's other regional landscapes. The citizen-led watershed councils that are now emerging in Iowa can be invited to consider biodiversity protection as a goal.

Goal 3: Extend Nature's Benefits into the Working Landscape

Iowa's natural integrity is best reclaimed by restoring remnants and reconstructing a diversity of native communities. But even with concerted effort, land coverage by intact native communities is likely to remain relatively small. Does this mean that the vast majority of Iowa — our working agricultural lands, cities, and suburbs — must remain devoid of nature's functions and native species? Not at all. To an extent, nature can be extended into working lands by dissecting natural communities and reinserting individual elements anywhere. Those elements may be individual native species or small clusters of natives. They may be nonnative plant communities that mimic nature sufficiently to serve as habitat for native animals. Or they may be structures that substitute for natural objects or organisms. By identifying and promoting any such individual elements of the natural world, nature's benefits can be extended throughout the working landscape. Recognizing and seeking ways to make these piece-by-piece extensions will be far cheaper, easier, and more effective than struggling to replace nature's functions artificially.

Thus two mandates should guide us. First, wherever possible, use native plants and encourage native animals rather than exotic species imported from other parts of the globe. Selectively plant natives anywhere and everywhere, in small or large plantings, simple or diverse associations, and urban or rural landscapes.

Second, identify specific processes or functions carried out by native communities and seek environmentally friendly methods to mimic these in human-transformed landscapes. To clarify this concept, consider the following example that focuses on birds and insect control. Today nuisance insects are commonly controlled by pesticides and electronic mechanisms. Such modern devices are mimics of the services that have been provided by birds and bats for thousands of years. Native Americans realized the benefits of insect-feeding purple martins and attracted them to villages by hanging gourds that the birds used for nesting. The martins' preference for nesting near humans later encouraged Iowa's farmers to erect martin houses near their gardens, a practice that is still common among the Amish. The building of martin and bat houses would be an environmentally friendly way of replacing artificial bug-controllers with natural ones.

Consider also a second bird-related example. Many of Iowa's birds now nest and feed in human-created landscapes, which serve as mimics of the birds' original habitat. For some birds, original savannas have been replaced by the scattered trees of urban areas. For others, woody in-filling on pastureland and suburban outlots has replaced prairie thickets of hazelnut and wild plum. Some prairie nesters seek out open pasturelands, alfalfa fields, hayfields, or rural set-aside plantings, including those dominated by exotic plants.

When human landscapes are recognized as substitutes for native habitat, bird-friendly management practices become more obvious. For example, setting back the cutting of hayfields until after July 15 would allow the fledging of the first brood of bobolink chicks and other grassland nesters that are killed by earlier mowings; the water level in reservoirs could be managed for migrating shore-birds that now probe their muddy shorelines rather than those of natural marsh-lands. (Reservoir levels currently are managed primarily for migrating ducks and geese that are desired by hunters.) Again, partially undeveloped suburban yards could be recognized and maintained as nurseries for birds and butterflies. Following such simple guidelines as well as other commonsense practices (keeping cats indoors, retaining dead trees for nesting, reducing pesticide use) could transform exotic landscapes into bird-friendly mimics of presettlement Iowa.

CITYSCAPES

Urban areas, with their compact populations and high use of resources, place tremendous demands on surrounding rural lands for food, energy, waste absorption, and the like. The urban landscape itself is often cleared of native species and natural processes, exacerbating the city's inability to handle basic environmental processes such as flowing stormwater and insect outbreaks.

In some locales, green developments, smart growth, and a variety of other approaches are attempting to guide land development in a more environmentally sustainable fashion. Traditional low-density subdivisions are giving way to developments that allow the landscape to retain and express its native features. The new developments tend toward compact arrangements of houses. Roadways and other paved surfaces as well as extensive stormwater drainage systems are minimized, reducing use of resources and costs of infrastructure construction and maintenance.

In conservation subdivisions, small lot sizes are counterbalanced by large common areas. These areas provide room for protection and restoration of native remnants and installation of native plantings, especially along streams and wetlands. Trail systems encourage alternative transportation such as biking and walking. These features allow ample interaction with nature and passive outdoor recreation and typically provide substantial open space and natural beauty. Home values rise accordingly.

Low impact development (LID) engages techniques that mimic the prairie's handling of precipitation. These techniques can be applied to new developments but also can be retrofitted to existing urban or suburban landscapes, including relatively dense housing or commercial developments. In conventional cities and suburbs, rainwater and its pollutants are flushed off the land into storm sewers and streams as rapidly as possible, creating a variety of environmental problems. In contrast, LID uses small-scale, decentralized management practices and structures to deal with stormwater close to its source. LID adopts an infiltration-based hydrology rather than the conventional runoff-driven hydrology. This shift reduces the volume of runoff, recharges groundwater, and cleanses the water, thus reducing water pollution and the flooding potential of small storms even while providing valuable wildlife habitat.

LID's prairie-mimicking systems start by protecting, buffering, and restoring

Fig. 44. Rain gardens are one of low impact development's many ways of infiltrating water into the land and thus helping to minimize the impact of housing developments. Here stormwater from the street feeds into a roadside garden planted in part with native species, which both coax the runoff deep into the soil and transpire it into the atmosphere rather than channeling it into sewers and rivers. Photograph courtesy Barr Engineering Co., Minneapolis, reproduced with permission. Project location: Burnsville, Minnesota.

the land's natural drainage systems, riparian corridors, ravines, and wetlands rather than reshaping or eliminating them. Natural infiltration systems are then supplemented by landscaped depressions. Designed to catch and infiltrate runoff from impervious surfaces, these depressions occur in various forms. Small, carefully planted depressions, or rain gardens (fig. 44), are complemented by more highly engineered bioretention cells capable of servicing impervious surfaces such as parking lots. Bioswales — vegetated water-conveyance systems — provide an alternative to storm sewers. Impermeable ground covers (for example, paved surfaces, asphalt roofing, compacted turf) yield to pervious surfaces that soak up water, such as permeable paving blocks, porous asphalt, pervious concrete, and green roofs. New LID techniques emerge regularly in this rapidly developing field (Girling et al. 2000).

Other methods for restoring the land's functionality focus on reintegrating native plantings into city and suburban landscapes. Gardening and landscaping with natives can be done nearly anywhere to advantage. For example, simple native plantings often cover LID infiltration structures as well as other types of sites. Wherever established, native plants pump organic matter into the soil, which further increases permeability. The dense, deep roots of prairie plants do this especially well and also help rebuild compacted urban soils. Here and elsewhere perennial plantings of prairie grasses and forbs are low in care and maintenance. Because of prairie plants' adaptations to Iowa's climate and soils, they seldom need the watering, mulching, or protection from frost required by other garden plants. Native low-fuss prairie gardens allow people to get to know prairie plants and the wildlife they attract on a small scale, one species at a time. They offer a gentle introduction to prairies as a whole, often opening the door to more intensive prairie involvement. Butterfly gardens and plantings specifically for birds are variations of native garden and landscaping efforts.

In cities and suburbs, broadly spaced trees and shrubs mimic Iowa's presettlement savannas. Here again native plantings are generally more attractive to native wildlife, which recognize these plants and are adapted to their use. Birds frequently nest and feed in these settings and use them as travel corridors. In addition, woody plantings add beauty and ecological function to urban areas. When knowledgeably placed, urban trees and shrubs produce multiple benefits: they reduce heating and air-conditioning demands, shelter buildings from the wind, cleanse the air, and decrease water and noise pollution. They increase water infiltration and storage and eventually may serve as a harvestable natural resource (Mark Vitosh, personal communication).

Nonnative plantings may share only a portion of these advantages and also can introduce problem species that eventually spread into wildlands. In towns, even mildly invasive plants threaten nearby wooded lands and parks, which often have exceedingly high concentrations of Japanese barberry, bush honeysuckle, oriental bittersweet (not the lovely native bittersweet), and other exotic landscaping shrubs. Modern subdivisions and rural housing sites that interfinger with wooded lands encourage major spread of invasives into nearby natural areas.

Using natives for landscaping and gardening will go a long way toward eliminating such invasive spread from managed to native lands. However, doing native plantings well requires knowledge and care. Good general rules include making sure you know what you are buying. Buy only from reputable nurseries, and question landscaping firms and nurseries about whether their stock is native to Iowa or includes potentially problematic exotics. Remind them about the problem of invasives. Request a sterile potting medium when ordering nursery stock. Avoid discount stores, which not uncommonly sell problem species. And watch carefully for invasives inadvertently introduced by contaminated equipment, in soils clinging to rootstock or in planting soils, and in seed mixtures. Avoid cultivars of native plants. Additional comments on seed and stock selection are given in chapters 4 and 6.

Individuals can help control the spread of invasives by getting to know problem plants and watching for them in yards and parks. Eradicate them as soon as they appear. Encourage your neighbors to do likewise. Some invasives (such as reed canarygrass) are already so widespread that restricting them is nearly impossible; these species are usually eliminated only in high-quality preserves. But invasives that are not yet commonplace in Iowa can be halted by alert landowners who attack them with knowledge and energy.

Given native plants' obvious advantages, city governments should encourage their planting both by example and by ordinance. For example, governments can plant natives on city-owned lands and along roadsides and require that all city shade trees be native species. Cities can improve water quality by encouraging buffer plantings of natives along urban streams and wetlands. At the very least, city governments should forbid planting of known invasives and allow the carefully controlled burns that stimulate prairie plantings. Subdivisions can follow suit — for example, by adopting a policy of landscaping only with natives. This stipulation could also be written into a subdivision's covenants, as could an agreement to reconstruct native plant communities on a given percentage of outlots or common lands.

A COUNTRY VIEW

Agricultural lands, like their urban counterparts, pose tremendous challenges to sustainability. Many believe that current midwestern farming practices not only are incapable of maintaining environmental integrity and a healthy rural social structure but also are incongruous with the long-term perpetuation of agriculture itself. Signs of these concerns frequent the news media: manure spills and fish kills, excessive nitrogen fertilizer in surface water and groundwater, loss of topsoil, human respiratory illnesses and annoying odors associated with confined animal feeding operations, native wildlife and prairies teetering on the brink. The personal and social costs of our shrinking rural towns and farming population are tremendous. Proposed solutions to these problems are abundant and complex. This discussion considers only a few that relate to biodiversity:

diversifying the agricultural landscape through returning prairie-mimicking perennial plantings to farms and redirecting the mammoth program of federal agricultural subsidies to better support environmental health. Both suggest that farming practices can be tempered by natural processes to the advantage of agriculture and native species alike.

Since the mid 1900s, environmental degradation in Iowa has been strongly linked to the tremendous quantities of inorganic fertilizers, pesticides, and fossil fuels that have been used for growing expanses of corn and soybeans (fig. 45). These inputs stand in stark contrast to the self-sufficiency of Iowa's original prairie ecosystems and to the more limited demands of Iowa's earlier, more diversified agricultural systems that interwove livestock production, row crops, and perennial grasslands. Many think that the key to agricultural sustainability depends on converting a substantial portion of today's row crops back to perennial growth, thus reinstating such plants' inherent functional benefits.

Would it be excessive to work toward covering half of Iowa with perennial growth? Already, one-third of Iowa's land is under the permanent cover of grasslands, woody growth, and wetlands, the other two-thirds being corn and soybeans. What about then striving to transform one-fifth of the permanent cover (10 percent of Iowa) into native vegetation? Inserting permanent cover into Iowa's largest expanses of corn and soybeans — for example, as buffer strips along drainages — would be especially important. Retirement of vulnerable row-cropped land makes common sense as a means of safeguarding our land's future agricultural productivity and environmental integrity.

A variety of approaches for increasing Iowa's perennial cover have been proposed. The most forthright promotes increasing the diversity of crops and farming systems as well as native biodiversity. It uses pre-1950s farming systems as a starting point and suggests the widespread reintegration of livestock as well as perennial grasslands. Pastures and hayfields would once again provide havens for prairie-mimicking plants and wildlife. Examining historic integrated farming systems and supplementing them with judicious use of modern agricultural techniques could point us toward an economically and environmentally sustainable future, one that becomes even more appealing when the true costs of today's environmental degradation are acknowledged.

As an added benefit, reinstating well-managed grasslands could provide habitat for native plants, just as in earlier decades. Research is showing that native perennial grasses and legumes can be seeded directly into existing exotic pastures, producing a win-win result: they increase native biodiversity and work

Fig. 45. Iowa's homogeneous croplands, which on the state's flattest regions cover the land to the near-total exclusion of self-sufficient native communities, stand in stark contrast to smaller pre–World War II farms, which incorporated livestock and far greater crop diversity. Today's expanses of row crops require tremendous investments of chemical fertilizers, pesticides, and fossil fuels, all of which exact a high environmental cost. Photograph by Carl Kurtz.

their magic, integrating carbon and water deep into soils. And the pasture's grazing value increases: native grasses, which grow mostly during warm summer months, provide forage during those months when spring- and fall-growing exotic grasses grow slowly. Warm-season natives also are better at withstanding drought (Jackson and Jackson 2002).

The value of diverse pasturelands that contain native grasses can be enhanced even more through carefully managed rotational grazing: the practice of regularly moving cattle (or pigs or poultry) from one temporarily fenced pasture area to another. Various schemes dictate the frequency and pattern of animal movements. Suffice it to say that this practice (which mimics the grazing patterns of large prairie ungulates) produces additional benefits for grazing animals, their owners, and wildlife. Rotational grazing reduces trampling, provides more and higher-quality forage than continuously grazed pastures, is less labor and re-source intensive than utilizing confinement structures, and when properly managed provides excellent nesting habitat for grassland birds and other animals (Undersander et al. 2000).

Iowa's agricultural lands also can be perennialized without livestock. For example, federally sponsored programs support the return of perennial growth in conservation plantings, which pull farmland out of use. The Conservation Reserve Program subsidizes native prairie or tree plantings and buffer strips on erodible lands removed from agricultural production. Other programs offer cost-sharing for broad buffer strips along creeks and wetlands, to help keep sediments and agricultural chemicals out of surface waters. With all such programs, diverse plantings of natives should be pushed to the greatest degree possible. However, the limited duration of government contracts for such lands can serve as a disincentive for investing diverse seed and money in high-quality reconstructions.

In coming years, perennial crops may be grown for production of an expanding number of chemicals and fibers, and perennial crops will likely be planted to sequester carbon in an attempt to help combat global warming. The most far-reaching attempt to reinstitute perennial plant growth focuses on perennializing our cropland itself — that is, developing deep-rooted perennial grains that would reduce agriculture's tremendous input of inorganic fertilizers, synthetic pesticides, and fossil fuels and would manage water, nutrients, and soils far better than shallow-rooted annuals like corn. The Land Institute in Salina, Kansas, has been working since 1976 to breed perennial grains that could be grown in diverse production systems. Its success would be nothing less than revolutionary.

Agriculture is moving toward growing biofuels, such as ethanol produced from corn, as renewable energy sources. Increasing the quantity of annual row crops to produce biofuels will only exacerbate Iowa's environmental problems. New techniques may soon allow biofuel production from corn stalks or other crops, but the removal of the total corn plant from croplands could degrade soils. Using monocultures of switchgrass could be a marginal improvement. On the other hand, promoting perennial polycultures of native plants for use as biofuels could profit the farmer while leading to partial restoration of ecosystems and ecological functions on far more land. Biofuel production could potentially lead to major shifts in Iowa's agriculture. However, considering only biofuels' economic benefits is bound to produce new environmental problems. The total environmental costs of any biofuel scheme will need to be carefully assessed to avoid additional environmental degradation.

A small but growing number of Iowa farms produce organic foods and specialty products such as bison meat for niche markets. These farms typically promote environmental quality and also help maintain rural society. Each of us can support their operations by buying locally produced vegetables and meats, such as those sold through farmers' markets and Community Supported Agriculture operations.

Discussions about promoting perennial growth will do little good as long as the federal farm program continues to subsidize a small number of specific crops. With a multibillion-dollar farm subsidy that ties payments to production of corn, soybeans, and a few other crops, the trend toward vast row-crop monocultures interrupted only by massive animal confinement buildings is bound to persist, along with its correlates of ever-larger farms and heavy use of environmentally damaging chemicals and techniques. And with the current growth of industrial farming and multinational food-producing corporations, sensitive attention given by individual farm owners to environmental problems is bound to decrease. Many argue that the living soils and natural systems that produce our food cannot be manipulated by massive machinery and intensely treated with synthetic chemicals without forever losing integrity. In the end, the current industrial farm may condemn Iowa's fine agricultural soils to the same fate as the prairie itself or the northern white pine forests that allowed settlement of the prairie: commodities that were used up and largely forgotten.

The bottom line is to recognize that farms produce far more than food and to shape governmental policy accordingly. Farms produce clean (or polluted) water and air, healthy (or degrading) soil, and sites for hunting and fishing and other recreational uses (or the absence thereof). They renew (or deplete) wildlife and biodiversity and sequester (or release) greenhouse gases that change our climate. They create (or destroy) an aesthetically pleasing landscape. And on Iowa's vast agricultural landscape, they do all of these on a massive scale.

Because farms have the potential of affecting environmental health in so many ways, many have long argued that federal programs should subsidize farmers not just for filling grain bins but also for providing a healthy natural environment — an asset as crucial to human health as food itself. Subsidies could be reformed, for example, to encourage conversion of economically marginal cropland to grass-based livestock production. Or a significant portion of Iowa's working landscape could be redefined as environmental-services land rather than food-producing land. Subsidies might be awarded for managing and monitoring these lands to encourage certain of the beneficial natural functions mentioned above. Or perhaps a given percentage of each county, or each watershed, could be classified as a sustainability zone for propagating native biodiversity. Such goals would be furthered by the creation and passage of legislation that would establish a federal program to assist farmers and other private citizens who want to work to improve the environmental health of their land (Leopold Center for Sustainable Agriculture Task Force 2005: 32). Even on Iowa's richest farmlands, such a program would comprise an investment in the land's continued productivity rather than a restriction of present production. A revised federal farm policy that clearly promotes nonmarket public goods could send a clear signal to farmers and jumpstart the creation of more sustainable agricultural systems.

Government promotion of nonmarket public goods proved its worth in England in the 1990s, when farmers were required to set aside land as part of a European Community compensation program. The 11 percent of England's arable land that was removed from production reaped substantial benefits for declining species of both wintering and breeding birds (Firbank et al. 2003). In the United States, farm programs have since their inception been tied to conservation through their land-retirement programs and cost sharing for conservation practices. Funding is sometimes low, and some programs have been narrowly focused, but the public benefits of conservation have been accepted.

The 2002 federal farm bill made a promising move by establishing the nation's first green payment program: the Conservation Security Program (CSP). Moving away from subsidizing specific row crops and toward supporting farmers with diverse operations, the CSP proposes to award cash payments to producers for environmental products and benefits furnished by their working land — for improved water quality, enhanced native plants and animals, soils sustainably managed, and similar public goods. The CSP has the potential of boosting sustainability practices and becoming Iowa's most powerful conservation tool, but only if it is well funded and fully implemented.

In summary, food is our most basic human need, and in postsettlement Iowa its production has always been the basis of our society, economy, and culture. Agriculture's course, like the land itself, has been ever changing. The forces rewriting agriculture's definition lie increasingly beyond our boundaries, in the offices of multinational corporations with little direct knowledge or concern for our state or our land. Is this what we want? What exactly do we expect our farms to give us, and what are we willing to give in return?

Today Iowans are being challenged to reclaim our land and restore a harmonious balance between farming, the natural world, and human society. Real progress toward more sustainable farms will likely occur only with changes in values, priorities, agricultural paradigms, and government programs. It will require a turn from the large-scale, fossil fuel–based, heavy-input farming that emphasizes profit above all else back to farming that values nature-mimicking processes and relies on complex biotic interactions. Now, more than at any time in the past, we must be active in shaping agriculture's evolution, rather than simply reacting to the consequences of negative changes that otherwise are bound to occur.

Goal 4: Implement and Activate

We may dream about preserving, restoring, and mimicking native landscapes across the state, but none of our goals will be met without people, programs, policies, and values that push the goals forward. Implementation and activation are the subject of this last section — creating a nature-centered infrastructure, supported fully by a nature-sensitive populace, which ensures that our government and culture are working to advance native biodiversity, stability, and sustainability. Implementation depends on six activities: engagement, encouragement, investigation, funding, governance, and education.

ENGAGE

A concerned and engaged populace that advocates funding of environmental programs is prerequisite to all of this book's suggestions. People will advocate things they know well and love. While in past decades most Iowans had daily contact with nature on their farms, today's urban majority will profit from purposeful efforts to reconnect them with the natural world.

Engagement with nature begins in childhood, with acts as simple as wandering outside or playing in the soil. Such activities have great power. Parents and grandparents should take time to walk with children and talk with them about nature's beauty and wonder, realizing that these acts become beloved rituals that shape our future. Concerned adults can reach out more broadly to children by volunteering at nature centers or county conservation boards or initiating nature-focused activities with church, Scout, and other youth groups. Nature-based experiential public school programs for children were extremely popular earlier in the 1900s; it's time for their renewal.

Adults can be encouraged to connect with nature in any number of ways. Some may jump into local restoration efforts, while others will be more comfortable gardening with prairie plants or photographing wildflowers. Sketching or writing a nature journal hones observation skills. Nature is addictive. It has a way of drawing people in. Start wherever you are comfortable — attend field days, join nature seminars, read the literature, plant a few prairie plants — and trust that you will soon be contributing to nature's health in a manner that is right for you.

Participation in fishing, hunting, and trapping should be encouraged. And people engaged in these sports should be welcomed as members of the conservation community who provide valuable services and are political and financial mainstays for conservation efforts.

Organizations such as the Iowa Prairie Network, the Iowa Native Plant Society, local birding clubs, nature centers, county conservation boards, and the Iowa Natural Heritage Foundation and other land trusts offer excellent field experiences that introduce nature lovers to specific sites and topics as well as to one another. And several volunteer programs now train individuals to conduct simple nature-monitoring efforts. NatureMapping (an Iowa State University Extension program) engages the general public in monitoring common wildlife. The Iowa DNR administers the Frog and Toad Survey through its Wildlife Diversity Program. IOWATER (operated through the Iowa Geological Survey) engages citizen volunteers in simple water-quality monitoring efforts. The Audubon Society conducts the Christmas Bird Count and other local bird-monitoring efforts. These programs, which involve straightforward techniques, can be conducted by nearly anyone who is willing to step outside the front door. They are excellent ways of engaging children in intentional nature observation.

ENCOURAGE

People undertaking remnant restorations and reconstructions need support and encouragement about many issues. They may not recognize native plants, know how to assess their land's environmental quality, see its potential for restoration, or know how to produce a management plan. This is true of the growing number of people buying rural land for recreational purposes, but it also may describe long-term landowners: the majority need information and help with land management. Even those aware of restoration practices may falter before the enormity of the task. False starts based on inadequate knowledge may be made. Or landowners may take initial steps and then, when success does not seem imminent or time and resources ebb, drop the project. Invasive populations may be fought for a few years and then allowed to resurge. Prairie plantings that fail to thrive because of inadequate management are not uncommon.

Encouragement and aid can be sought from the types of professional advisers and assistants suggested throughout this chapter and in chapter 6. Public agency personnel do a noble job of providing necessary services but are typically overworked. With the majority of Iowa's land remaining in private hands, new well-funded programs to assist landowners with recognizing and managing remnants and reconstructions are much needed.

As the interest in biodiversity and the need for field professionals grow, counties or the Iowa DNR might consider hiring a new type of professional, a "native biodiversity specialist," to coordinate and encourage positive restoration efforts within a given region. The efforts of biodiversity specialists could supplement those of more specialized advisers such as district foresters and private land wildlife biologists. Biodiversity specialists, focusing broadly on the health of our native lands, could provide the long-term vision required for sustaining native species and communities on a landscape scale. They could pull together the efforts of other programs and maintain lists of local sources of labor and demonstration sites, thus serving as centralized information sources who would surely raise consciousness about biodiversity and restoration efforts. The number and quality of field restoration advisers could also be increased through county conservation boards, if these entities were to become more involved in promoting restoration activities.

Demonstration sites that showcase various native communities and reconstructions will help engage others in restoration efforts and educate them about restoration techniques. County conservation boards or any other conservation groups would do well to establish such sites across the state, advertise them actively, and feature them on field days. Individuals involved in restoration can do the same by talking to their neighbors about their plantings and efforts. Through demonstration sites, even casual viewers could learn to distinguish healthy oak woodlands from degenerating forests and come to appreciate the texture and diversity of prairie plantings.

INVESTIGATE

Although we know a great deal about restoring nature's health, we still have much to learn. Doing so requires both formal and informal research. Formal research, carried out under controlled conditions and directed toward answering specific questions, is conducted by professionals at educational institutions and research centers but also is done by self-trained Iowans who have become experts in a given topic. Informal research encompasses the efforts of the masses — those who try a certain invasive-control method, or burn in a nontraditional manner, or apply any other restoration technique and witness its effects. The results of informal researchers are often shared by word of mouth. A broader sharing of positive or negative results — for example, by posting a note in the journal *Ecological Restoration* or describing results on the Internet — would save future restorationists much effort.

What restoration questions need to be answered? They span the imagination and cover everything from how to restore oak woodland understory, to regeneration of oaks, to using cattle for prairie management. List almost any area of concern, and more knowledge would be beneficial. Research on controlling invasives is badly needed. So is research on melding native species successfully into agriculture and integrated pest control. Efforts could be better directed if we had ongoing statewide inventories of Iowa's remnants and a rating system to rank these remnants or (as Minnesota is now doing) detailed inventories for each county. To trace the health of nature in Iowa, we need more information on the distribution and population trends of individual native species. These, our miners' canaries, will not be heard if we don't listen in ordered fashion by conducting inventories that record changes from one year or one generation to the next.

Research on basic natural history questions — for example, the interplay of prairie plants and their pollinators — will yield significant prairie management information. Because nature is complex and interrelated, research needs to be the same. Thus the trend toward comprehensive, long-term, interdisciplinary research on hydrologic and other issues is welcome. Economics is also important. We need research on calculating the real costs of environmental degradation and the financial benefits of nature's healthy functions, so that they can be routinely integrated into governmental policies and personal decisions.

Both research and restoration are forwarded by initiatives such as the landmark Iowa Wildlife Action Plan (Zohrer 2005). This comprises the first comprehensive inventory of Iowa's vertebrate and selected invertebrate animals since 1933. Completion of this plan allows Iowa to receive federal grants to improve and double wildlife habitat on public and private lands over the next twenty-five years. Statewide monitoring of wildlife is a major component of the plan.

FUND

Efforts to preserve and restore nature in Iowa often stumble along, held together by the dedication of citizens who care passionately about native species and communities. Their activities are almost always limited by lack of funding. In Iowa, in the early twenty-first century only about 1.5 percent of all state revenues went to natural resource protection. In that same time period, Iowa ranked forty-ninth in the amount of land set aside for public use, with Kansas being the only state to rank lower.[1]

Programs at all levels are poorly financed, with more money needed by the State Preserves System, Iowa's state parks, county conservation boards, and private conservation and land trust organizations for all efforts: purchasing land and equipment, developing programs, hiring staff, and managing land by restoring its natural features and native communities. Additional funding would energize landowners stymied by restoration costs, park and preserve managers overwhelmed by brushy or exotic invasions, agencies struggling to manage and monitor remnants, and teachers hoping to bus students to field sites. Increased funding could be used to produce educational materials, manage conservation easements, cost-share restoration efforts with landowners, and support research and monitoring programs. More personnel are desperately needed to restore and manage public lands and to fight invasive species.

County, state, and federal governments would profit from strongly expressed public support for conservation and biodiversity programs. County conservation boards often struggle to manage the lands they currently own and thus

1. Information on Iowa's state funding of natural resources protection was provided through personal communication with Diane Ford-Shivvers, legislative liaison for the Iowa DNR, and was based on her experience with Iowa's state budget. She stated that in 2006, for several years, the Iowa DNR and Iowa Department of Agriculture and Land Stewardship together had received about $40 million from Iowa's General Fund and $35 million from gambling revenues, out of a total state budget of over $5 billion. In that same time period, Iowa was forty-ninth in the nation in public natural areas, as stated in multiple sources, including the *Des Moines Register* lead editorial, February 25, 2007.

are financially unable to acquire, restore, and manage new public parks and preserves. At the state level, citizen advocates would do well to push for full funding of the Resource Enhancement and Protection (REAP) program, along with other programs administered through the Iowa DNR and Iowa Department of Agriculture and Land Stewardship. At the federal level, Iowans should encourage full funding and complete implementation of programs such as the Wildlife Habitat Incentive Program (WHIP), the CSP, and the Landowner Incentive Program (LIP). These programs are exemplary for their promotion of native communities and long-term land management, but federal cost-sharing allocations for conservation programs consistently fall short of funding those who want to enroll. Other federal cost-sharing programs could move beyond traditional conservation efforts such as hillside terrace construction and instead target biodiversity as a high priority. Programs that fund agricultural set-aside plantings should require long-term management for native biodiversity.

Individuals can contribute to private conservation groups and support state-administered programs such as the Chickadee Checkoff (on state income tax forms) and natural resource automobile license plates, which fund biodiversity efforts. These important and worthy programs deserve broader public backing than they receive. But a more robust plan for sustainably funding state natural resource programs is needed. Some Iowans have been looking to Missouri as a model. That state, starting in 1976, dedicated a one-eighth-cent sales tax to its Department of Conservation and a one-tenth-cent sales tax to its Department of Natural Resources, generating millions of dollars annually for parks, wildlife, and biodiversity efforts.

Other funding possibilities include charging user fees for parks, fishing tournaments, and the like and redirecting some funds traditionally directed toward hunting and fishing into biodiversity programs. Demographic statistics show that early in the twenty-first century, an increasing number of Iowans were interested in nature, hiking, watchable wildlife, and family-oriented outdoor recreation, while hunting and fishing license sales were declining (Iowa Department of Natural Resources 2006b; U.S. Fish and Wildlife Service 2002). Enhancing amenities for nature lovers would broaden the constituency supporting native communities. Whatever approach is taken, an organized campaign involving grassroots efforts will be prerequisite to adequate, sustainable conservation funding.

GOVERN

Politicians implement policies and programs. Thus political involvement is necessary to promote restoration and biodiversity management. The promotion of environmental sustainability should become a baseline for all governmental decisions concerning use of the land. Programs to inventory, restore, and monitor native biodiversity need to be adequately financed and given regulatory backing.

To encourage these goals, advocates need to attend governmental policy hearings, monitor legislation, raise environmental issues at election time, and encourage votes that are environmentally positive. We need to educate our politicians about the deep connections between nature's health, biodiversity, and environmental and agricultural sustainability and our own well-being and economy. Comprehensive policies regarding invasive exotics are desperately needed. These suggestions will be more appealing if politicians realize that a healthy environment, more abundant public lands, and well-managed natural areas are key quality-of-life issues. Because they are important in drawing employers to Iowa and keeping young adults here, these factors are crucial to the state's economic health. Trail systems, scenic and wild areas, and other nature-oriented recreational facilities, including ecotourism destinations, are major drawing cards for the state and economic assets for local businesses. Investments in these are returned many times over and magnify the health and happiness of Iowa's residents.

Iowa's city dwellers, who provide much of the state's tax revenues, need to willingly fund programs that boost nature's health in both urban areas and surrounding rural areas. Increased funding to improve water quality is a move in the right direction. In addition, city dwellers as well as rural residents should track the positions of county boards of supervisors on land-use issues and become involved in the election of environmentally knowledgeable supervisors. These officials set the tone for the rural land-use policies, ordinances, and zoning decisions that are crucial to the survival of remnants and to restoration efforts. Land-use regulations, for example, stipulate whether prairie plantings will be allowed as lawns and whether prescribed fire can be applied within city limits. By encouraging new construction on existing city lots, supervisors can discourage suburban sprawl and fragmentation of outlying native remnants. Cities and counties will profit from adopting and consistently applying zoning ordinances and land-use plans that maximize preservation of biodiversity. The provision of model documents to our city and county governments would encourage this goal.

State and federal legislators routinely make decisions without realizing their links to the survival of native plants and animals. The nation's complex and ever-shifting farm programs will benefit from the involvement of an alert, observant conservation community. For example, conservationists have pointed out that federal programs intended to increase perennial grasslands have inadvertently led to native prairie remnants being plowed or planted with trees. Present wisdom points toward a farm bill that favors a shift toward perennial cover and diverse, prairie-mimicking crop rotations. The more decision makers understand the valuable functions of natural systems, the more intelligently they can design programs that preserve and mimic these systems.

EDUCATE

As Thomas Macbride stated in this chapter's opening epigraph, "The people would act today if the situation were clearly understood." Thus discussion of goal 4, which opened with engaging the human spirit, ends with training the mind.

Education implies that the general public will come to understand that Iowa's natural processes are important and are currently endangered. Without such awareness, people will not support biodiversity initiatives. Any effort to raise public awareness about ecological sustainability — whether by public service announcements, news coverage, or simply talking with one's neighbors — is valuable. Facts about nature can be injected into daily life in numerous creative ways. For example, in 2005 the Iowa Geological Survey produced brochures for RAGBRAI bicyclers that described natural features along each day's course. A broader audience could be reached via television, such as through a program that repeatedly revisited the same restoration sites to display the dramatic changes occurring over time. More targeted outreach might include the creation of picture-rich brochures or booklets for persons moving into rural subdivisions, perhaps handed out by real estate agents, on the value of native plantings and residents' responsibilities to the land.

Some people will want to dig deeper into facts about nature and its restoration. Their education often begins with recognizing nature's elements. Learning to identify plants or birds requires patience, time for observation, and the courage to plunge into guidebooks and keys. Fortunately, the number of Iowa nature guidebooks has increased tremendously in recent years. Guides to Iowa's plants include Christiansen and Müller 1999 for prairie plants and van der Linden and Farrar 1993 for forest and shade trees. Runkel's books, with Bull (1987) or Roosa (1989, 1999), give detailed descriptions of woodland, prairie, and wetland wildflowers, including their historic uses. Eilers and Roosa 1994 remains Iowa's comprehensive reference for Iowa's vascular plants. A few of the many treatises on Iowa animals include Schlicht et al. 2007 for butterflies; Christiansen and Bailey 1990, 1991, and 1997 for reptiles and amphibians; Harlan et al. 1987 for fish; Laubach et al. 1994 for bats; and Jackson et al. 1996 for birds. Those who want to visit native communities can consult Herzberg and Pearson's 2001 guide to Iowa's State Preserves, while Dinsmore 1995 locates wildlife-viewing sites.

Getting to know Iowa's native elements is greatly eased by attending field trips with knowledgeable leaders (fig. 46). Additional innovative programs or field trips to teach about native organisms and restoration could be organized by many groups — for example, the Iowa State Extension Service and its Master Gardeners, gardening clubs, and community colleges. The field experiences and volunteer opportunities listed earlier lead participants toward a deeper understanding of nature's complexities, as do the excellent Master Conservationist classes, also offered through the Extension Service.

Integrating more nature-based education into the public school system will instill both factual understanding and respect for the complex world that supports all life. As Bohumil Shimek argued decades ago, students who learn botany "will have a source of wholesome physical, mental, and ethical influence throughout their lives" (1931a: 8). Greater classroom emphasis on nature could be encouraged in many ways: linking teachers to conservation organizations, bringing in naturalists to give talks in schools, greater utilization of county conservation boards and nature centers, holding teacher education workshops, and increasing funding for all such efforts. Children's positive experiences on the land, led by enthusiastic guides, are crucial. None of these will occur without school systems putting biology and nature studies higher on the educational priority list and supporting teachers who are enthusiastic about our land and its creatures.

Education needs to extend to professionals who work in the field, such as park rangers and managers, and to those who transmit nature-based information to the general public, such as Natural Resources Conservation Service employees. These personnel need ongoing training in the latest restoration techniques, biodiversity issues, techniques for controlling invasives, and similar issues.

Fig. 46. The fate of nature in Iowa depends on the concern of Iowans. Caring about the land is enhanced by getting to know its natural features, a process encouraged by the growing number of field trips offered by varied organizations and agencies. Photograph by Carl Kurtz.

And our educational system must work to produce a continuing stock of future professionals: well-trained Iowans capable of carrying out restoration of our lands. That means that our high schools, colleges, and universities need ample field-based coursework in biology and environmental studies. Some schools are doing a fine job here. To name a few, in 2005 the Des Moines Area Community College offered the course "Restoration of Native Plant Communities," which won the national Take Pride in America award; Drake University offered extensive field-based coursework and the Prairie Rescue and Restoration Internship Program; and the University of Northern Iowa was teaching field courses in ecological restoration and conservation biology. At the same time, other institutions such as the University of Iowa, past home of Shimek, Macbride, and other of our finest natural historians, were largely relinquishing field-based biological studies and systematics in favor of molecular biology. This shift, occurring in many institutions across the country, bodes poorly for our environmental future.

In recent years a number of training programs and internships have been developed primarily for college students. These programs, offered by the Nature Conservancy, the Iowa Natural Heritage Foundation, certain colleges and universities, and others, place young adults in the field where they help with native seed production and ecological restoration activities. AmeriCorps also has placed individuals in key conservation programs across Iowa. The labor of these young adults is extremely beneficial to the land. But even more valuable may be the students' increased interest in native communities and restoration techniques, and their acquisition of the practical knowledge and hands-on experience necessary to continue in resource management and restoration careers. The challenges and rewards of these programs are described by Chad Graeve, land manager at Hitchcock Nature Center in the Loess Hills: "How do you teach a young person [being trained in restoration techniques] that there is no glamour in developing calluses on your hands and sweating so much that your boots slosh and your leather belt turns white? . . . Your ultimate reward is knowing you have done what you can to leave the land in better condition, and that your grandfather who preached 'it's better to wear out than rust out' will smile from above" (Chad Graeve, personal communication).

A Vision for the Future

If all these suggested activities were magically implemented, what would Iowa look like? How would our landscape and culture change?

The answer pivots around a single word: diversity. A restored Iowa landscape would hold a diversity of native communities, which housed a diversity of native plants and animals, governed by diverse processes, managed with diverse techniques, carrying out a diversity of natural functions. These would be encouraged by a diversity of people connecting to the natural world in diverse ways.

This diversity would reflect a new balance between agricultural and conservation interests. Farmlands and cities would intergrade with native communities and species associations. Croplands would form a mosaic with oak copses and perennial grasslands. Strings of wooded lands and wetlands would weave a maze across intensively managed lands, and prairie plants would line our roadsides and waterways. Our land's health and pastoral beauty would be boosted by native plant associations providing surrounding lands with birds and bats to restrain insect pests and weed seeds and to pollinate their flowers, and with predators to control their rodents. Both cities and rural areas would provide sites for nature-based physical, emotional, and spiritual rejuvenation, places of beauty where adults release the stresses of everyday life and children bond with nature.

With such an interweaving of natural and human landscapes, our native plants and animals could maintain their populations. Utilizing their superb adaptations to Iowa's climate and soils, native species would feed the sun's energy into complex molecules that flowed through a large number of species. Native associations would hold and rebuild soil, capture and filter water, cleanse air while sequestering carbon dioxide, detoxify pollutants, moderate local climate, cycle minerals, provide raw materials, and rid us of our organic wastes. In carrying out a full range of free ecological goods and services, native communities and species would make Iowa's intensively modified lands environmentally sustainable and resilient in the face of change.

Such a landscape would be a living negation of current trends. It would say no to overt destruction of remaining high-quality remnants and no to their ongoing degradation and fragmentation. No to the resulting environmental problems. No to declining genetic strains, species, and community types. No to the ecological shifts predicted to accompany the loss of our oak woodlands. A healthy Iowa landscape would negate the globalization of the world's flora. And it would reject the homogenization of specialized, distinctive native communities or, worse still, the fading of Earth's biological rainbow, its reduction to species-poor associations of aggressive exotic generalists.

Iowa's citizens would be intimately involved in monitoring and restoring nature's health through volunteer efforts on private and public tracts. The clearing of brush, use of prescribed fire, fighting of invasive exotics, and the like would become as routine as mowing the lawn. The lay public and politicians would be knowledgeable about and supportive of efforts to stimulate natural processes and minimize nature's degradation. They would understand the value of nature's services and would resist the temptation to choose short-term windfalls at the expense of long-term environmental and economic health.

This vision may never be fully realized in Iowa. But that possibility should not restrain our efforts. Today's activities dictate tomorrow's options. Every step we take toward optimizing Iowa's natural diversity, flexibility, and functionality will work toward keeping nature's pathways open and clear. Each step will expand our future resources and choices. In the current period of rapid environmental change, working thus to maintain nature's health, resilience, and predictability remains the wisest and the most practical direction we can choose.

Epilogue

Amid all the refinements of modern life there rises often doubtless a longing unconfessed, a keen desire for the old-time freedom and the wild beauty of that earlier day when the State was new.... Once only in recorded time has nature turned over to the hands of civilized man a world in newness, freshness, absolute. Has destiny made us in any sense partakers of the gift unique, ours be the joy, ours too the peculiar responsibility of use. — Thomas Macbride, 1895

Coming generations may well characterize the last half of the twentieth century as the time when long-standing human relationships with nature were turned inside out. When the natural order, which had always surrounded and nurtured human life, was reduced to islands, and when cities, agriculture, and industrial lands assumed dominance around the globe. When routine contact with nature, once an assumed part of daily life, dissolved for soaring numbers of urban dwellers. During this time, the human population more than doubled, rising from 2.6 billion people in 1950 to 6.1 billion people in 2000 (U.S. Census Bureau 2006). With rising resource use, by 2000 humans were appropriating over 40 percent of the globe's terrestrial plant productivity (new growth) and over half of Earth's accessible freshwater runoff (Pimm 2001: 6). The relationships between humanity and nature that had always governed life on Earth were being redefined (Millennium Ecosystem Assessment 2005; Raven 2002).

Can elements of the natural world survive this tightening human embrace? That question will be answered in the first half of the twenty-first century. During this next fifty-year span, Earth's human population is projected to rise by another three to four billion and then level off, with resource consumption increasing accordingly (U.S. Census Bureau 2006).

The question will be answered first and most emphatically where our transformation of the natural world has been most intense — in places like Iowa. Thus the door is open for Iowans once again to take the lead and to demonstrate that forward-looking land use can partner with environmental healing and wholeness. Here, where nature has been so very compromised, we can show that utilization of the land can be refocused so that it also provides for native species. We can demonstrate that natural communities and their inherent functions can be reestablished for the benefit of all.

Doing so will achieve homeland security in its most elementary form — by guaranteeing that our planet can sustainably support human life. It will be a way of revisiting the past and fulfilling what our ancestors came here to achieve: a life of abundance, harmony, and stability. And doing so will be a way to honor the future, to leave our children and grandchildren with something more basic and necessary than goods and economic benefits: a predictable, nurturing environment that will carry them, and their offspring, toward a renewed emerald horizon.

Appendix. Common and Scientific Names of Native and Naturalized Plants in the Text

Anemone, Canada — *Anemone canadensis*
 rue — *Thalictrum thalictroides*
 wood — *Anemone quinquefolia*
Arrowheads — *Sagittaria* spp.
Ash, black — *Fraxinus nigra*
 green — *Fraxinus pennsylvanica*
 white — *Fraxinus americana*
Ashes — *Fraxinus* spp.
Aspen, bigtooth — *Populus grandidentata*
Aster, hairy — *Symphyotrichum pilosum*
 New England — *Symphyotrichum novae-angliae*
 skyblue — *Symphyotrichum oolentangiense*
Asters — *Symphyotrichum* spp.

Baneberry, white — *Actaea pachypoda*
Barberry, Japanese — *Berberis thunbergii*
Barley, little — *Hordeum pusillum*
Basswood — *Tilia americana*
Bedstraws — *Galium* spp.
Bellflower, American — *Campanulastrum americanum*
Bellwort (largeflower) — *Uvularia grandiflora*
Betony, wood (Canadian lousewort) — *Pedicularis canadensis*
Birch, river — *Betula nigra*
Birches — *Betula* spp.
Bishop's cap (twoleaf miterwort) — *Mitella diphylla*
Bittersweet (native) — *Celastrus scandens*
Bittersweet, oriental — *Celastrus orbiculatus*
Blackeyed Susan — *Rudbeckia hirta*
Blazing star, prairie — *Liatris pycnostachya*
Blazing stars — *Liatris* spp.
Bloodroot — *Sanguinaria canadensis*
Bluebells, Virginia — *Mertensia virginica*
Blue cohosh — *Caulophyllum thalictroides*
Blue-eyed grass, prairie — *Sisyrinchium campestre*

Bluegrass, Kentucky	*Poa pratensis*
Bluejoint	*Calamagrostis canadensis*
Bluestem, big	*Andropogon gerardii*
little	*Schizachyrium scoparium*
Boneset, common	*Eupatorium perfoliatum*
Boxelder	*Acer negundo*
Brome, smooth	*Bromus inermis*
Buckthorn, common (exotic)	*Rhamnus cathartica*
native	*Rhamnus lanceolata, R. alnifolia*
Bulrushes	*Scirpus* spp.
Burdock	*Arctium minus*
Burningbush	*Euonymus alatus*
Bur-reed	*Sparganium eurycarpum*
Bush clover, round-headed	*Lespedeza capitata*
Buttercup	*Ranunculus* spp.
Butternut	*Juglans cinerea*
Buttonbush	*Cephalanthus occidentalis*
Cardinalflower	*Lobelia cardinalis*
Cattail (hybrid)	*Typha angustifolia* x *T. latifolia*
Cattails	*Typha* spp.
Cherry, black	*Prunus serotina*
wild: see Cherry, black	
Chicory	*Cichorium intybus*
Chokecherry	*Prunus virginiana*
Clearweed	*Pilea pumila*
Clover, red	*Trifolium pratense*
Clovers	*Trifolium* spp.
Compassplant	*Silphium laciniatum*
Coneflower, (eastern) purple	*Echinacea purpurea*
gray-headed	*Ratibida pinnata*
pale purple	*Echinacea pallida*
Coneflowers	*Echinacea* spp., *Ratibida* spp., *Rudbeckia* spp.
Cordgrass, prairie (slough grass)	*Spartina pectinata*
Coreopsis, prairie (stick tickseed)	*Coreopsis palmata*
Cottongrasses	*Eriophorum* spp.
Cottonwood	*Populus deltoides*
Crowfoot, water (water buttercup)	*Ranunculus flabellaris* and *R. longirostris*
Crownvetch	*Securigera varia*
Culver's root	*Veronicastrum virginicum*
Cup plant	*Silphium perfoliatum*

Daisy, oxeye	*Leucanthemum vulgare*
Dame's rocket	*Hesperis matronalis*
Dandelion, common	*Taraxacum officinale*
Daylily	*Hemerocallis fulva*
Dogwood, gray	*Cornus racemosa*
roughleaf	*Cornus drummondii*
Dogwoods	*Cornus* spp.
Dropseed, prairie	*Sporobolus heterolepis*
rough (composite dropseed)	*Sporobolus compositus*
sand	*Sporobolus cryptandrus*
Dutchman's breeches	*Dicentra cucullaria*
Elm, American	*Ulmus americana*
Siberian	*Ulmus pumila*
slippery	*Ulmus rubra*
Elms	*Ulmus* spp.
Evening primrose, common	*Oenothera biennis*
Fern, interrupted	*Osmunda claytoniana*
lady	*Athyrium filix-femina* var. *angustum*
maidenhair	*Adiantum pedatum*
ostrich	*Matteuccia struthiopteris*
Fir, balsam	*Abies balsamea*
Fleabane, eastern daisy	*Erigeron annuus*
Fleabanes	*Erigeron* spp.
Foxglove, slender false	*Agalinis tenuifolia*
Foxtails	*Setaria* spp.
Gentian, cream	*Gentiana alba*
fringed	*Gentianopsis crinita*
Gentians	*Gentiana* spp.
Geranium, wild	*Geranium maculatum*
Golden Alexanders	*Zizia aurea*
Goldenrod, Canada	*Solidago canadensis*
elmleaf	*Solidago ulmifolia*
Missouri	*Solidago missouriensis*
stiff	*Oligoneuron rigidum* var. *rigidum*
Goldenrods	*Solidago* spp.
Gooseberries	*Ribes* spp.
Goosefoot	*Chenopodium* spp.
Grama, blue	*Bouteloua gracilis*
sideoats	*Bouteloua curtipendula*

Grape, riverbank — *Vitis riparia*
Grass, bottlebrush — *Elymus hystrix*
   broad-leaved panic — *Dichanthelium latifolium*
   long-awned wood
     (bearded shorthusk) — *Brachyelytrum erectum*
   porcupine — *Hesperostipa spartea*
   sandreed (prairie sandreed) — *Calamovilfa longifolia*
Grass of Parnassus — *Parnassia glauca*

Hackberry (common) — *Celtis occidentalis*
Hawthorns — *Crataegus* spp.
Hazelnut (American) — *Corylus americana*
Hepatica — *Hepatica nobilis*
Hickories — *Carya* spp.
Hickory, bitternut — *Carya cordiformis*
   shagbark — *Carya ovata*
Hogpeanut — *Amphicarpaea bracteata*
Honewort — *Cryptotaenia canadensis*
Honeylocust — *Gleditsia triacanthos*
Honeysuckle, amur (exotic) — *Lonicera maackii*
   exotic bush: see Honeysuckle,
     amur and tartarian
   native bush — *Diervilla lonicera*
   native vinelike — *Lonicera dioica, L. reticulata*
   tartarian (exotic) — *Lonicera tatarica*
Horse gentians — *Triosteum* spp.

Indiangrass — *Sorghastrum nutans*
Indian pipe — *Monotropa uniflora*
Indigo, cream wild — *Baptisia bracteata* var. *leucophaea*
   white wild — *Baptisia alba* var. *macrophylla*
Indigos, wild — *Baptisia* spp.
Iris, blueflag (Shreve's iris) — *Iris virginica* var. *shrevei*
Ironweed, prairie — *Vernonia fasciculata*
Ironwood (hophornbeam) — *Ostrya virginiana*
Isopyrum, false rue anemone — *Enemion biternatum*

Jack-in-the-pulpit — *Arisaema triphyllum*
Jacob's ladder — *Polemonium reptans*
Joepyeweed — *Eupatorium purpureum*
Junegrass — *Koeleria macrantha*
Juniper, common — *Juniperus communis*

Knapweed, spotted	*Centaurea stoebe* ssp. *micranthos*
Knotweed	*Polygonum erectum*
Japanese	*Polygonum cuspidatum*
Ladies' slippers: see Orchids,	
lady's slipper	
Leadplant	*Amorpha canescens*
Lespedeza, sericea	*Lespedeza cuneata*
Lily, white trout (dogtooth violet)	*Erythronium albidum*
Locoweed, purple	*Oxytropis lambertii*
Locust, black	*Robinia pseudoacacia*
Loosestrife, purple	*Lythrum salicaria*
Maple, black	*Acer nigrum*
hard: see Maple, black and	
sugar	
Norway	*Acer platanoides*
silver	*Acer saccharinum*
soft: see Maple, silver	
sugar	*Acer saccharum*
Marigold, yellow marsh	*Caltha palustris*
Mayapple	*Podophyllum peltatum*
Milkweed, butterfly	*Asclepias tuberosa* ssp. *interior*
common	*Asclepias syriaca*
green	*Asclepias viridiflora*
poke	*Asclepias exaltata*
purple	*Asclepias purpurascens*
swamp	*Asclepias incarnata*
Monkshood, northern (blue)	*Aconitum noveboracense*
Mulberry, white	*Morus alba*
Mustard, garlic	*Alliaria petiolata*
Nettle, stinging	*Urtica dioica*
Nightshade, enchanter's	*Circaea lutetiana* ssp. *canadensis*
Oak, black	*Quercus velutina*
bur	*Quercus macrocarpa*
(northern) red	*Quercus rubra*
swamp white	*Quercus bicolor*
white	*Quercus alba*
Oaks	*Quercus* spp.
Olive, autumn	*Elaeagnus umbellata*
Russian	*Elaeagnus angustifolia*

Orchids, lady's slipper | *Cypripedium* spp.
lady's tresses | *Spiranthes* spp.
Osage orange | *Maclura pomifera*
Oxeye | *Heliopsis helianthoides*

Parsnip, wild | *Pastinaca sativa*
Pasqueflower | *Pulsatilla patens* ssp. *multifida*
Penstemon, foxglove | *Penstemon digitalis*
Phlox | *Phlox* spp.
prairie (downy phlox) | *Phlox pilosa* ssp. *fulgida*
Pine, (eastern) white | *Pinus strobus*
Plantain, prairie Indian | *Arnoglossum plantagineum*
Plum, wild (American plum) | *Prunus americana*
Poison ivy | *Toxicodendron radicans, T. rydbergii*
Pondweed, curly | *Potamogeton crispus*
Poplar, white | *Populus alba*
Prairie clover, purple | *Dalea purpurea*
white | *Dalea candida*
Prairie clovers | *Dalea* spp.
Pricklyash, common | *Zanthoxylum americanum*
Privet | *Ligustrum* spp.
Puccoon, hoary | *Lithospermum canescens*
Puccoons | *Lithospermum* spp.
Pussytoes (field) | *Antennaria neglecta*

Quackgrass | *Elymus repens*
Queen Anne's lace | *Daucus carota*

Ragweed, annual | *Ambrosia artemisiifolia*
giant | *Ambrosia trifida*
Ragweeds | *Ambrosia* spp.
Ragwort, prairie | *Packera plattensis*
Raspberries | *Rubus* spp.
Rattlesnake master | *Eryngium yuccifolium*
Redcedar, eastern | *Juniperus virginiana*
Reed, common | *Phragmites australis*
Reed canarygrass | *Phalaris arundinacea*
Rose, multiflora | *Rosa multiflora*
sunshine (prairie rose) | *Rosa arkansana*

Saxifrage, Iowa golden | *Chrysosplenium alternifolium* var. *sibiricum*
Sedge, Pennsylvania | *Carex pensylvanica*
tussock | *Carex stricta*

Sedges	*Carex* spp.
Shootingstar	*Dodecatheon meadia*
Showy orchis	*Galearis spectabilis*
Skeleton weed	*Lygodesmia juncea*
Snakeroot, white	*Ageratina altissima*
Sneezeweed	*Helenium autumnale*
Solomon's seal	*Polygonatum biflorum*
false	*Maianthemum* spp.
Spiderwort, common	*Tradescantia ohiensis*
Spring beauty	*Claytonia virginica*
Spring cress (bulbous bittercress)	*Cardamine bulbosa*
Spurge, leafy	*Euphorbia esula*
Stickseed	*Hackelia* spp.
Sumac, smooth	*Rhus glabra*
Sunflower, common (annual sunflower)	*Helianthus annuus*
pale-leaved	*Helianthus strumosus*
prairie (stiff sunflower)	*Helianthus pauciflorus* ssp. *pauciflorus*
sawtooth	*Helianthus grosseserratus*
Sunflowers	*Helianthus* spp.
Sweet cicely	*Osmorhiza claytonia*
Sweetclover, yellow and white	*Melilotus officinalis*
Switchgrass	*Panicum virgatum*
Sycamore (American)	*Platanus occidentalis*
Teasel	*Dipsacus fullonum, D. laciniatus*
Thimbleweed, tall (tall anemone)	*Anemone virginiana*
Thistle, Canada	*Cirsium arvense*
field	*Cirsium discolor*
Thistles	*Cirsium* spp.
Ticktrefoils	*Desmodium* spp.
Timothy	*Phleum pratense*
Toothwort	*Cardamine concatenata*
Touch-me-nots (jewelweeds)	*Impatiens* spp.
Tree-of-heaven	*Ailanthus altissima*
Trefoil, bird's-foot	*Lotus corniculatus*
Trilliums	*Trillium* spp.
Vervain, hoary	*Verbena stricta*
Vetch, American	*Vicia americana*
Violet, birdfoot	*Viola pedata*
Violets, prairie	*Viola pedatifida* spp.
Virginia creeper	*Parthenocissus quinquefolia*

Walnut, black   *Juglans nigra*
Waterleaf, Virginia   *Hydrophyllum virginianum*
Watermilfoil, Eurasian   *Myriophyllum spicatum*
Waternymph, brittle (brittle naiad)   *Najas minor*
Wild ginger (Canadian)   *Asarum canadense*
Wildrye, Canada   *Elymus canadensis*
Willow, black   *Salix nigra*
    peachleaf   *Salix amygdaloides*
    sandbar   *Salix interior*
Willows   *Salix* spp.
Woodnettle   *Laportea canadensis*

Yew, American (Canada yew)   *Taxus canadensis*
Yucca (soapweed)   *Yucca glauca*

Taxonomy follows "The PLANTS Database" (U.S Department of Agriculture 2007) as based on Kartesz. Common names also follow this source, except when the "Database" common names diverge greatly from those familiar to Iowans; in these cases, the Iowa names were retained to avoid confusion.

Bibliographic Acknowledgments

The references cited below served as broad information sources for the listed subjects. Citations also include personal communications, which were in the form of discussions, e-mail exchanges, and reviews of manuscript drafts. The entire manuscript was reviewed by John Pearson (Iowa DNR), and an early draft was reviewed by Tom Rosburg (Drake University). Citations for specific facts or topics are given in the text and in the notes.

Major information sources for chapter 1 included Anderson 1998 and Prior 1991 and personal communications with Raymond Anderson and Brian Witzke (both Iowa Geological Survey) and Richard Baker (University of Iowa) for geology; Anderson 1990, Baker et al. 1992, chapter 3 of Risser et al. 1981, and personal communications with Richard Baker and Holmes Semken (University of Iowa) for paleoecology; Alex 2002, Delcourt and Delcourt 2004, and Peterson 1997, and personal communications with Lynn Alex (Office of the State Archaeologist) for archaeology; Anonymous 1883, Bogue 1963, Schwieder 1996, and Smith 1992, for Iowa's settlement and state history; Conard 1997 and Penna 1999 for history of conservation in Iowa; and Anderson 2005, Beeman and Pritchard 2001, Bogue 1963, Gardner 2002, Hurt 1994, Jackson and Jackson 2002, and discussions with Laura Jackson (University of Northern Iowa) and Fred Kirschenmann (Leopold Center for Sustainable Agriculture) for agricultural history. Kirschenmann 2002 and other articles on the Leopold Center for Sustainable Agriculture Web site explained current agricultural trends and sustainable alternatives. My understanding of soils and climate was much enhanced by discussions with Michael T. Sucik (Iowa's State Soil Scientist) and Harry Hillaker (Iowa's State Climatologist).

Information on prairies in chapters 2 and 4 came from extensive reading of historic documents and modern research and from personal communications with John Pearson, Thomas Rosburg, Daryl Smith (University of Northern Iowa), and Paul Christiansen (Cornell College). Descriptions of multiple aspects of prairies, their inhabitants, and other features (such as soils, hydrology, fire, plant adaptations, and human use and its effects) were provided by Costello 1969, Mutel 1989, Risser et al. 1981, and Weaver 1954. Although Curtis 1959 and Schroeder 1982 focus on adjacent states, they were helpful in understanding Iowa's prairies. Other broader information sources included Cooper 1982, Rosburg 2001, Shimek 1948, and Steinauer and Collins 1996. Details of prairie types and community variations came from Conard 1952, Eilers and Roosa 1994, Howe et al. 1984, Pearson 1998, Shimek 1911, and White and Glenn-Lewin 1984; Novacek et al. 1985, and Rosburg and Glenn-Lewin 1996 (Loess Hills prairies); Pearson and Leoschke 1992 (fens); Rosburg 1999 (dry prairies); and Ugarte 1987 (northeastern

Iowa hill prairies). Information on the history, use, and results of tallgrass prairie and wetland transformation by plowing and grazing came from many of these sources as well as from Bogue 1963 and Smith 1981, 1992, 1998, and 2001. Natural Resources Conservation Service 1996 presents a good summary of the resulting soil and water problems. Discussions of prairie soil traits and changes were based largely on Blumberg 1999, Miller 2005, Risser et al. 1981, Weaver 1954, and personal communications with Wayne Petersen (Natural Resources Conservation Service) and Michael T. Sucik.

Wetland and water discussions in chapters 2 and 4, including Iowa's hydrologic regime, water quality, and the processes and effects of agricultural transformation and wetland conversion, were based on personal communications with Wayne Petersen, Susan Galatowitsch (University of Minnesota), and Richard Baker, and on Galatowitsch and van der Valk 1994, Riessen 2002, Runkel and Roosa 1999, Simpkins et al. 2004, Weaver 1954, and Zedler 2003, as well as sources cited in the text.

Information on woodlands and forests in chapters 2 and 5 came from numerous field observations and from historic documents and modern research publications, with heavy reliance on discussions primarily with Paul Christiansen, John Pearson, and Thomas Rosburg, but also with Mark Vitosh (Iowa DNR) and Cathy Mabry (Iowa State University). Sources important in understanding the character and distribution of historic wooded lands, their fire regime, and human use and subsequent alterations included Abrams 2003, Bogue 1963, Delong and Hooper 1996, Ebinger and McClain 1991, Ladd 1991, Macbride 1895 and 1897, McClain and Elzinga 1994, Mutel 1996, Packard 1993, Pammel 1896, and Shimek 1899, as well as the mid 1800 General Land Office survey records housed at the State Historical Society of Iowa, Iowa City. Sources important to understanding present-day woodlands and forests included Abrams 2003, Conard 1952, Haney and Apfelbaum 1995, Jungst et al. 1998, Leach and Ross 1995, Pearson 1998, and van der Linden and Farrar 1993. Johnson-Groh 1985, Johnson-Groh et al. 1987, and Raich et al. 1999 were significant sources for central Iowa, as was Glenn-Lewin et al. for northeastern Iowa and Mutel 1989 and Novacek et al. 1985 for the Loess Hills. Curtis 1959 and Kotar and Burger 1996 were also useful, even though they focus on Wisconsin.

Discussions of native animals are primarily in chapter 3, with shorter animal sections in chapters 2, 4, and 5. General descriptions of presettlement animal populations in chapter 2 were from Bowles 1975, Dinsmore 1994, Shimek 1883, and extrapolations from the research publications listed below. Chapter 3's descriptions of trends and changes in specific native plant as well as animal groups were from these sources and from the proceedings of Declining Flora and Fauna symposia published in *Proceedings of the Iowa Academy of Science* 1981, vol. 88, no. 1, and the *Journal of the Iowa Academy of Science* 1998, vol. 105, nos. 2 and 3, as well as from Jackson et al. 1996 and Kane et al. 2002. The arrival and effects of exotic and invasive organisms and stories of specific species, topics discussed in several chapters, came from a special invasive species edition of the *Journal of the Iowa Academy of Science* 108, no. 4 (2001), as well as from Bogue 1963, Westbrooks 1998, and other sources cited above.

Modern animal populations are described primarily in chapters 3, 4, and 5. Iowa's threatened and endangered species lists are posted at Iowa Department of Natural Resources 2006a. Details specific to butterflies were from Schlicht and Orwig 1998 and personal communications with Dennis Schlicht (Iowa Lepidoptera Project). Reptiles and amphibians sections were based primarily on Christiansen 1981 and 1998, Hemesath 1998, and personal communications with James Christiansen (Drake University), Neil Bernstein (Mount Mercy College), and Bruce Ehresman (Iowa DNR). The bird section was based largely on Dinsmore 1981 and 1998, with personal communications with James Fuller, Tom Kent, and Bruce Ehresman also providing information. Bird statistics and trends were mostly confirmed by *The Iowa Breeding Bird Atlas* (Jackson et al. 1996) and the Web site of the North American Breeding Bird Survey (Sauer et al. 2004), although the latter's statistics vary from source to source and may appear contradictory. Mammals discussion was based on Bowles 1975 and 1981, Bowles et al. 1998, Dinsmore 1994, the Iowa Department of Natural Resources 2005 and earlier years, and personal communications with David McCullough (Wartburg College) and Pat Schlarbaum (Iowa DNR), with information on deer coming from Stone 2003 and Iowa DNR 2005.

Much of chapter 6 was written from personal experience, with reliance on Kurtz 2001 and Packard and Mutel 2005 for details. My understanding of oak woodland restoration was greatly expanded by personal communications with Karl Delong (Grinnell College) and John Pearson, both of whom have been instrumental in raising awareness of the need for oakland restoration, and also with Paul Christiansen, Don Farrar (Iowa State University), and Thomas Rosburg; Iowa DNR district foresters Gary Beyer, Stan Tate, and Mark Vitosh; Larry Gnewikou, Amana Society forester; and Paul Nelson (Mark Twain National Forest) and Ken McCarty (Missouri Department of Natural Resources). Useful references included Abrams 2003, Brose et al. 2001 for shelterwood forestry treatments, McCarty 1998 for dry woodlands, and Packard 1988 and 1993. Wetland restoration was based primarily on Galtowitsch and van der Valk 1994, Zedler 2000 and 2003, and discussions with Susan Galatowitsch, Wayne Petersen, and Terry VanDeWalle (Natural Resources Consulting, Inc.). Personal communications with James Martin (Johnson County Soil and Water Conservation District), Jim Munson (U.S. Fish and Wildlife Service), Kelly Smith (Iowa DNR), and Wayne Petersen helped me understand conservation and restoration assistance programs.

As the culmination of my reading and research for this book, chapter 7 utilized nearly every source I have cited. But while some of the chapter's ideas have been presented elsewhere, their synthesis here remains my own. The following persons and publications were especially important in shaping the chapter: John Pearson and Marlene Ehresman (Iowa Natural Heritage Foundation) for the entire chapter; Wayne Petersen and Janette Thompson (Iowa State University) for minimizing impacts of urban and housing developments; Diane Ford-Shivvers (Iowa DNR) for conservation funding; Laura Jackson, Fred Kirschenmann, Wayne Petersen, Banks 2004, Jackson and Jackson 2002, and the publications and Web site of the Leopold Center for Sustainable Agriculture for agricultural practices, their impacts, and sustainable farming; and Duane Sand (Iowa Natural Heritage Foundation), Helms 2003, and the last chapter of Jackson and Jackson 2002 for the history and critique of the farm subsidy programs. Participants in "Iowa's Ecological Future," a session of the Iowa Prairie Conference held July 2005 at the Indian Creek Nature Center, Cedar Rapids, made numerous suggestions helpful to this chapter, especially concerning education and public involvement.

References Cited

Abrams, M. D. 2003. "Where Has All the White Oak Gone?" *BioScience* 53:927–939.

Alex, L. M. 2000. *Iowa's Archaeological Past*. Iowa City: University of Iowa Press.

Allison, S. K. 2002. "When Is a Restoration Successful? Results from a 45-Year-Old Tallgrass Prairie Restoration." *Ecological Restoration* 20:10–17.

Andersen, K. L. 2000. "Historical Alterations of Surface Hydrology in Iowa's Small Agricultural Watersheds." Master's thesis, Iowa State University.

Anderson, J. L. 2005. "Industrializing the Corn Belt: Iowa Farmers, Technology, and the Midwestern Landscape, 1945–1972." Ph.D. diss., Iowa State University.

Anderson, P. F. 1996. "Final Report: GIS Research to Digitize Maps of Iowa 1832–1859 Vegetation from General Land Office Township Plat Maps." Iowa State Preserves Advisory Board, Iowa Department of Natural Resources, and Iowa State University, Ames. www.public.iastate.edu/~fridolph/dnrglo.html.

Anderson, R. C. 1990. "The Historic Role of Fire in the North American Grassland." In *Fire in North American Tallgrass Prairies*, ed. S. L. Collins and L. L. Wallace, 8–18. Norman: University of Oklahoma Press.

Anderson, W. A. 1936. "Progress in the Regeneration of the Prairie at Iowa Lakeside Laboratory." *Iowa Academy of Science Proceedings* 43:87–93.

Anderson, W. I. 1998. *Iowa's Geological Past: Three Billion Years of Changes*. Iowa City: University of Iowa Press.

Andreas, A. T. 1875. *A. T. Andreas' Illustrated Historical Atlas of the State of Iowa*. Chicago: Andreas Atlas.

Anonymous. 1883. *History of Johnson County, Iowa, 1836–1882*. Reprinted 1973, Evansville, Ind.: Unigraphic.

Arbuckle, K. E. 2000. "Statewide Assessment of Freshwater Mussels (Bivalvia: Unionidae) in Iowa Streams." Master's thesis, Iowa State University.

Ashfall Fossil Beds State Historical Park, Nebraska. 2006. http://ashfall.unl.edu/index.html.

Aurner, C. R. 1912. *Leading Events in Johnson County Iowa History*. Cedar Rapids, Iowa: Western Historical Press.

Baker, R. G., L. J. Maher, C. A. Chumbley, and K. L. Van Zant. 1992. "Patterns of Holocene Environmental Change in the Midwest." *Quaternary Research* 37:379–389.

Baker, R. G., D. P. Schwert, E. A. Bettis III, and C. A. Chumbley. 1993. "Impact of Euro-American Settlement on a Riparian Landscape in Northeast Iowa, Midwestern USA: An Integrated Approach Based on Historical Evidence, Floodplain Sediments, Fossil Pollen, Plant Macrofossils, and Insects." *Holocene* 3, no. 4: 314–323.

Balmford, A., A. Bruner, P. Cooper, et al. 2002. "Economic Reasons for Conserving Wild Nature." *Science* 297:950–953.

Banks, J. E. 2004. "Divided Culture: Integrating Agriculture and Conservation Biology." *Frontiers in Ecology and the Environment* 2:537–545.

Beeman, R. S., and J. A. Pritchard. 2001. *A Green and Permanent Land: Ecology and Agriculture in the Twentieth Century.* Lawrence: University Press of Kansas. History, approaches, and importance of sustainable agriculture.

Bettis, E. A., III. 1992. "Soil Morphologic Properties and Weathering Zone Characteristics as Age Indicators in Holocene Alluvium in the Upper Midwest." In *Soils in Archaeology,* ed. V. T. Holliday, 119–144. Washington, D.C.: Smithsonian Institution Press.

Bishop, R. A. 1981. "Iowa's Wetlands." *Proceedings of the Iowa Academy of Science* 88:11–16.

Bishop, R. A., J. Joens, and J. Zohrer. 1998. "Iowa's Wetlands, Present and Future, with a Focus on Prairie Potholes." *Journal of the Iowa Academy of Science* 105:89–93. History of wetland restoration, including incentives for preservation and restoration.

Blaustein, A. R., and P. T. J. Johnson. 2003. "The Complexity of Deformed Amphibians." *Frontiers in Ecology and the Environment* 1:87–94.

Blewett, T. J., and G. Cottam. 1984. "History of the University of Wisconsin Arboretum Prairies." *Wisconsin Academy of Sciences, Arts and Letters* 72:130–144.

Blumberg, A. 1999. "Adventures in the Rhizosphere: Life Underground." *Chicago Wilderness* (Spring Edition): 10–14. Excellent and understandable description of the complexity of prairie soil processes.

Bogue, A. L. 1963. *From Prairie to Cornbelt: Farming on the Illinois and Iowa Prairies in the Nineteenth Century.* Chicago: Quadrangle Paperbacks.

Bowles, J. B. 1975. *Distribution and Biogeography of Mammals in Iowa.* Special Publication #9. Lubbock: The Museum, Texas Tech University.

———. 1981. "Iowa's Mammal Fauna: An Era of Decline." *Proceedings of the Iowa Academy of Science* 88:38–43.

Bowles, J. B., D. L. Howell, R. P. Lampe, and H. P. Whidden. 1998. "Mammals of Iowa: Holocene to the End of the 20th Century." *Journal of the Iowa Academy of Science* 105:123–132.

Boykin, J. T. 2003. *Iowa's Forest Resources in 2000.* Resource Bulletin NC-211. St. Paul, Minn.: USDA Forest Service, North Central Research Station.

Brand, G. J., and J. T. Walkowiak. 1991. *Forest Statistics for Iowa, 1990.* Resource Bulletin NC-136. St. Paul, Minn.: USDA Forest Service, North Central Experiment Station.

Brose, P., T. Schuler, D. Van Lear, and J. Berst. 2001. "Bringing Fire Back: The Changing Regimes of the Appalachian Mixed-Oak Forests." *Journal of Forestry* (November): 30–35.

Bulkley, R. V. 1975. "A Study of the Effects of Stream Channelization and Bank

Stabilization on Warm Water Sport Fish in Iowa." In *Inventory of Major Stream Alterations in Iowa.* Contract 14-16-0008–745. Washington, D.C.: U.S. Fish and Wildlife Service.

Calvin, S. 1893. "Prehistoric Iowa." In *Iowa Historical Lectures,* 5–29. Iowa City: Iowa State Historical Society.

Christiansen, J. L. 1981. "Population Trends among Iowa's Amphibians and Reptiles." *Proceedings of the Iowa Academy of Science* 88:24–27.

———. 1998. "Perspectives on Iowa's Declining Amphibians and Reptiles." *Journal of the Iowa Academy of Science* 105:109–114.

———. 2001. "Non-native Amphibians and Reptiles in Iowa." *Journal of the Iowa Academy of Science* 108:210–211.

Christiansen, J. L., and R. M. Bailey. 1990. *The Snakes of Iowa.* Des Moines: Iowa Department of Natural Resources.

———. 1991. *The Salamanders and Frogs of Iowa.* Des Moines: Iowa Department of Natural Resources.

———. 1997. *The Lizards and Turtles of Iowa.* Des Moines: Iowa Department of Natural Resources.

Christiansen, P. 1996. "Frequency Study of Hayden Prairie, 1995." Unpublished report prepared for the Iowa State Preserves Advisory Board, Iowa Department of Natural Resources, Des Moines.

Christiansen, P., and M. Müller. 1999. *An Illustrated Guide to Iowa Prairie Plants.* Iowa City: University of Iowa Press.

Cochrane, T. S., and H. H. Iltis. 2000. *Atlas of the Wisconsin Prairie and Savanna Flora.* Technical Bulletin 191. Madison: Wisconsin Department of Natural Resources.

Conard, H. S. 1952. "The Vegetation of Iowa: An Approach toward a Phytosociologic Account." *State University of Iowa Studies in Natural History* 19:1–166.

Conard, R. 1997. *Places of Quiet Beauty: Parks, Preserves, and Environmentalism.* Iowa City: University of Iowa Press. Excellent history of conservation efforts in Iowa and Iowa's leadership role therein.

Conservation Design Forum. 1998. "Floristic Inventory and Habitat Assessment for the Clear Creek Corridor, Coralville, Iowa." Elmhurst, Ill: Conservation Design Forum.

Cooper, T. C. 1982. *Iowa's Natural Heritage.* Des Moines: Iowa Natural Heritage Foundation and Iowa Academy of Science.

Costanza, R., R. d'Arge, R. de Groot, et al. 1997. "The Value of the World's Ecosystem Services and Natural Capital." *Nature* 387:253–259.

Costello, D. F. 1969. *The Prairie World — Plants and Animals of the Grassland Sea.* New York: Thomas Y. Crowell.

Cruden, R. W., and O. J. Gode Jr. 1998. "Iowa's Odonata: Declining and/or Changing?" *Journal of the Iowa Academy of Science* 105:67–81.

Curtis, J. T. 1959. *The Vegetation of Wisconsin.* Madison: University of Wisconsin Press.

Czarapata, E. J. 2005. *Invasive Plants of the Upper Midwest: An Illustrated Guide to Their Identification and Control*. Madison: University of Wisconsin Press.

Dahl, T. E. 1990. *Wetlands Losses in the United States 1780's to 1980's*. Washington, D.C.: U.S. Department of the Interior, Fish and Wildlife Service.

Daily, G. C., S. Alexander, P. R. Ehrlich, et al. 1997. "Ecosystem Services: Benefits Supplied to Human Societies by Natural Ecosystems." *Issues in Ecology* 2. Washington, D.C.: Ecological Society of America. Good summary of ecosystem goods and services and their value.

Damschen, E. I., N. M. Haddad, J. L. Orrock, et al. 2006. "Corridors Increase Plant Species Richness at Large Scales." *Science* 313:1284–1286.

Delcourt, P. A., and H. R. Delcourt. 2004. *Prehistoric Native Americans and Ecological Change: Human Ecosystems in Eastern North America since the Pleistocene*. Cambridge: Cambridge University Press.

Delong, K., and C. Hooper. 1996. "A Potential Understory Flora for Oak Savanna in Iowa." *Journal of the Iowa Academy of Science* 103:9–28. Detailed savanna and woodland species lists from historic and modern research.

Dick-Peddie, W. A. 1953. "Primeval Forest Types in Iowa." *Journal of the Iowa Academy of Science* 60:112–116.

Dinsmore, J. J. 1981. "Iowa's Avifauna: Changes in the Past and Prospects for the Future." *Proceedings of the Iowa Academy of Science* 88:28–37.

———. 1994. *A Country So Full of Game: The Story of Wildlife in Iowa*. Iowa City: University of Iowa Press. Traces the settlement-induced decline of game birds and mammals in a highly readable and entertaining fashion.

———. 1998. "Iowa's Avifauna: Recent Changes and Prospects for the Future." *Journal of the Iowa Academy of Science* 105:115–122.

———. 2001. "Invasive Birds in Iowa: Status, Problems, and Threats." *Journal of the Iowa Academy of Science* 108:212–220.

Dinsmore, S. J. 1995. *Iowa Wildlife Viewing Guide*. Helena, Mont: Falcon Press.

Dornbush, M. 2004. "Plant Community Change Following Fifty Years of Management at Kalsow Prairie Preserve, Iowa, U.S.A." *American Midland Naturalist* 151:241–250.

Drury, M. R. 1931. "Reminiscences of Early Days in Iowa." Toledo, Iowa: Toledo Chronicle Press.

Ebinger, J. E., and W. E. McClain. 1991. "Forest Succession in the Prairie Peninsula of Illinois." *Illinois Natural History Survey Bulletin* 34:375–381.

Egan, D., and E. A. Howell, eds. 2005. *The Historical Ecology Handbook: A Restorationist's Guide to Reference Ecosystems*. Washington, D.C.: Island Press. Methods for determining an area's site history and prehistoric ecosystems.

Ehresman, M. 2003. *A Bird's Eye View: A Guide to Managing and Protecting Your Land for Neotropical Migratory Birds in the Upper Mississippi River Blufflands*. Des Moines: Iowa Natural Heritage Foundation. Specifies land management techniques for neotropical migratory birds.

Eilers, L. J., and D. M. Roosa. 1994. *The Vascular Plants of Iowa: An Annotated Check-list and Natural History.* Iowa City: University of Iowa Press.

Falk, D. 1990. "Discovering the Future, Creating the Past: Some Reflections on Restoration." *Restoration and Management Notes* 8:71–72.

Farrar, D. R. 2001. "Exotic and Invasive Woody Plant Species in Iowa." *Journal of the Iowa Academy of Science* 108:154–157.

Firbank, L. G., S. M. Smart, J. Crabb, et al. 2003. "Agronomic and Ecological Costs and Benefits of Set-Aside Land in England." *Agriculture, Ecosystems and Environment* 95:73–85.

Frazer, Sir J. G. 1922. *The Golden Bough: A Study in Magic and Religion.* New York: Macmillan.

Galatowitsch, S. M., and A. G. van der Valk. 1994. *Restoring Prairie Wetlands: An Ecological Approach.* Ames: Iowa State University Press. Describes wetland communities in their native and altered states, as well as restoration.

———. 1996. "Characteristics of Recently Restored Wetlands in the Prairie Pothole Region." *Wetlands* 16:75–85.

Gardner, B. L. 2002. *American Agriculture in the Twentieth Century: How It Flourished and What It Cost.* Cambridge, Mass.: Harvard University Press.

Gerken, M. E. 2005. "Effects of Disturbance on the Floristic Composition and Functional Ecology of the Herbaceous Layer in Central Hardwood Forests of Iowa." Master's thesis, Iowa State University.

Gibbon, D. L., ed. 1999. *Impact of Deer on the Biodiversity and Economy of the State of Pennsylvania: Conference Proceedings.* Darby, Pa.: Diane. See also http://www.deerandforests.org/resources for additional information.

Girling, C., R. Kellett, J. Rochefort, and C. Roe. 2000. *Green Neighborhoods — Planning and Design Guidelines for Air, Water, and Urban Forest Quality.* Eugene: University of Oregon Center for Housing Innovation. Provides techniques for limiting environmental impacts of housing developments.

Glenn-Lewin, D. C., R. H. Laushman, and P. D. Whitson. 1984. "The Vegetation of the Paleozoic Plateau, Northeastern Iowa." *Proceedings of the Iowa Academy of Science* 91:22–27. Part of the proceedings of the 1983 symposium "Iowa's Driftless Area," which includes several other articles helpful in understanding the natural history of northeastern Iowa.

Haney, A., and S. I. Apfelbaum. 1995. "Characterization of Midwestern Oak Savannas." In *Proceedings of the 1993 Midwest Oak Savanna Conference*, ed. F. Stearns and K. Holland. Washington, D.C.: U.S. Environmental Protection Agency. www.epa.gov/glnpo/ecopage/upland/oak/index.html. Web site includes many additional Oak Savanna Conference articles useful for defining traits and restoration of oak woodlands.

Harlan, J. R., E. B. Speaker, and J. Mayhew. 1987. *Iowa Fish and Fishing.* Des Moines: Iowa Department of Natural Resources.

Helms, J. D. 2003. "The Evolution of Conservation Payments to Farmers." In *Com-*

pensating Landowners for Conserving Agricultural Land, ed. N. De Cuir et al., 123–132. Davis: University of California. http://www.aic.ucdavis.edu.

Hemesath, L. M. 1998. "Iowa's Frog and Toad Survey, 1991–1994." In *Status and Conservation of Midwestern Amphibians*, ed. M. J. Lannoo, 206–216. Iowa City: University of Iowa Press.

Herzberg R., and J. Pearson. 2001. *The Guide to Iowa's State Preserves*. Iowa City: University of Iowa Press. Guide to Iowa's best remaining native remnants.

Hillaker, H. 2005a. "Climates of the States, Climatography of the United States No. 60: Iowa." National Climatic Data Center, U.S. Department of Commerce, Asheville, N.C., http://hurricane.ncdc.noaa.gov/climatenormals/clim60/states/Clim_IA_01.pdf.

————. 2005b. "Iowa Statewide Average Precipitation 1873–2005 and Iowa Statewide Average Temperature (F), 1873–2005." Unpublished data provided by the author.

Howe, R. W., M. J. Huston, W. P. Pusateri, et al. 1984. *An Inventory of Significant Natural Areas in Iowa: Two Year Progress Report of the Iowa Natural Areas Inventory*. Des Moines: Iowa Conservation Commission and the Nature Conservancy.

Howell, E. A., and W. R. Jordan III. 1991. "Tallgrass Prairie Restoration in the North American Midwest." In *The Scientific Management of Temperate Communities for Conservation*, ed. I. F. Spellerberg et al., 395–414. Oxford: Blackwell Scientific Publications. Excellent summary of the goals, history, techniques, and results of prairie reconstruction efforts.

Hurt, R. D. 1994. *American Agriculture: A Brief History*. Ames: Iowa State University Press.

Hyde, A. J. 1902. "How the First Farmers Labored, 36th Annual Reunion, August 21, 1902." In *Old Settlers' Association Yearbooks 1866–1925, Johnson County, Iowa*. Reprinted 1977, Coralville, Iowa: Johnson County Historical Society.

Iltis, H. H. 2000. "Humans and Mother Nature: The Unbreakable Bond." In *Atlas of the Wisconsin Prairie and Savanna Flora, Technical Bulletin 191*, ed. T. S. Cochrane and H. H. Iltis, 47. Madison: Wisconsin Department of Natural Resources.

Iowa Department of Agriculture and Land Stewardship. 2006. "Facts about Iowa Agriculture." http://www.agriculture.state.ia.us/agfacts.htm.

Iowa Department of Natural Resources. 2005. *Trends in Iowa Wildlife Populations and Harvest — 2004*. Des Moines: Iowa Department of Natural Resources — Wildlife Bureau. Annual publication on game species and wildlife restoration advances.

————. 2006a. "Iowa's Threatened and Endangered Species Program." http://www.iowadnr.com/other/threatened.html.

————. 2006b. "State Conservation and Outdoor Recreation Plan." http://www.iowadnr.com/grants/scorp.html.

Iowa Natural Heritage Foundation. 1996. "Estimates of Land Use in Comparison to Population for the Des Moines Metropolitan Area." Unpublished report prepared for Iowa Natural Heritage Foundation, Des Moines.

Iowa State University. 2000. *Iowa's Land and Environment — Serving Competing*

Needs. Ames: College of Agriculture Experiment Station and Iowa State University Extension. www.econ.iastate.edu/research/webpapers/landuse/landuse.pdf.

Iowa State University Extension. 1998. "Final Report on the 1998 Pilot Land Use Inventory." Unpublished report prepared for Iowa State University Extension, Ames.

Irish, Captain F. M. 1868. "History of Johnson County, Iowa." *Annals of Iowa* 6:302–328.

Irish, Mrs. C. W. [Abigail]. 1922. "Iowa in 1846, 1922–1923 Yearbook." In *Old Settlers' Association Yearbooks 1866–1925, Johnson County, Iowa*. Reprinted 1977, Coralville, Iowa: Johnson County Historical Society.

Jackson, D. L., and L. J. Jackson. 2002. *The Farm as Natural Habitat: Reconnecting Food Systems with Ecosystems*. Washington, D.C.: Island Press. Discusses interaction between agriculture and native communities and suggestions for mitigating resulting impacts.

Jackson, L. S., C. A. Thompson, and J. J. Dinsmore. 1996. *The Iowa Breeding Bird Atlas*. Iowa City: University of Iowa Press.

Jacobson, R. L. 2006. "Guidelines for Restoring and Managing Native Wetland Vegetation." St. Paul: Minnesota Board of Soil and Water Resources. http://www.bwsr.state.mn.us/wetlands/publications/nativewetveg.pdf. Promotes some species not native to Iowa.

Johnson County Secondary Roads Department. 2006. "Johnson County (Iowa) Native Plant Community Policy." http://www.johnson-county.com/secondaryroads/index.shtml.

Johnson-Groh, C. L. 1985. "Vegetation Communities of Ledges State Park, Boone County, Iowa." *Proceedings of the Iowa Academy of Science* 92:129–136.

Johnson-Groh, C. L., D. Q. Lewis, and J. F. Shearer. 1987. "Vegetation Communities and Flora of Dolliver State Park, Webster County, Iowa." *Proceedings of the Iowa Academy of Science* 94:84–88.

Jungst S. E., D. R. Farrar, and M. Brandrup. 1998. "Iowa's Changing Forest Resources." *Journal of the Iowa Academy of Science* 105:61–66. Traces variations in amount and type of Iowa's forest coverage since settlement.

Kalkhoff, S. J., K. K. Barnes, K. D. Becher, et al. 2000. *Water Quality in the Eastern Iowa Basins, Iowa and Minnesota, 1996–98*. Circular 1210. Denver: U.S. Geological Survey.

Kane K. L., E. E. Klaas, K. L. Andersen, et al. 2003. *The Iowa Gap Analysis Project Final Report*. Ames: Iowa Cooperative Fish and Wildlife Research Unit, Iowa State University.

Kirschenmann, F. 2002. "The Future of Agrarianism: Where Are We Now?" Ames: Leopold Center for Sustainable Agriculture, Iowa State University. http://www.leopold.iastate.edu/pubs/pubs.htm. Web site contains many additional publications useful in understanding current agricultural trends.

Knutson, M. G., J. R. Sauer, D. A. Olsen, et al. 2000. "Landscape Associations of Frog and Toad Species in Iowa and Wisconsin, U.S.A." *Journal of the Iowa Academy of Science* 107:134–145.

Kotar, J., and T. Burger. 1996. "A Guide to Forest Communities and Habitat Types of Central and Southern Wisconsin." Madison: Department of Forestry, University of Wisconsin.

Kurtz, C. 2001. *A Practical Guide to Prairie Reconstruction.* Iowa City: University of Iowa Press. Straightforward, excellent guide for anyone planting a prairie from scratch.

Ladd, D. 1991. "Reexamination of the Role of Fire in Missouri Oak Woodlands." In *Proceedings of the Oak Woods Management Workshop*, ed. G. V. Burger, J. E. Ebinger, and G. S. Wilhelm, 76–80. Charleston: Eastern Illinois University.

———. 2005. "Vascular Plants of Midwestern Tallgrass Prairies." In *The Tallgrass Restoration Handbook*, ed. S. Packard and C. F. Mutel, 351–399. Washington, D.C.: Island Press.

Lannoo, M. J. 2000. "Conclusions Drawn from the Malformity and Disease Session, Midwest Declining Amphibian Conference, 1998." *Journal of the Iowa Academy of Science* 107:212–216.

Laubach, C. M., J. Bowles, and R. Laubach. 1994. *A Guide to the Bats of Iowa.* Des Moines: Iowa Department of Natural Resources.

Leach, M. K., and T. J. Givnish. 1996. "Ecological Determinants of Species Loss in Remnant Prairies." *Science* 273:1555–1558.

Leach, M. K., and L. Ross. 1995. "Midwest Oak Ecosystems Recovery Plan: A Call to Action." Washington, D.C.: U.S. Environmental Protection Agency. www.epa .gov/glnpo/ecopage/upland/oak/oak95/call.htm.

Leatherberry, E. C., S. M. Roussopoulos, and J. S. Spencer. 1992. *An Analysis of Iowa's Forest Resources, 1990.* Resource Bulletin NC-142. St. Paul, Minn.: USDA Forest Service, North Central Experiment Station.

Lentz, D. L., ed. 2000. *Imperfect Balance: Landscape Transformations in the Precolumbian Americas.* New York: Columbia University Press.

Leopold, A. 1949. *A Sand County Almanac, and Sketches Here and There.* New York: Oxford University Press.

Leopold Center for Sustainable Agriculture Task Force. 2005. *Toward a Global Food and Agricultural Policy, Draft Report.* Ames: Leopold Center for Sustainable Agriculture, Iowa State University.

Lewis, D. Q. 1998. "A Literature Review and Survey of the Status of Iowa's Terrestrial Flora." *Journal of the Iowa Academy of Science* 105:45–54.

Lewis, D. Q., and R. O. Pope. 2001. "An Overview and Management Plan of Iowa's Non-native, Invasive, Terrestrial Forbs." *Journal of the Iowa Academy of Science* 108:116–123.

Lindig-Cisneros, R., and J. B. Zedler. 2002. "*Phalaris arundinacea* Seedling Establishment: Effects of Canopy Complexity in Fen, Mesocosm, and Restoration Experiments." *Canadian Journal of Botany* 80:617–624.

Mabry, C. 2000. "Floristic Analysis of Central Iowa Woodlands, and Comparison of Reproduction and Regeneration in Common and Restricted Herbaceous Species." Ph.D. diss., Iowa State University.

———. 2002. "Effects of Cattle Grazing on Woodlands in Central Iowa." *Journal of the Iowa Academy of Science* 109:53–60.

Macbride, T. H. 1895. "The Landscapes of Early Iowa." *Iowa Historical Record* 11:341–349.

———. 1897. "Forests in Iowa." *Proceedings of the American Forestry Association* 12:170–173.

———. 1898. "The President's Address." *Proceedings of the Iowa Academy of Science for 1897* 5:12–23.

———. 1925. *On the Campus.* Cedar Rapids, Iowa: Torch Press.

Madson, J. 1972. "The Running Country." *Audubon* 74: 4–19.

Mansheim, G. 1989. *Iowa City: An Illustrated History.* Norfolk, Va.: Donning.

Martin, H., H. Zinn, and A. Nelson. 1951. *American Wildlife and Plants — A Guide to Wildlife Food Habits, the Use of Trees, Shrubs, Weeds, and Herbs by Birds and Mammals of the United States.* New York: McGraw-Hill.

McCarty, K. 1998. "Landscape-Scale Restoration in Missouri Savannas and Woodlands." *Restoration and Management Notes* 16, no. 1: 22–32. Practical approaches for dry sites.

McClain, W. E., and S. L. Elzinga. 1994. "The Occurrence of Prairie and Forest Fires in Illinois and Other Midwestern States, 1679 to 1854." *Erigenia* 13:79–90.

McKinley, V. L., and R. Wolek. 2003. "The Effects of Tallgrass Prairie Restoration on Soil Quality Indicators." In *Proceedings of the 18th North American Prairie Conference: Promoting Prairie,* ed. S. Fore, 138–149. Kirksville, Mo.: Truman State University Press.

Millennium Ecosystem Assessment. 2005. *Ecosystems and Human Well-Being: Synthesis.* Washington, D.C.: Island Press. Major United Nations analysis of worldwide changes in natural ecosystems, ecosystem services, and human well-being, 1950 to 2000.

Miller, M. C. 1995. "Analysis of Historic Vegetation Patterns in Iowa Using Government Land Office Surveys and a Geographic Information System." Master's thesis, Iowa State University.

Miller, R. M. 2005. "Prairie Underground." In *The Tallgrass Restoration Handbook,* ed. S. Packard and C. F. Mutel, 23–27. Washington, D.C.: Island Press.

Mottl, L. 2000. "Woodland Herbaceous Layer Restoration in Iowa." Master's thesis, Iowa State University.

———. 2001. "Woodland Herb Restoration Using Transplants and Nursery Plugs (Iowa)." *Ecological Restoration* 19:172–174.

Mutel, C. F. 1989. *Fragile Giants: A Natural History of the Loess Hills.* Iowa City: University of Iowa Press.

———. 1996. "The Historic Role of Iowa's Trees." In *Famous and Historical Trees of Iowa,* ed. W. A. Farris, 4–16. Des Moines: Iowa Department of Natural Resources. Describes postsettlement history and use of Iowa's woodlands.

Naeem, S., F. S. Chapin, R. Costanza, et al. 1999. "Biodiversity and Ecosystem Functioning: Maintaining Natural Life Support Processes." *Issues in Ecology* 4. Washington, D.C.: Ecological Society of America. Good summary of the benefits of biodiversity.

National Agricultural Statistics Service. 2002. "Census of Agriculture." Washington, D.C.: U.S. Department of Agriculture.

———. 2005a. "Iowa Agricultural Statistics." Washington, D.C.: U.S. Department of Agriculture.

———. 2005b. "Iowa State Agricultural Overview — 2005." Washington, D.C.: U.S. Department of Agriculture.

———. 2006a. "Agricultural Chemical Usage, 2005 Field Crops Summary." Washington, D.C.: U.S. Department of Agriculture.

———. 2006b. "Iowa's Rank in Agriculture." Washington, D.C.: U.S. Department of Agriculture.

———. n.d. (ongoing). USDA-NASS Quick Stats. National Agricultural Statistics Service, U.S. Department of Agriculture, Washington, D.C. www.nass.usda.gov:8080/QuickStats/PullData_US.jsp.

National Audubon Society. 2004. "State of the Birds USA." *Audubon Magazine*, September–October, with details at http://www.audubon.org/bird/stateofthebirds/index.html.

National Park Service. 2002. *The Loess Hills of Western Iowa — Special Resource Study and Environmental Assessment*. Omaha, Neb.: U.S. Department of Interior, National Park Service Midwest Regional Office.

Natural Resources Conservation Service. 1996. *America's Private Land: A Geography of Hope*. Washington, D.C.: U.S. Department of Agriculture.

———. 2000. *Summary Report: 1997 National Resources Inventory* (revised). Washington, D.C., and Ames, Iowa: U.S. Department of Agriculture and Statistical Laboratory, Iowa State University.

Newhall, J. B. 1841. *Sketches of Iowa or the Emigrant's Guide*. New York: J. H. Colton, Merchant's Exchanges.

———. 1846. *A Glimpse of Iowa in 1846*. Reprinted 1957, Iowa City: State Historical Society of Iowa.

Norris, W. R., D. Q. Lewis, M. P. Widrlechner, et al. 2001. "Lessons from an Inventory of the Ames, Iowa, Flora (1858–2000)." *Journal of the Iowa Academy of Science* 108:34–63.

Norris W. R., M. P. Widrlechner, D. Q. Lewis, et al. 2001. "More Than a Century of Change in the Ames, Iowa Flora (1859–2000)." *Journal of the Iowa Academy of Science* 108:124–140.

Novacek, J. M., D. M. Roosa, and W. P. Pusateri. 1985. "The Vegetation of the Loess Hills Landform along the Missouri River." *Proceedings of the Iowa Academy of Science* 92:199–212.

Nuzzo, V. 1986. "Extent and Status of Midwest Oak Savanna: Presettlement and 1985." *Natural Areas Journal* 6:6–36.

Oschwald, W. R., F. F. Riecken, R. I. Dideriksen, et al. 1965. *Principal Soils of Iowa*. Special Report 42. Ames: Iowa State University Cooperative Extension Service.

Packard, S. 1988. "Just a Few Oddball Species: Restoration and the Rediscovery of the Tallgrass Savanna." *Restoration and Management Notes* 6, no. 1: 13–22. Describes the discovery of savannas as unique communities and lists savanna restoration techniques.

———. 1993. "Restoring Oak Ecosystems." *Restoration and Management Notes* 11, no. 1: 5–15.

Packard, S., and C. F. Mutel, eds. 2005. *The Tallgrass Restoration Handbook for Prairies, Savannas, and Woodlands*. Washington, D.C.: Island Press. Comprehensive restoration manual.

Pammel, L. 1896. "Iowa." *Proceedings of the American Forestry Association* 11:77–78.

———. 1926. "Our Highways and Railway Right-of-ways for Bee Pasturage." *Report of the Iowa State Horticultural Society* 61:305–310.

Patterson, L. B. n.d. "Address." In *Old Settlers' Association Yearbooks 1866–1925, Johnson County, Iowa*. Reprinted 1977, Coralville, Iowa: Johnson County Historical Society.

Pearson, J. 1989. "Ancient Record Keepers." *Iowa Conservationist* (February): 14–15.

———. 1998. "Assessment of the Representation of Natural Communities in the Iowa State Preserve System." Unpublished report prepared for the Iowa State Preserves Advisory Board, Iowa Department of Natural Resources, Des Moines.

Pearson, J., and M. J. Leoschke. 1992. "Floristic Composition and Conservation Status of Fens in Iowa." *Journal of the Iowa Academy of Science* 99:41–52.

Penna, A. N. 1999. *Nature's Bounty — Historical and Modern Environmental Perspectives*. Armonk, N.Y.: M. E. Sharpe.

Peterson, C. L. 1997. "Sand Road Heritage Corridor, Johnson County, Iowa: Archaeology and History of Indian and Pioneer Settlement." Contract Report 492. Iowa City: Office of the State Archaeologist.

Pimental, D., L. Lach, R. Zuniga, and D. Morrison. 2000. "Environmental and Economic Costs of Non-indigenous Species in the United States." *Bioscience* 50:53–65.

Pimm, S. L. 2001. *The World According to Pimm: A Scientist Audits the Earth*. New York: McGraw-Hill.

Pirog, R., and A. Benjamin. 2003. "Checking the Food Odometer: Comparing Food Miles for Local versus Conventional Produce Sales to Iowa Institutions." Ames: Leopold Center for Sustainable Agriculture, Iowa State University.

Plumbe, J., Jr. 1839. *Sketches of Iowa and Wisconsin*. Reprinted 1948, Iowa City: State Historical Society of Iowa.

Porter, E., K. Tonnenssen, J. Sherwell, and R. Grant. 2000. "Nitrogen in the Nation's Rain." NADP Brochure 2000-01c (revised) 2M-05. Champaign, Ill: National Atmospheric Deposition Program.

Prior, J. C. 1991. *Landforms of Iowa*. Iowa City: University of Iowa Press.

———. 2003. *Iowa's Groundwater Basics*. Educational Series 6. Iowa City: Iowa Geological Survey.

Raich, J. W., D. R. Farrar, R. A. Herzberg, et al. 1999. "Characterization of Central Iowa Forests with Permanent Plots." *Journal of the Iowa Academy of Science* 106:40–46.

Raven, P. H. 2002. "Presidential Address: Science, Sustainability, and the Human Prospect." *Science* 297:954–958. Overview of human-imposed ecological costs and statistics for changes in the twentieth century.

Riessen, J. 2002. "A Matter of Quality." *Iowa Conservationist* (January/February): 6–11. Summary of Iowa's water quality changes and status.

Risser, P. G., E. C. Burney, H. D. Blocker, et al. 1981. *The True Prairie Ecosystem.* US/IBP Synthesis Series 16. Stroudsburg, Pa.: Hutchinson Ross.

Robinson, Solon. 1842. "Something About Western Prairies." *American Agriculturist* 1:14–16.

Rock, H. W. 1977. *Prairie Propagation Handbook.* Milwaukee, Wis.: Wehr Nature Center, County Park System.

Rosburg, T. R. 1996. "A Quantitative Plant Inventory of Sheeder Prairie and a Comparison with its Composition in 1968." Unpublished report prepared for the Iowa State Preserves Advisory Board, Iowa Department of Natural Resources, Des Moines.

———. 1999. "Community Composition of Dry Prairie in Iowa and Southeast Nebraska." *Journal of the Iowa Academy of Science* 106:69–81. Includes species lists helpful in planning prairie restorations.

———. 2001. "Iowa's Non-native Graminoids." *Journal of the Iowa Academy of Science* 108:142–153.

———. 2001. "Iowa's Prairie Heritage: From the Past, through the Present, and into the Future." In *Proceedings of the 17th Annual North American Prairie Conference, Seeds for the Future, Roots of the Past,* ed. N. P. Bernstein, and L. J. Ostrander, 1–14. Mason City: North Iowa Area Community College.

———. 2003. "The Grand River Grasslands Project: An Inventory of the Remnant Prairies of Southeast Ringgold County, Iowa." Unpublished report prepared for the Nature Conservancy, Iowa Field Office, Des Moines.

———. 2004. "Effects of Deer Browse on Woody Vegetation in Forests at Coralville Lake, Iowa: Final Report 1998 to 2002." Unpublished report prepared for the U.S. Army Corps of Engineers, Coralville Lake Project, Iowa City, Iowa.

Rosburg, T. R., and D. C. Glenn-Lewin. 1996. "Species Composition and Environmental Characteristics of Grassland and Ecotonal Plant Communities in the Loess Hills of Western Iowa (USA)." *Natural Areas Journal* 16:318–334.

Runkel, S. T., and A. F. Bull. 1987. *Wildflowers of Iowa's Woodlands.* Ames: Iowa State University Press.

Runkel, S. T., and D. M. Roosa. 1989. *Wildflowers of the Tallgrass Prairie: The Upper Midwest.* Ames: Iowa State University Press.

———. 1999. *Wildflowers and Other Plants of Iowa Wetlands.* Ames: Iowa State University Press. Includes introduction to Iowa's wetland plants and communities.

Samson, F., and F. Knopf. 1994. "Prairie Conservation in North America." *Bioscience* 44:418–421.

Sauer, J. R., J. E. Hines, and J. Fallon. 2004. "The North American Breeding Bird

Survey, Results and Analysis 1966–2003, Version 2004.1." Laurel, Md.: U.S. Geological Survey Patuxent Wildlife Research Center. http://www.mbr-pwrc.usgs .gov/bbs/bbs.html.

Schilling, K. E., and R. D. Libra. 2003. "Increased Baseflow in Iowa over the Second Half of the 20th Century." *Journal of the American Water Resources Association* 39:851–860.

Schlicht, D. W., and T. T. Orwig. 1998. "The Status of Iowa's Lepidoptera." *Journal of the Iowa Academy of Science* 105:82–88.

Schlicht, D. W., J. C. Downey, and J. C. Nekola. 2007. *The Butterflies of Iowa*. Iowa City: University of Iowa Press.

Schroeder, W. A. 1982. *Presettlement Prairie of Missouri*. Natural History Series 2. Jefferson City: Missouri Department of Conservation.

Schwieder, D. 1996. *Iowa: The Middle Land*. Ames: Iowa State University Press.

Scudder, S. H. 1869. "A Preliminary List of the Butterflies of Iowa." *Chicago Academy of Science Transactions* 1:326–337.

Shimek, B. 1883. "Natural History, Mr. Shimek's Report; Native Animals." In *History of Johnson County, Iowa, 1836–1882*, 561–579. Reprinted 1973, Evansville, Ind.: Unigraphic.

———. 1899. "The Distribution of Forest Trees in Iowa." *Proceedings of the Iowa Academy of Science* 7:47–59.

———. 1911. "The Prairies." *Bulletin of the State University of Iowa New Series 35, Contributions from the Laboratories of Natural History* 6:169–240.

———. 1925. "The Persistence of the Prairie." *University of Iowa Studies in Natural History* 11:3–24.

———. 1931a. "Common Names of Plants." *University of Iowa Studies in Natural History* 14:3–9.

———. 1931b. "The Relation between the Migrant and Native Flora of the Prairie Region." *University of Iowa Studies in Natural History* 14:10–16.

———. 1948. "The Plant Geography of Iowa." Ed. H. S. Conard. *University of Iowa Studies in Natural History* 18:1–178. A comprehensive but unfinished vegetation analysis that Shimek was writing at the time of his death; published posthumously.

Simpkins, W. W., M. R. Burkart, R. Horton, et al. 2004. "The Hydrology of Intensively Managed Landscapes (IML) in the Glaciated Midwest U.S., CUAHSI Vision Paper." In *Proceedings of a Vision Paper Workshop*. Ames: Iowa State University. Good summary of presettlement hydrology and impacts of agricultural transformation.

Smith, D. D. 1981. "Iowa Prairie — An Endangered Ecosystem." *Proceedings of the Iowa Academy of Science* 88:7–10.

———. 1992. "Tallgrass Prairie Settlement: Prelude to the Demise of the Tallgrass Ecosystem." In *Proceedings of the Twelfth North American Prairie Conference*, ed. D. D. Smith, and C. A. Jacobs, 195–199. Cedar Falls: University of Northern Iowa.

———. 1998. "Iowa Prairie: Original Extent and Loss, Preservation and Recovery Attempts." *Journal of the Iowa Academy of Science* 105:94–108.

———. 2001. "America's Lost Landscape: The Tallgrass Prairie." In *Proceedings of the 17th North American Prairie Conference*, ed. N. P. Bernstein, and L. J. Ostrander, 15–20. Mason City: North Iowa Area Community College.

Springer, J. 1924. "Reminiscences, 1924–1925 Yearbook." In *Old Settlers' Association Yearbooks 1866–1925, Johnson County, Iowa*. Reprinted 1977, Coralville, Iowa: Johnson County Historical Society.

State Data Center Program. 2006. "Total Population and Housing Units for Iowa and Its Counties: 2000; Land Area and Population Density for Iowa: 1850–2000; Urban and Rural Population (1850–2000) for Iowa." Prepared by the State Library of Iowa from U.S. Bureau of the Census, Decennial Censuses. http://data.iowa-datacenter.org/indexlinks/browse.html.

Steinauer, E. M., and S. L. Collins. 1996. "Prairie Ecology — The Tallgrass Prairie." In *Prairie Conservation: Preserving North America's Most Endangered Ecosystem*, ed. F. B. Samson and F. L. Knopf, 39–52. Washington, D.C.: Island Press.

Stone, L. 2003. *Whitetail: Treasure, Trophy or Trouble? A History of Deer in Iowa*. Des Moines: Iowa Department of Natural Resources.

Sullivan, D. J. 2000. *Fish Communities and Their Relation to Environmental Factors in the Eastern Iowa Basins in Iowa and Minnesota, 1996*. Water Resources Investigations Report 00-4194. Denver: U.S. Geological Survey.

Thomson, G. W. 1987. "Iowa's Forest Area in 1832: A Reevaluation." *Proceedings of the Iowa Academy of Science* 94:116–120.

Thornton, P. L., and J. T. Morgan. 1959. "The Forest Resources of Iowa, U.S. Forest Survey Release 22." Columbus, Ohio: Central States Forest Experiment Station.

Tiffany, L. H. 2001. "Introduced Fungi: Some Cause Significant Plant Disease Problems." *Journal of the Iowa Academy of Science* 108:112–115.

Transeau, E. N. 1935. "The Prairie Peninsula." *Ecology* 16:423–437.

Ugarte, E. A. 1987. "The Hill Prairies of Northeast Iowa: Vegetation and Dynamics." Ph.D. diss., Iowa State University.

Undersander, D., S. Temple, J. Bartlet, et al. 2000. *Grassland Birds: Fostering Habitats Using Rotational Grazing*. Publication A3715. Madison: University of Wisconsin Cooperative Extension Service. Available from Wisconsin County Extension Service offices and Web sites.

Union of Concerned Scientists. 2004. "Climate Change in the Hawkeye State: Impacts on Iowa Communities and Ecosystems." www.ucsusa.org/iowa.

U.S. Census Bureau. 1900. *Census of Agriculture*. Washington, D.C.: U.S. Department of Commerce.

———. 1978. *Census of Agriculture*. Washington, D.C.: U.S. Department of Commerce.

U.S. Census Bureau, Population Division/International Programs Center. 2006. "Total Midyear Population for the World: 1950–2050." http://www.census.gov/ipc/www/worldpop.html.

U.S. Department of Agriculture. 2007. "The PLANTS Database." Baton Rouge, La.: National Plant Data Center, Natural Resources Conservation Service. http://

plants.usda.gov, March 20, 2007. The taxonomic checklist for vascular plants in this database was prepared by John Kartesz of the Biota of North America Program.

U.S. Fish and Wildlife Service. 2002. "2001 National Survey of Fishing, Hunting, and Wildlife-Associated Recreation, State Overview." http://library.fws.gov/Pubs/State_overview01.pdf.

———. n.d. (ongoing). "National Wetlands Inventory." http://www.ag.iastate.edu/centers/iawetlands/NWIhome.html.

U.S. Geological Survey. 2006. "The Gulf of Mexico Hypoxic Zone." http://toxics.usgs.gov/hypoxia/hypoxic_zone.html.

van der Linden, P. J., and D. R. Farrar. 1993. *Forest and Shade Trees of Iowa*, 2nd ed. Ames: Iowa State University Press.

Van Lear, D. H. 1991. "Fire and Oak Regeneration in the Southern Appalachians." In *Fire and the Environment — Ecological and Cultural Perspectives*, General Technical Report SE-69, ed. S. C. Nodvin, and T. A. Waldrop, 15–21. Asheville, N.C.: U.S. Department of Agriculture Forest Service, Southeastern Forest Experiment Station.

Walkowiak, J., and J. Haanstad. 2001. "Forest Invasives in Iowa: Current Problems and Future Issues." *Journal of the Iowa Academy of Science* 108:181–184.

Weaver, J. E. 1954. *North American Prairie*. Lincoln, Neb: Johnsen. Applies primarily to drier, more western prairies.

Westbrooks, R. 1998. *Invasive Plants, Changing the Landscape of America: Fact Book*. Washington, D.C.: Federal Interagency Committee for the Management of Noxious and Exotic Weeds.

White, J. A., and D. C. Glenn-Lewin. 1984. "Regional and Local Variation in Tallgrass Prairie Remnants of Iowa and Eastern Nebraska." *Vegetatio* 57:65–78.

Wilhelm, G. S. 1991. "Implications of Changes in Floristic Composition of the Morton Arboretum's East Woods." In *Proceedings of the Oak Woods Management Workshop*, ed. G. V. Burger, J. E. Ebinger, and G. Wilhelm, 31–54. Charleston: East Illinois University. Traces woodland changes with increasing density and shade.

Wilson, J. H. C. 1901. "Letter, August 12, 1901 Yearbook." In *Old Settlers' Association Yearbooks 1866–1925, Johnson County, Iowa*. Reprinted 1977, Coralville, Iowa: Johnson County Historical Society.

Zedler, J. B. 2000. "Progress in Wetland Restoration Ecology." *Tree* 15:402–407.

———. 2003. "Wetlands at Your Service: Reducing Impacts of Agriculture at the Watershed Scale." *Frontiers in Ecology and the Environment* 1:65–72. Wetland and hydrologic decline, and restoration strategies.

Zedler, J. B., and L. Shabman. 2001. "Compensatory Mitigation Needs Improvement, Panel Says." *Ecological Restoration* 19:209–211.

Zohrer, J. J. 2005. *Iowa Wildlife Action Plan, Securing a Future for Fish and Wildlife: A Conservation Legacy for Iowans*. Des Moines: Iowa Department of Natural Resources.

Index

Numbers in italics indicate an illustration or photograph.

Selected Bur Oak Books/Natural History

Butterflies in Your Pocket:
A Guide to the Butterflies of the
Upper Midwest
By Steve Hendrix and Diane Debinski

The Butterflies of Iowa
By Dennis Schlicht, John C. Downey,
and Jeffrey C. Nekola

A Country So Full of Game:
The Story of Wildlife in Iowa
By James J. Dinsmore

Fragile Giants:
A Natural History of the Loess Hills
By Cornelia F. Mutel

An Illustrated Guide to Iowa
Prairie Plants
By Paul Christiansen and Mark Müller

The Iowa Breeding Bird Atlas
By Laura Spess Jackson, Carol A.
Thompson, and James J. Dinsmore

Iowa's Archaeological Past
By Lynn M. Alex

Iowa's Geological Past:
Three Billion Years of Change
By Wayne I. Anderson

Iowa's Minerals:
Their Occurrence, Origins,
Industries, and Lore
By Paul Garvin

Landforms of Iowa
By Jean C. Prior

A Practical Guide to Prairie
Reconstruction
By Carl Kurtz

Prairie:
A North American Guide
By Suzanne Winckler

Prairie in Your Pocket:
A Guide to Plants of the Tallgrass
Prairie
By Mark Müller

Prairies, Forests, and Wetlands:
The Restoration of Natural Landscape
Communities in Iowa
By Janette R. Thompson

Restoring the Tallgrass Prairie:
An Illustrated Manual for Iowa and
the Upper Midwest
By Shirley Shirley

The Vascular Plants of Iowa:
An Annotated Checklist and
Natural History
By Lawrence J. Eilers and
Dean M. Roosa

Where the Sky Began:
Land of the Tallgrass Prairie
By John Madson